# BEER AND RACISM

# Sociology of Diversity series

*Series Editor:* **David G. Embrick,**
University of Connecticut, US

---

The Sociology of Diversity series brings together the highest quality sociological and interdisciplinary research specific to ethnic, racial, gender and sexualities diversity.

## Forthcoming in the series:

*Racial Diversity in Contemporary France: Rethinking the French Model*
**Marie des Neiges Léonard**, June 2021

*Craft Food Diversity: Challenging the Myth of a U.S. Food Revival*
**Kaitland M. Byrd**, June 2021

*Disproportionate Minority Contact*
**Paul Ketchum** and **B. Mitchell Peck**, September 2021

## Out now in the series:

*The Death of Affirmative Action? Racialized Framing and the Fight Against Racial Preference in College Admissions*
**J. Scott Carter** and **Cameron Lippard**, March 2020

## Find out more at

bristoluniversitypress.co.uk/sociology-of-diversity

# BEER AND RACISM

## How Beer Became White, Why It Matters, and the Movements to Change It

Nathaniel G. Chapman and David L. Brunsma

Foreword by
Anthony Kwame Harrison

First published in Great Britain in 2020 by

Bristol University Press
University of Bristol
1–9 Old Park Hill
Bristol
BS2 8BB
UK
t: +44 (0)117 954 5940
e: bup-info@bristol.ac.uk

Details of international sales and distribution partners are available at bristoluniversitypress.co.uk



British Library Cataloguing in Publication Data
A catalogue record for this book is available from the British Library

ISBN 978-1-5292-0175-8 hardcover
ISBN 978-1-5292-0179-6 paperback
ISBN 978-1-5292-0177-2 ePub
ISBN 978-1-5292-0176-5 ePdf



Cover design by blu inc.
Front cover image: Unsplash/Elevate

This book is dedicated to the people and their communities whose voices, experiences, and stories related to beer and brewing in the US have been erased and ignored. Beginning to uncover and recover such stories along with the people who lived them is a central part of 'why it matters.' It is our hope that this book will shed light on those stories and provide a broader context for understanding the deep-rooted racism that was, and still is, so prevalent in the brewing industry. It is but a beginning—a preface of sorts—to a larger narrative of our troubled history with race and beer. We hope that this is the beginning of a conversation.

The movements to change the dynamics of race and racism in the brewing industry have their roots in the social movements of the past. The contemporary movements taking place today across social media and within the industry itself—and those movements yet to come—have helped to craft the narrative of *Beer and Racism*. There are many stories yet to be told, and even more yet to be written. As we wrote this book, a new narrative was being crafted. It is actively being crafted as you read this. It is a narrative that is hopeful, optimistic, engaged, critical, and, most of all, diverse. It is our hope that, in some small way, this book will be a passage written in this #newnarrative. Onward and cheers!

# Contents


About the Authors viii
Acknowledgments ix
Foreword by Anthony Kwame Harrison xi
Series Editor Preface xv

1 Brewing Up Race 1

2 Racism, Brewing, and Drinking in US History 27

3 The Making of the (White) Craft Beer Industry 49

4 The Paths to Becoming a Craft Brewer and Craft Beer Consumer 75

5 Exposure, Marketing, and Access: Malt Liquor and the Racialization of Taste 103

6 Gentrification and the Making of Craft Beer White Spaces 131

7 #WeAreCraftBeer: Contemporary Movements to Change the Whiteness of Craft Beer 155

Appendix A: Respondents to the Semi-Structured Interviews 181
Appendix B: Interview Protocol 183
References 185
Index 203

# About the Authors

**David L. Brunsma** is Professor of Sociology at Virginia Tech, USA, where he researches race, racism, and whiteness. He is founding co-editor of *Sociology of Race and Ethnicity* and has a book series by the same name at University of Georgia Press. He lives, loves, and drinks beer in Blacksburg, VA.

**Nathaniel G. Chapman** is Assistant Professor of Sociology at Arkansas Tech University, USA. His research examines the ways in which craft beer consumption relates and intersects with race, class, and gender. He is co-editor of *Untapped: Exploring the Cultural Dimension of Craft Beer* (West Virginia Press, 2017).

# Acknowledgments

We would first like to thank our friends, families, and colleagues, without whose support, expertise, and endless hours of conversations—along with a few beers—this book would not have been possible. We would also like to thank our colleagues who took time from their lives to review the book and provide invaluable feedback. There were many of you, and your feedback on the original draft of the manuscript provided validation for what we were doing, critically pushed us to think harder about a wide variety of angles, and presented us with new insights that we had not considered. Thank you for this. While the peer reviews (some 15 of them!) made the book stronger, they also laid bare just how much work there is yet to do regarding the inquiry into race, racism, and beer. While we could not incorporate all of the ideas, critiques, and insights, we look forward to the next iterations in this ongoing research and hope to do much of that work in collaboration with you all.

Most importantly, we would like to thank our informants. From its inception, the entire book was inspired by following and watching the groundbreaking work that you were all doing across the spectrum of the brewing industry. Your innovations, your tenacity, your drive against all odds in an industry that has worked exceedingly hard to exclude your communities for hundreds of years is awe-inspiring. We hope that this book helps to socially and culturally contextualize your experiences with beer and brewing, especially as they pertain to historical and contemporary structures of racism in the industry. Thank you for sharing your stories, experiences, and passion with us. Your voices resonate throughout this book and we are humbled to be a small part of telling your stories.

Nathaniel G. Chapman would like to thank David L. Brunsma, Anthony Kwame Harrison, and Slade Lellock. Your mentorship, friendship, and support have made a lasting impact. In many ways, this book is a testament to your influence on my scholarship. Thank

.or encouraging me to explore the sociology of craft beer and ,porting me throughout my journey as a scholar.

David L. Brunsma would like to thank Nate Chapman for, in many ways, introducing me to the intricacies of craft beer, and for his friendship. There are far too many people to thank for their support of this manuscript, its development, and its publication. The conversations, the published scholarship, the conference presentations, the ways in which the community pushes us all to more fully understand the social life of beer as a social and cultural object, the work it does, and the work it has yet to do, I am thankful for all of these and more.

# Foreword

*Anthony Kwame Harrison*

I started drafting the foreword for this important book on a Saturday in late March 2020—the end of a trying week, both societally and personally. The grave reality of the COVID-19 virus had finally (and inevitably) reached Southwest Virginia and the small college town that I call home. All around Blacksburg, stores were closing and restaurants were scrambling to convert to takeout-only service. In the coming weeks, the governor would issue a stay-at-home order as the number of confirmed COVID-19 cases in the US soared to the highest in the world. Amid all this, at a more personal level, an organization I led was in crisis. Over a 24-hour period, I had received roughly two dozen emails or phone calls in response to a lengthy memo (having nothing to with COVID-19) that I had sent out to the organization's governing committee. Under any circumstances, this would have been a difficult situation—that much more in the midst of a global pandemic.

Since receiving the gracious invitation from Nate Chapman and Dave Brunsma to introduce *Beer and Racism*, I had been eager to get started. However, with all that was happening, in order to write, I needed to disengage: shut down my phone and internet, turn off the television, put on Fleetwood Mac's greatest hits, crack a beer, and enter my happy place of writing. For many Americans—and I would venture to add Europeans and Australians (white people the world over)—the notion of 'cracking a beer' (opening a beer) calls to mind a state of disengaged happiness that is simultaneously a product of enduring privilege (having the luxury to disengage) and a response to circumstantial stressors. Even the rich, famous, and powerful regularly call on 'beer' for a sense of release during a difficult moment (as in, 'I need one') or as a social elixir to help cooperatively negotiate an uncomfortable situation (as in, 'let's get one'). President Obama's 2009 'beer summit,' in response to racially saturated tensions surrounding the arrest of Harvard Professor

Henry Louis Gates Jr (while entering his own home), is just one prominent example.

Using the beer summit as an exemplar, few would dispute that the images associated with beer consumption in the US have historically placed it in spaces of cisgender male privilege (Obama, Gates, and the arresting Cambridge police officer were all men). Important work by Chapman, Megan Nanney, Slade Lellock, and Julie Mikles-Schluterman (2018) documents and theorizes the ways in which gender is done, undone, and redone through women's increasing presence in these hegemonic beer spaces.

Using the beer summit as a foil, few would question that the images surrounding beer in America, and craft beer in particular, have historically located its consumption within white spaces (Anderson, 2015). In *Beer and Racism*, Chapman and Brunsma do a masterful job of documenting how this correlation between beer and whiteness came into being, how it has been maintained, how the pre-Civil Rights movement introduction of malt liquor later led to its rebranding as the black antithesis to beer during the post-Civil Rights era, and how the commendable efforts of activists and progressives to decouple the enduring association between beer and whiteness are beginning to ferment.

*Beer and Racism* unequivocally demonstrates the sturdy entanglements of race and marketplace (Johnson et al, 2019) surrounding one of the USA's choicest beverages and most rapidly expanding industries. In Clint Eastwood's 2008 film *Gran Torino*, 70-something white savior Walt Kowalski guzzles beer prior to taking on the Hmong gangstas who are destroying his neighborhood. Throughout the movie, the constant crushed beer cans on his porch come to symbolize his character: a flawed (circumstantial) hero (enduring), who regularly cracks a beer on the porch to disengage from all that is wrong with the world.

The beer I cracked as I began to write was a regional India Pale Ale (IPA). In their pioneering edited volume *Untapped*, Chapman, Lellock, and Cameron Lippard (2017) highlight the astounding explosion of craft beer over the past few decades. Mine comes from Foothills Brewing of Winston Salem, North Carolina—specifically, their 'Craft Happiness IPA Project,' with its heart-centered hop logo. The beer is a U B U IPA, 'brewed to embrace individuality and acceptance.'

My practice of almost always ordering/buying IPAs started from the assumption (correct or incorrect) that in the esoteric field of craft beer knowledge, being an IPA drinker would suggest to people that I am an insider: a real 'beer guy.' A few weeks before writing this, at an (otherwise) all-white ski-après happy hour at Black Mountain ski resort, a friendly New Yorker with expressed anti-IPA tastes convinced me to order a particular Hefeweizen with my dinner later that evening—he assured me that they carried it at the restaurant next door. An hour later, when I asked the bartender for one, she responded: "What? We don't have that!" I felt outed. It is one thing to be a black man in all-white Jackson, New Hampshire; it is quite another to be exposed as either a non-beer guy or, even worse, a pompous ass who shows up in the White Mountains of Northern New England asking for Hefeweizen. Any chance at honorary white status was gone (please get my sarcasm here)!

Returning to my 'U B U' refreshment, the rhetoric of individualism that permeates craft brewing's progressive character is at once disturbing and inspiring. Pondering it, I cannot help but think of misguided colorblind convictions that America's blatantly racist history has no bearing on material inequalities (income and wealth) between different racial groups, nor the existing laws, policies, and norms through which such inequalities endure and are even extended. Racially speaking, we neither start from nor play on a level playing field. At the same time, when I look around and see the multiple expressions of black, Latinx, Asian-American, and Native American identities, as well as the ever-growing movements to break free from the expectations and constraints of the racial categories that bind us (Appiah, 2018), I wonder how a historically and sociologically informed embrace of 'U B U' might make headway in eroding race's enduring significance. *Beer and Racism* documents and grapples with these critical intersections of concern and hope—of the meanings of race and how race *means*—in the popular but rarely racialized field of craft beer. In writing this book, Chapman and Brunsma have done a tremendous service for anyone interested in beer, race, and American society.

I tend to attend a lot of regional conferences and, as a result, regularly find myself driving on Southern interstates—routes 81, 64, 77, 95, and 85 in particular. Over the years, I have developed a practice of documenting Southern material culture through buying bits of local flavor at different service station gift shops. By and large, I try to keep my personal politics out of these purchasing decisions and occasionally even delight in unsettling racial expectations by selecting something that, for a black academic, may seem out of character. For instance, a few weeks ago, I bought a beautiful red trucker's hat with a red American flag on it. It was likely a symbol of Red America but the hat was too beautiful not to buy.

A few years ago, in a service station just off Route 81 in Shenandoah County, Virginia, I found a cobalt blue T-shirt in the five-dollar rack reading, 'BEER, Helping White Men Dance Since 1863.' From the moment I saw the shirt, I wondered about the potentially racist connotations of its slogan. The year 1863 is unquestionably a monumental one in American racial history. The Emancipation Proclamation, freeing more than three-and-a-half million enslaved African-Americans, took effect on January 1, 1863. As one friend remarked, any effort to link emancipation with humor is suspect for that fact alone. Later that year, Union forces led by George Meade would defeat Robert E. Lee's Confederate Army in the Battle of Gettysburg—the largest single battle of the Civil War, which many historians regard as its decisive turning point. Despite these highly suggestive associations, and following several conversations with colleagues, friends, and students, I have still not arrived at a definitive position on how to read the T-shirt's humor. One measure might be the white store clerk's reaction when I showed up at the counter with it, along with five bucks to hand her: she swallowed her gum.

Ultimately, I have to credit the T-shirt designers (or slogan makers) for locating, what by my reading seems to be, the liminal space between the abhorrent history of racism in America and the encouraging notion that white dominion is not what it used to be—a situation that not all white men are happy about. However, beer apparently makes them happy. If the slogan on my T-shirt reflects an Alt-Right coded transcript, it is too hidden for this outsider to see. Once again, I am outed. Instead, I would like to believe that the association between 'BEER' and 'White Men' symbolizes the fleeting efforts, on the parts of some white people, to hold on to traditional spaces of white exclusivity and dominance. Such efforts can be conscious or unconscious. Rebel flag waving white supremacists are not the only ones invested in preserving white spaces in the interests of prosperity, privilege, and comfortableness. The most sociologically interesting questions concern how cultural fields like craft beer will constitute themselves around competing incentives to preserve the conveniences of exclusive whiteness or to pursue the generative but sometimes inconvenient possibilities of embracing inclusion, equity, and genuine cooperation, both across and within racial groups. These are the kinds of crucial questions that *Beer and Racism* takes on. Let us crack a beer together and enjoy our reading.

# Series Editor Preface

As I write this, cities across the US are lined with protesters seeking justice for what has continued to be a never-ending attack against blacks. This anti-blackness violence is not new, nor is it just about the murder of George Floyd by Minneapolis police officer Derek Chauvin, who placed his knee on Floyd's neck, while Floyd was handcuffed and lying face down on a city street, for 8 minutes and 42 seconds. Nor is it just about the murder of Breonna Taylor, who was gunned down while sleeping in her apartment by plainclothes police officers on the southside of Louisville, KY. Rather, what we are witnessing is yet another moment in history where people are fed up. It is not enough to sit idly by and demand (hope for) justice; peaceful protests and the calls for civility are often used by whites (and their supporters) to quell public unrest—an acknowledgment that some lives are worth more than others. Racism and anti-blackness are real in America, and not figments of our imagination. Nor are they relegated to one political party over another, unique to one institution over another, or just the seeds of a few bad apples. Racism and anti-blackness are systemic. As sociologist Eduardo Bonilla-Silva has argued, we live in a racialized social system in which privileges are afforded to some over others, and in which our very institutions are racialized (and gendered, etc.) and work to maintain the current racial order. Yet, the world is not that simple, still. We are governed by intersecting and global systems of oppression. Late political scientist Cedric Robinson, expanding on the profound works of sociologist Oliver Cromwell Cox, warned us of the dangers of an evolving system of oppression that would be dependent on violence, racism, imperialism, and so forth. Racial capitalism is saturated in our society and our culture; it informs us of who belongs and who might tag along so long as they do not disrupt the current social and racial order. Some would argue that the COVID-19 pandemic is a result of racial capitalism.[1] Certainly, we have clear data that the disease has overwhelmingly affected folx of color more so, and in ways that differ from their white counterparts. The point is that while we give lip-service to diversity or how much we care about diversity, the truth is we are a nation that continues to be divided. As I mentioned in the inaugural book, the aim of the *Sociology of Diversity* series is to interrogate the contradictions of diversity and inclusion as they are currently manifested in our social institutions and everyday lives. Books in this series equip and challenge the reader to think critically about racism, sexism, ableism, or other persistent inequalities and their interactions, connections, and embeddedness within our society, institutions, and culture.

Professors Nathaniel Chapman and David L. Brunsma do just this. Their book, *Beer and Racism: How Beer Became White, Why It Matters and the Movement to Change It*, the second published book in the *Sociology of Diversity* series, is a tour de force that upends many questions about the craft beer industry and its historical (and current) role in fueling white America. While there have been other scholarly books written on the beer industry, this is the first of its kind—one that offers deep and critical analysis not about who is allowed to purchase beer, but the racialization and culture of the beer industry. In this book, Chapman and Brunsma, in seven chapters, present a sociohistorical testament that uncovers the whiteness of beer, and its impact in shaping American culture in society as well as in institutions such as media, business (bars, restaurants, etc.). Further, this is not just a book about beer, the beverage of choice for millions of Americans. Chapman and Brunsma take the reader through a journey that uncovers how whiteness and racism have operated and continue to operate in all aspects of the beer industry, from origin stories and myths, to the three-tiered distribution system, to the process of becoming a brewer, to production, consumerism, and more. Most importantly, the authors weave their research through the framework of critical diversity, illustrating time and time again the need to challenge whiteness, racism, and the oft thrown about notions of diversity itself.

*David G. Embrick*
University of Connecticut

## Note

1 See: Whitney, N. Laster Pirtle (2020) 'Racial capitalism: a fundamental cause of novel coronavirus (COVID-19) pandemic inequities in the United States,' *Health Education & Behavior*. Available at: https://doi.org/10.1177/1090198120922942.

# 1

# Brewing Up Race

## The whiteness of craft beer in the US

Take a look around: at your local grocery store; the posts on your friends' social media; one of your favorite restaurants; the advertisements posted around you; fueling up at the gas station; watching an international soccer tournament; or a friendly drive down a main street of your town or city. Beer, more particularly, craft beer, is everywhere. There are more breweries in operation now than at any other time in the history of the US—with the vast majority of these operating as local microbreweries (60.7 per cent) and brewpubs (34.8 per cent) (Brewers Association, 2019a). The beer produced by the almost 8,000 total US breweries is distributing to a broader spectrum of outlets than ever before (NBWA, 2019a). Ultimately, the consumption of beer and craft beer is at an all-time high, capturing some 49 per cent of alcohol consumption, with the proportion of craft beer consumption growing the fastest within total beer consumption (BI, 2019). Craft beer has centrally established itself within the US brewing landscape within a fairly short period of time and is becoming an interwoven aspect of social, cultural, economic, and political life—much like beer, brewing, and drinking was at earlier points in US history.

The contemporary landscape of brewing is one of: beer tastings at your local grocery store; beer festivals throughout the year; an increase of homebrewers, homebrewing clubs, and homebrewing competitions; beer trading; online craft beer social media; breweriana collectors and the rise of beer history tours and museum collections; the building of new breweries, brewpubs, and gastropubs in the development of neighborhoods; collaborations between musicians and brewers; online beer, brewing, and beer culture discussion groups; local and regional beer tours; an increase in the gastronomy and culinary import of craft beer and food pairings; family-friendly beer spaces; and an increasing presence in colleges and universities through fermentation science programs. Craft beer seemingly provides so much more than just variety in the experience of consuming this historic beverage—it is now becoming woven into the fabric of the lives of Americans—yet, this has always been the case. Indeed, as the pioneers of craft beer have helped craft beer carve out its space within the US brewing industry, its reach into the everyday lives of Americans is becoming something of sociological interest.

Whether one is a casual observer of the craft beer industry (the beers, the increased reach, the increase space on grocery shelves, and so on), craft beer spaces (the local microbrewery or beer festival, the guest lecture at the library, the posts on your Instagram feed, and so on), or craft beer culture (the advertising, the iconography, the labels, and so on), or whether one is a craft beer aficionado (a 'beer nerd'), who attends the festivals, who 'checks in' and 'rates' each and every beer they try on Untapped, who 'cellars' beers in their basement, who frequents their local bottle shop (or who drives 30 minutes to the closest one), who frequents the local breweries when they are vacationing in a new town or city, or who, perhaps, dabbles (or excels) in homebrewing, one cannot help but notice one central image: the bearded white man. This image has become so ubiquitous that Anheuser Busch (now AB-Imbev) used the trope in commercials making fun of craft beer and craft drinkers. Put another way, beer, particularly craft beer, seems fundamentally brewed by, owned by, catered to, distributed by (and to), invested in by, advertised to, bought by, discussed by, and consumed by white men. By extension, it appears that craft beer, its industry, its sales force, its consumers, its celebrations, its heroes, its stories, its spaces and places, perhaps even its very identity is white and male. It does not take a sociologically trained eye to note that craft beer is a predominantly white and male phenomenon. However, it might take a sociological lens to understand why this is the case, why it matters, and what might be done about it. This is the goal of *Beer and Racism*.

In December 2015, food and drink blogger Dave Infante asked the question 'Why is craft beer … so white?' in his *Thrillist* article 'There are almost no black people in craft beer. Here's why' (Infante, 2015). This article came across our desks as one of us had just finished his dissertation on the rise of craft beer in the US (Chapman, 2015) and the other one of us (Brunsma) had just finished his first year editing the journal he co-founded, *Sociology of Race and Ethnicity*. Infante asked a question that we had asked each other many, many times before as we—the craft beer lovers that we are—explored the various virtual and literal spaces of its culture of consumption, and as we—at the same time, as trained scholars who cannot but help to be critical of our own experiences—looked through our critical lenses and scratched our heads at the obvious, in-your-face, whiteness (and hetero-masculinity) of the scene. As sociologists trained to see the ways in which what appears as 'normal' is not at all normal, but an accomplishment, trained to see the ways in which social inequality structures everyday existence (including the beer that we drink), and trained to always 'make the familiar strange' and the 'invisible visible,' we asked critical questions, just like Infante's article. In his 'call-out' article, Infante called out craft beer's production and consumer culture for its whiteness, and identified some basics with the limited data he had: the industry has always been white, being underwritten by racism and racial discrimination, and the difficulty for racialized minorities to get loans. He is certainly right about these (and, of course, the comments from readers in the comments section provide very useful insights into the issue, as well as into the ways in which race, racism, and beer are structurally, ideologically, and culturally intertwined and wrapped up with the identities, experiences, and meanings of whiteness). However, there is a much fuller story to tell here in order to understand the whiteness of craft beer.

In *Beer and Racism*, we hope to dig much deeper with an interdisciplinary and critical lens into this seemingly basic question of the whiteness of craft beer. When one looks at the deep history of beer and its origin stories in the 'new world,' when one asks critical questions about the country that race and racism built and beer's role in that process, when one understands the relationship between temperance, Prohibition, capitalism, imperialism, and whiteness in the building of the racial state, when one digs into the social structure of becoming a brewer in the US historically and contemporarily, when one looks at the exploitation of racialized minorities within and by the brewing industry in the US, and when one assesses the meanings of and experiences within the spaces of craft beer production, distribution, and consumption, then one realizes that beer in the US has always been bound up with race, racism, and the construction of white institutions and identities. Given the very quick and meteoric rise of the craft beer industry, especially in the US, as well as the myopic scholarly focus on economic and historical trends in the industry, there is an urgent need to take stock of the intersectional inequalities that such realities gloss over. This book will carve a much-needed critical and interdisciplinary path to examine and understand the racial dynamics in the craft beer industry and the popular consumption of its primary product: beer.

As the craft beer industry continues to grow, questions about the racial dynamics within the craft beer industry and culture will continue to become more salient.

## The social object of beer

Beer is basically water, grain, yeast, and, hops. Perhaps. One cannot think about beer without thinking about these ingredients and how they come together, chemically, to produce it. One would not want to drink a beer that was made from milk, or one that was yeastless, or even one that had no grain fermentables in the mix because it would not be legible as beer. Beer *is*, then, because those basic ingredients *are*. Alter the ingredients, the chemical context, and alter the beer. To some, beer is the beverage of choice after a long day at work. To others, it is something to be meticulously pondered over and to be enamored with, to analyze and scrutinize, and to enjoy and savor. At the heart of beer lies four basic ingredients: water, grain, yeast and hops. As a material object, a prepared drink, perhaps this is all one needs to know to understand it. That is all. But is it? While beer may simply be a way to relax, a means to a numbing of the self and life's problems, a beverage to be enjoyed at dinner, or a bottle shared with friends, it is much more complex than that.

Beer is not just a material object; it is a historical, social, cultural, political, and economic object—an 'occasion of symbolism' (Bennett and Ames, 1985: xv). Furthermore, beer has been (and remains) quite important in the human experience: understanding beer is important in the understanding of ourselves, who we are, and who we can become. Beer itself also comes in a wide variety of profiles, as do those who drink the storied beverage. While the craft beer revolution in the US began to make its climb in the 1980s, there have always been brewers of this concoction, for centuries, millennia even. The distinction between craft beer now and at the dawn of the craft beer movement, as well as the social and cultural implications of the distinction, have grown increasingly more complex and sociologically fascinating. Some look at craft beer with disdain; others celebrate its every variance. Some would not want to drink a beer without its basic ingredients because it would be rendered somewhat unintelligible as a culinary object; others might not care. Either position has the potential to detach beer from its historical, social, cultural, political, and economic contexts, and, in doing so, increase the potential of not fully understanding beer. There is an ever-present risk of misunderstanding beer, and, as such, the story of beer, brewing beer, and brewers, as well as of those who distribute, market, and consume it. Ultimately, beer is a social and cultural product because of the shape of the social, cultural, political, and economic context that is structured in particular ways, at particular times, and in particular locations. Capitalism has been the defining context for beer in the US. Beer and brewing have shaped US capitalism and its relations to its production, and US capitalism has shaped beer and brewing.

The story of beer, especially in the context of the US, is as dizzyingly rich and complex as some of the craft beers that are currently being made at the apex of the craft beer revolution in the US (for example, consider Funky Bhudda's brew Morning Wood, a whiskey barrel-aged, imperial maple bacon coffee porter). However, very few of the prominent histories of US beer and brewing, very few of the leading beer periodicals and online blogs, very little of the emerging academic and scholarly attempts to theorize and understand beer and brewing in the US, and certainly very few industry analysts have attempted to fully understand, theorize, or engage with the importance of race, racism, and racial inequality in the story of beer and brewing in the US. In the American project, racialized (as well as gendered) capitalism (read: white supremacy) has been the dominant project. Like other cultural products, beer was not immune to this, nor was racialized capitalism detached from beer and brewing. Thus, one must engage with such marginalized stories and histories to answer the fundamental question at the core of this book: why are beer, brewing, and the attendant industries and structures of beer and brewing so white?

In investigating the sociological object that is craft beer, we are necessarily enmeshed in the structures that shape our relationship with that object of beer and the relationships that are solidified, legitimized, and encouraged as one engages with that object. This means that one cannot walk down the historical, political, cultural, and often mythological, imagined, and manipulated path of beer, brewing, and craft beer without also having honest conversations along the way with experiences of racial inequality, exclusion, and outright exploitation, as well as listening to the stories of ideas stolen, dreams deferred, and potential unfulfilled. We must make the turn from the material object of beer, the logistical practice of brewing it, and the simple act of imbibing it, to thinking hard about the relationship structures that make those things happen and make them meaningful, and the shape of those relationships across class, gender, sexuality, and, for our primary purposes in this book, racial lines. Acknowledging these relational realities within which beer, brewing, and the craft beer culture are fundamentally embedded will allow us to be more able to talk about the whiteness of beer, why it matters, and why one should work to change such structures surrounding the material culture that is craft beer—where material culture is concerned 'with the relationship between artefacts and social relations [with] aims to systematically explore the linkage between the construction of social identities and the production and use of culture' (*Journal of Material Culture*, 2019). Indeed, as we will see later in the book, many of the individuals we talked to in researching beer and racism are indeed at the front lines of crafting the new narratives and new realities of craft beer, which are centrally responding to the core arguments of this book: that the old narratives and realities of beer have, continue, and will portend a future that rests firmly on the racialized realities of beer and brewing. In order to even begin to understand what is going on here, one needs some kind of way to anchor oneself and to provide a set of frames with which to read the dizzying array of debates, the varying data trend lines, and the myriad and often conflicting histories and narratives that are swirling in the fermenter that is the structure and culture of beer in the US.

## The quest for answers: racism, whiteness, production, and resistance

While one can start with assumptions about beer, brewing, and its attendant cultures that are derived from its various imagined communities and surrounding mythos—as bringing people together, as the location of sociability, as common symbol and sustenance, as local and national identity, as greasing the wheels of interaction, as opportunity, as community-building, and as bringing people together—such starting points and the origin myths that they are embedded in will not get us very far in understanding the realities of beer production, distribution, and consumption in the US, and even less far in understanding the craft beer revolution, which may have been part of the solidification of white dominance after the Civil Rights Act 1964. As such, in order to understand our central question—'Why is beer, in particular, craft beer, so white?'—we must start with the realities of the classed, gendered, and fundamentally racialized social structure that has served (and continues to serve) as an organizing principle in the US upon which all other institutions and interaction orders are built and sustained. Additionally, along this path, one must engage with critical notions of whiteness—as structure, as an ideology, and as identity—in order to have a fighting chance at understanding the real story of craft beer's whiteness. It is our contention that readers must have a fairly solid grounding in the sociological and cultural understanding of how cultural products (including beer) emerge and gain social, political, economic, and cultural currency; thus, the production of culture perspective is key. Finally, critical understanding of the importance of diversity and inclusion in historically (as well as contemporary) exclusionary industries is key to why all of this ultimately matters for craft beer and its future. Therefore, since knowledge is built through struggling with the lenses we use (or use us), the following are our guiding theoretical perspectives.

## *Race and the founding of the US*

In order to think through the whiteness of beer and brewing, our analytic vantage point begins with the sober and deeply evidenced recognition that the arc of history in the US was launched from a position of white domination through the establishment of three prominent white settler colonies (Glenn, 2015)—British, French, and Spanish—where white personhood, authority, placemaking, and governance shaped the blueprint for white supremacy (Coates et al, 2017). White supremacy is 'a political system, a particular power structure of formal or informal rule, socioeconomic privilege, and norms for the differential distribution of material wealth and opportunities, benefits and burdens, rights and duties' (Mills, 1997: 3), as well as a racialized social structure (Bonilla-Silva, 1997) that benefits its central beneficiaries—white people—in the 'maintenance of, and acquiescence in, racialized hierarchies governing resource distribution' (Gunier, 2004: 98). Underwritten by a white God and narrated by a collective white belief in their own superiority through such early ideological tools as the Great Chain of Being (see Mills, 1997; Zuberi, 2001), all other ethnic groups that the early state encountered were either exploited, enslaved, killed, or dispossessed of their land, culture, and dignity so as to bolster white social, political, economic, and cultural structures of domination. The US was and continues to be a society structured by white supremacy, with the idea of race taking central stage and the realities of racism maintaining the racial status quo. Thus, in this society, brewing beer has always been and continues to be part and parcel of both reproducing (and resisting) this over 400-year-old racial project.

In addition to straight-up violent exclusion, white people secured a privileged place in society by embedding their tastes, norms, and practices into the culture, policies, and operating procedures of US organizations and institutions (Bonilla-Silva et al, 2006; Feagin,

2013). Indeed, sociologists and race scholars across a wide swath of disciplines have shown the role of institutions in shaping the racialized social structure of the US. Such work reveals how white supremacist institutions develop white supremacist structures and identities to maintain a system whereby its primary constituents (that is, white people) are privileged, and therefore collectively and individually complicit in that privilege. This institutionalization of white norms and practices buttresses white power by positioning white norms and practices as normal and objective (Doane and Bonilla-Silva, 2003). In this way, the white structuring of institutional life becomes hegemonic and thus mostly invisible to white people and people of color (Jackman, 1994). The consequence is that few people question or challenge the institutional policies and practices that benefit white people and disadvantage people of color, including historical and contemporary brewers, beer distributors, and consumers.

In this book, we keep in mind that under white supremacy, the state provides the scaffolding that supports white life, white community, white mobility, and white stories, which thereby perpetuates the rhetoric and reality of white superiority. Thus, in a departure from McIntosh (1988), we argue that white privilege has been 'earned' by white people via the pursuit of hundreds of years of violent and exclusionary policies designed to uplift white people and subjugate and exploit people deemed 'non-white.' Perhaps the same goes for beer and brewing in the US—a matrix of social inequalities coming together through a combination of exploitation and opportunity hoarding, enacting a kind of social closure that has excluded and continues to exclude minority participation in institutional and organizational life in the US. In questioning the whiteness of brewing and beer in US society, one would do well to consider the structures and practices of white opportunity hoarding as a key process in perpetuating racial privilege in society. By 'opportunity hoarding,' we mean the process by which a dominant social group—in this case, white people—work to gain, and ultimately acquire, near-to-exclusive access to valuable social goods and resources, and then in an effort to maintain the value of those resources, bar people of color from accessing said resources, thereby limiting their social mobility (Weber, 1978 [1968]; Tilly, 1998). Importantly, taking a perspective of social closure illuminates the inner workings of everyday opportunity hoarding as explicit intra-racial favoritism of white people for white people, instead of assuming a phenomenon of interracial discrimination. Thus, discrimination is not only based on protecting resources and opportunities, but also about maintaining status distinctions between groups (Stainback and Tomaskovic-Devey, 2012).

### *Racial ideology and the boundaries of Americanity: whiteness, white space, and belonging*

Sociological theory and the sociological method are well suited to interrogating norms and normative structures—the socio-cognitive-affective animating element of all social life. Norms are the blueprints, expectations, assumptions, and unwritten rules guiding social interactions, the building blocks of our identities, and the glue that holds societies, their institutions, and their organizations together. Sociologists of race and ethnicity, who take the aforementioned centrality of white supremacy as the starting point, excel at this inquiry as they place whiteness firmly at the normative center. This means that whiteness and its central constituents—white people—represent the unquestioned norm, the implicit bias/preference, the conceptual (and even linguistic) starting point, and the set of practices and cultural understandings that reign and support the structure of white supremacy. Perhaps, it would whisper, legitimate craft beer is produced by, distributed by, and consumed by white people. Whiteness is also about identity and belonging, and such identity work and boundary policing takes place within white spaces, which bolster white institutions and, ultimately, white supremacy. Far from 'name calling' and/or calling out all 'white people' as immediately to blame, sociologists of race and ethnicity are 'system calling' and ask us to understand the system of whiteness under white supremacy, as well as the myriad ways in which 'whiteness' has opened its doors to some and closed them to others—even those who may 'look white' (for example, German immigrant brewers).

The history of race, racism, and racial inequality is the history of the development of, maintenance of, and rationalization of white identities and white spaces; this is an everyday reality for people of color who navigate various white spaces. In the US, black scholars, indigenous scholars, and Chicano scholars—as well as poets, musicians, novelists, and so on—have articulated the realities of navigating the white space, whether that be in the white space of the white imagination (Morrison, 1993), white logic (Zuberi and Bonilla-Silva, 2008), white epistemologies/ignorance (Mills, 2007), or white affect (Matias, 2016) across a number of institutional arenas, including government (Feagin, 2012), media (Daniels, 2013), education (Leonardo, 2009), law (Moore, 2007), history

(Ladson-Billings, 2003), labor (Roediger, 1999), and family (Collins, 1998), to name but a few. Ethnographers have detailed the notions of white space as both socio-historical place, interactional space, and also perceptual space (Anderson, 2015). Although Anderson comes very close to a more cohesive understanding of the cultural pillar that is white space (and its counterpart: the iconic ghetto), whiteness has haunted (Gordon, 2008) cognition, identity (Rockquemore and Brunsma, 2007), interactions (Itzigsohn and Brown, 2015), institutions (Ray, 2019), and knowledge production (Mills, 1997).

Beer and brewing, particularly craft beer and brewing, has been and is largely a white space. In many ways, Wendy Moore's (2007) *Reproducing Racism* was one of the first sociological attempts to define and theorize the white space. In her important analysis of a crucial institution in all things racial—the law (white supremacy's moral code [see Jacobson, 1999]) and law schools (the training ground for, largely, white people to uphold, legitimately, such a code)—she theorizes both the institution (law), the organization (law school), and the practices as white spaces. The reality of race in the US is segregation and the creation and maintenance of white space. Racial segregation is politically, socially, legally, and economically upheld under white supremacy. It structures and determines the distribution of resources and opportunities. Racial segregation and white supremacy *constitute* the cultural soul of America (DuBois, 1903). Segregation, Moore (2007: 25) notes, serves as a central organizing principle of institutional racism as 'racist relations can be reproduced without individuals' intentional racist acts because racism is deeply entrenched within our institutions.' These arguments underpin her, as well as our, understanding of the logic of white space in brewing. In a white supremacist society, whiteness is the organizational logic of social, cultural, and economic institutions, social relationships, and social identities. Nowhere is the structure of whiteness and white domination more evident in all its manifestations than in interactional spaces, where institutions parameterize interaction, where identities are deployed and accomplished in interaction, and where meaning through our behaviors is the glue that holds these spaces together. Through processes of normalization, that is, through a particular matrix of assumptions, it is in such spaces—white spaces—that the interactional work is done to accomplish whiteness and its counterpart: racial exclusion.

Scholars have investigated numerous white spaces over the past several decades, though not always with a fully theorized and critical notion of white space. Research on the structure and functioning of white spaces can be seen in scholarship that has investigated sport

(Carrington, 2013), suburban schools (Lewis, 2003) and historically and predominantly white colleges and universities (Brunsma et al, 2013), electronic dance music (Brunsma et al, 2016; Motl, 2018), the craft beer industry (Withers, 2017), architecture (Kaplan, 2006), and other predominantly white fields, as well as the cultural fields of classical music (Yoshihara, 2007), gaming (Gray, 2014), art (Bowles, 2001), and the culinary world (Slocum, 2011), to name but a few. In this book, we use this lens of whiteness and white space to trace the history and contemporary realities of beer and brewing in the US as it is linked to even very central notions like 'Who is an American?' As such, it is about so much more than a legal process; rather, it is about identity, ideology, property, ownership, legitimacy, and so much more—all weighted at the center by whiteness. As we approach over 8,000 breweries in 2019, craft beer has a kind of historical, cultural, economic, and political amnesia about the role of race and racism in its industry. We seek to begin telling that story here.

### *Production of (beer as) culture*

In addition to polishing our lenses to center racism and whiteness, we are working with another analytic tool at our disposal: the production of culture perspective (Peterson, 1990; Peterson and Anand, 2004). This perspective is instrumental in understanding how the production of cultural products (like beer), the shape of those cultural products, and the structure of the dissemination of those cultural products occur within a given society. Developed by Richard Peterson, the production of culture perspective has, over decades, theoretically developed six factors that help sociologists understand and explain the production of cultural products: law, technology, industry structure, organizational structure, occupational careers, and markets. Such a perspective adopts a macro-level approach in order to examine how such social structures produce culture, including beer-as-cultural-product and beer-as-culture. The instructive case that Peterson uses to develop his approach is the emergence of rock and roll in the 1950s. In that now-classic article, he clearly shows how the six facets of law, technology, industry structure, organizational structure, occupational careers, and markets led to the advent of rock and roll in 1955 (Peterson, 1990), when consumers' tastes were changing and thus, in conjunction with the six facets, a new musical genre and an entire culture surrounding this music were created. This perspective provides an instructive key to unlocking the whiteness of beer and the six facets are important to consider when trying to grapple with the questions raised by this book.

First, laws and regulations can greatly constrain (or stimulate) the production of culture. Consider the effects of copyright law on the production of rap music in the 1990s as a parallel to the changes in US brewing. Over the course of US brewing history, there have been numerous laws that have significantly affected the production and consumption of alcoholic beverages. The second aspect of importance here is industry structure—the structural relationship between the degrees of oligopolistic control (a small set of firms that control the price, quantity, quality, and style of their cultural goods) and the levels of vertical and horizontal integration (Peterson, 1990). The constraining effects of industry structure can be seen as limiting and shaping the tastes of consumers through the promotion of homogeneous (or diverse) products. Third, a consideration of organizational structure—the number of decision levels, the specialization of tasks, and the level of vertical integration—is also important. Organizational structure can constrain the production of craft beer in ways similar to the production of popular music. The DIY nature of homebrewing is similar to the production of digital music in the home. Fourth, Peterson (1982) asks us to consider the importance of markets, where markets are the producer's perception of an audience's taste, resulting in the production of goods to be constrained in ways that reflect what is popular. Large macro-breweries helped to shape the tastes of Americans by predicting that we all wanted to drink beer and be healthy (for example, light beer), and that craft beer exists as a culturally produced alternative that strives for diversity in products. Fifth, the importance of technology cannot be underestimated. Technological advances and innovation have shaped the cultural products that we consume in many ways—advancements in brewing technology have increased the production of beer and craft beer in the US to achieve the same goals: increase audience, increase marketability, and increase profitability. Finally, Peterson (1982: 148) suggests that the 'ways that creative people define their occupations and organize their careers can influence the nature of the work they produce.' Thus, Peterson (1990) classifies occupational careers into four main groups—craftsman, showman, entrepreneur, and bureaucratic functionary—with each link in the structure influencing the cultural product produced, in this case, beer.

In general, the production of culture perspective will allow us to look carefully at the intertwined and changing relationships between law, technology, industry structure, organizational structure, occupational careers, and markets, and how these help us understand the emergence of craft beer in the US (an argument developed more fully in Chapter 3). This perspective has been used to explain a myriad of cultural phenomenon, from music (Peterson, 1990) and film (Platts, 2013), to food (Morris, 2013) and tattooing (Sanders and Vail, 2009), and has been a staple of the sociology of culture in the US sociological tradition. Although the perspective has been criticized largely for its lackluster integration of the consumer side of cultural products and their consumption/reception (Childress, 2017; Prior, 2011), it is also true that the approach has been 'race light' and less than critical in its engagement with the realities of intersectionality and deeply ingrained social inequalities in the functioning and shape of its very theoretical tools: law, technology, industry structure, organizational structure, occupational careers, and markets. Our analysis of the whiteness of beer and brewing will begin to remedy this theoretical shortcoming of an otherwise very powerful approach; indeed, others have argued that law is racialized (Moore, 2007), that technology hides racialized production (Benjamin, 2019), that institutions (Coates et al, 2017) and organizations (Ray, 2019) are racialized, that career paths are impacted by whiteness (Stainback and Tomaskovic-Devey, 2012), and that markets racially distribute their goods and services (Johnson et al, 2019). We see all happening in the story of craft beer.

### *Critical diversity and brewing*

'Diversity' is a buzzword now; laden with ideological weight, the center of most contemporary discussions of 'diversity' is the status quo of racism, racial inequality, whiteness, and the maintenance of white supremacy. Why? The short version is because diversifying an institution, in whichever institutional realm under discussion (for example, higher education, medicine, the House of Representatives, the brewing industry, and so on), more often than not leaves the structure of racialized opportunities, normative 'white frames' (Feagin, 2013), the historical and contemporary realities of discrimination and exclusion, and so much more that animates the racialized institution completely intact. This is akin to painting a deteriorating building, rather than rebuilding it through a completely inclusive community. Ultimately, it does not work to provide a better, more just, and equitable space for all. Our years of engaging with the brewing industry and craft beer culture leave us realizing the importance of more *critical diversities*.

Sociologists Cedric Herring and Loren Henderson (2012) provide the intellectual scaffolding for and theorization of a lens that also includes critical diversity as our study does. For them, 'a theory of critical diversity includes an analysis of exclusion, discrimination, and it challenges hegemonic notions of colorblindness and meritocracy'

(Herring and Henderson, 2012: 632). Therefore, while beer and brewing can (and should) seek the inclusion of those who have been excluded, seek investment in those who have been disinvested in, and seek the voices and experiences of those whose voices and experiences have been silenced, this will only be a starting point. For us, in this book, we wish to keep the theoretical lens of critical diversity as front and center as we can throughout in order to understand where we have been and portend a much more robust future for beer and brewing—particularly craft beer and brewing. In many ways, Herring and Henderson's (2012: 640) conclusion is our beginning:

> In short, we must work toward a critical diversity that is about inclusion and is necessarily linked to access, equity, parity, and opportunity. If we had critical diversity, there would be proportional representation of people from all groups (because it occurs when we get a true reflection of the talent pool available). Without linking diversity to such concerns, the usage of the term 'diversity' is hollow.

The frontiers of craft beer have indeed been pushed over the past 20 years, for example, the styles (largely from Europe, craft beer has indeed taken very old styles and reclaimed them while also creating completely new styles, such as New England Style and West Coast Style IPAs, Barrel-Aged Stouts, and Wild Ales), the ingredients (an increasing variety of hops and grains, as well as other non-traditional additives such as coffee, vanilla, and a host of other ingredients), the techniques (for example, barrel-aging), the marketing strategies, and so on. Yet, the frontiers have also plodded along largely familiar demographic paths, histories, and experiences, with consequences not only for the beer, but for its consumers and the culture that has bubbled up around all of this growth, spread, and development. Although there is a head of change in the pint, we are left wondering what the craft beer kaleidoscope would look like had it all been different, that is, had the true variety of diverse techniques, experiences, and histories of those whom craft beer (and beer writ large) actively marginalized, underdeveloped, and rendered invisible throughout US history been embraced.

There is a thread that runs through our theoretical scaffolding and motivating set of ideas in our inquiry into the whiteness of craft beer. The racialized social structure of the US has distributed opportunities differentially since the founding of the country to those deemed as 'other' and 'non-white.' This structure has been upheld by alliance to whiteness as a normative structure, as an ideology, and as a set of practices, tastes, categorizations, and assumptions. Furthermore, culture and cultural products are constructed through processes. As highlighted by the production of culture perspective, laws have been raced, technology has been raced, the contributions of minorities have been raced/erased, organizations are white, and so on. Ultimately, as racialized minorities push back and rewrite the reality that has been obscured by whiteness, what is necessary as a corrective is critical diversity.

## Contemporary patterns of beer and brewing: critical demographics

According to the Brewers Association (2019a), there are currently over 8,000 independent craft breweries operating in the US. Given that in order to be defined as 'craft,' a brewery must be small (no more than 6 million barrels of beer produced annually) and independent (maintaining at least 75 per cent ownership by craft producers), there is *a lot* of beer in the market. Since the initial craft beer boom of the early 1980s, the industry has grown to a 12.7 per cent market share of the total beer market (Brewers Association, 2018a). This translates to over 24 million barrels of beer produced, by over 8,000 breweries. These breweries produce a range of styles that reflect the changing tastes of craft consumers. But who exactly is the craft consumer? What do they look like? What is the social location of the craft drinker?

By and large, the craft beer drinker is white, male, age 21–34, college educated and middle class. The stereotypical image of the bearded hipster sipping a dark beer from a snifter glass is not far from the truth—a historically, socially produced truth. While studies have shown that women are increasingly drinking more and more craft beer (Chapman et al, 2018; Darwin, 2018), one factor remains constant: race. The craft beer drinker, whether man or woman, is overwhelmingly white. The Brewers Association reports that less than 2 per cent of craft drinkers are African-American—a fact that led to the proposal for this very book. Why do people of color not produce or drink craft beer? Furthermore, how are people of color excluded from craft beer and its attendant cultures? What are the mechanisms and structures that discourage marginalized groups from drinking craft beer? What is the historical context of this exclusion? In order to understand the racialization of craft beer, we must first look historically at the nature of whiteness and exclusion in the beer industry at large. Craft brewers and craft beer often symbolize progressive ideals, creativity, independence, and forward-thinking. If this is true, then why is the craft industry and culture exclusively white? In what ways are marginalized groups claiming a stake in the craft industry, creating their own culture, and being recognized as legitimate players in the craft game? What we currently know about the demographics of the making, distribution, and drinking of beer in the US context is telling.

In terms of craft beer consumers, a recent Nielsen report shows that the 'average weekly craft beer drinker is primarily male, between the ages of 21–44, and makes between $75,000 and $99,000 annually' (Kendall, 2019). The statistics demonstrate that, on average, the weekly craft beer drinker is male, younger, and makes a relatively higher income; however, less frequent craft beer drinkers are more diverse (Kendall, 2019). As chief economist for the Brewers Association, Bart Watson (2018) reports that 'changes in craft's demographics by race/ethnicity are less positive in recent years. Although data show a growth in minority craft drinkers in absolute terms, the changes over time show less movement in percentage terms.' According to 2015 Harris poll data, non-Hispanic white people constituted 86.3 per cent of craft drinkers, with 13.7 per cent coming from other races/ethnicities (Watson, 2018). In 2018, the white percentage dropped to 85.5 per cent and the percentage from other races/ethnicities increased to 14.5 per cent (Watson, 2018). However, as Watson (2018) suggests, when 'lining that up with the total population/craft drinker data, that means from 2015–2018, 81 per cent of new craft drinkers were white, and 19 per cent came from minority groups. Given that only 68.7 per cent of the 21+ US population is non-Hispanic white, that's not progress.' What these data suggest is that minority craft beer consumption is on the rise, but as Watson (2018) notes, 'only because the total population of craft drinkers is growing, not because craft drinkers are getting more diverse along racial lines.'

In order to assess the state of diversity in terms of employment in the industry, the Brewers Association conducted its 'Brewery Operations Benchmarking Survey,' of which Craft Beer Program Director Julia Herz (2019) stated, 'anyone scanning it will conclude there is work to be done, and we as a craft beer community can do better.' Prior to the completion of the survey, the Brewers Association had not collected any data about diversity in the craft beer industry. When reviewing the data at the annual industry conference, Watson suggested that 'the data show that similar to craft consumers, brewery employees are disproportionately white relative to both the general US population and where breweries are located' (quoted in Herz, 2019). According to data from the 2016 Craft Brewers Conference, Herz (2016) reports:

> With 120,000+ full- and part-time jobs actually tied to the craft brewing community, take into account the 1,700 brewpubs, and you have a totally different group. As of 2015, 78.5 percent of legal drinking-age adults lived within 10 miles of a brewery. These adults, of varying race and gender, are the ones sourced for jobs at brewery taprooms and brewpubs.

Since the conference in 2016, the Brewers Association has taken several steps toward making the industry more diverse and inclusive. These steps include: the formation of the Brewers Association Diversity Committee; updating the Marketing and Advertising Code to 'provide standards on inclusive beer advertising and marketing'; hiring the first ever diversity ambassador; developing social media campaigns to highlight diversity in the industry; creating the Diversity Event Grant Program to 'fund local and regional events that intentionally promote and foster a more diverse and inclusive craft beer community'; publishing a series of best practices to help businesses diversify; and collecting data on the state of diversity in the industry (Herz, 2019). Additionally, Brewers Association Diversity Ambassador Dr J. Nikol Beckham points to three key ways in which craft breweries can advance their diversity:

> Identify and address unconscious bias that may exist within yourself and your team, give people an anchor they can relate to by hiring a diverse set of staff and attracting a diverse set of customers, make sure everyone feels invited and welcome at your brewery and make sure everyone has a 'comparable experience.' (Quoted in Herz, 2019)

While these are certainly much-needed steps in the right direction, Watson (2018) notes that 'there is clearly work to be done in marketing the amazing beers and brands of small and independent brewers to different communities across the US. I won't pretend to have the answers as to how.' Herz (2016) also contends that 'it's fair to want beer to represent our diverse population in an equal manner. We need to do a better job of attracting a diverse group of consumers, community employees, and owners. Always.' In many ways, the purpose of this book is to do just that: to find answers as to how to make the industry and its culture more diverse. Certainly, the steps that the Brewers Association has taken are in the right direction; however, more needs to be done. A clearer understanding of the racialized structures and mechanisms within the industry needs to be brought to light. We hope to walk a bit further down that analytic path in *Beer and Racism*.

## A note on craft

With the recent rise in craft consumption (see Campbell, 2005; Ocejo, 2017), it is useful to better understand the term 'craft' and how it functions. In Becker's (1982: 862) view, craft conveys a:

> [Shorthand] conception of a distinctive way of organizing work: the characteristic activities that make up the work, the typical settings in which it is done, and the cast of characters with whom one usually associates while doing it, the kinds of people who do it, their typical careers, the problems that ordinarily arise, and the moral evaluations those inside and outside the occupation make of the people and activities which compose it.

Becker is suggesting that the idea of craft encompasses not only the actions involved, but also the processes, the individuals, and the aesthetic discourse involved with any given craft product. Kritzer (2007: 323) offers a more simplified 'folk' definition of craft as 'a body of knowledge and skill which can be used to produce useful objects.' According to Campbell (2005: 23): 'the term "craft" is used to refer to consumption activity in which the "product" concerned is essentially both "made and designed by the same person" and to which the consumer typically brings skill, knowledge, judgement and passion while being motivated by a desire for self-expression.' Furthermore, Campbell (2005: 23) suggests, the craft consumer is typically a person with 'both wealth and cultural capital.' One thing that these definitions have in common is an emphasis on knowledge, both in the production of craft goods and in the consumption of craft products. As we will argue, black people and other racialized minorities have been structurally and actively excluded from the production, distribution, and consumption of craft beer. We contend that social and cultural capital are vital to the development of cultural tastes as it relates to craft beer, the exposure to craft beer, homebrewing and other pathways into the industry, and the success of interactions in craft beer and white spaces.

In terms of beer, the definition of craft has shifted and morphed over the long arc of brewing history in the US. Indeed, the earliest brewers on the continent were craft brewers, with the DIY nature of brewing, the small batches, and the experimentation (much of it lost to the sands of time—or inequality—though some are recovering those craft recipes now [for an example see www.lostlagers.com]). The shifting nature of 'craft' is deeply embedded within the economics, politics, and culture surrounding beer. Founded in 1978, the Brewers Association (2019b), whose purpose is 'to promote and protect American craft brewers, their beers, and the community of brewing enthusiasts,' acts as the governing body of craft beer. According to their website:

> The Brewers Association is a 501(c)(6) not-for-profit trade association. The association is an organization of brewers, for brewers and by brewers. More than 5,264 US brewery members and 46,000 members of the American Homebrewers Association are joined by members of the allied trade, beer wholesalers, retailers, individuals, other associate members and the Brewers Association staff to make up the Brewers Association. (Brewers Association, 2019b)

In addition to providing resources for brewers, industry data and insight, marketing tools, education programs, and a host of other resources, the organization also defines what is considered to be a craft brewery and a craft brewer. The definition of 'craft' has changed as production has increased, breweries have been bought and sold, and innovative techniques have continued to push the boundaries of what beer can be. Early definitions of craft breweries required that they be 'traditional' in addition to being small and independent. This requirement meant that a craft brewery had to have a majority of its total beverage volume utilize traditional ingredients and techniques. The traditional requirement was recently dropped from the definition in order to allow breweries to produce other types of alcoholic beverages such as mead, wine, cider, and hard seltzer, as well as to allow for the use of new innovative ingredients and brewing techniques.

The most up-to-date definition simply defines a US craft brewer as small and independent. Currently, the Brewers Association classifies a brewery as small if its annual production does not exceed 6 million barrels of beer. This measure has shifted over time as larger producers such as the Boston Beer Company and Sierra Nevada Brewing Company—two of the longest-operating craft breweries, which are both owned by white people—have increased their production and distribution. Additionally, the classification of 'independent' has also shifted. Previous definitions allowed for a craft brewery to be 50 per cent owned by non-craft producers. For example, if Anheuser-Busch purchased half of Sierra Nevada, Sierra Nevada would still be considered to be craft beer. Now, the Brewers Association defines independent as less than 25 per cent of a brewery being owned by a non-craft entity. In order to further distinguish craft beer from domestic beer, the Brewers Association has created a logo that can be affixed to cans and bottles as part of the label. This logo—an upside-down beer bottle that reads 'Brewers Association Certified: Independent Craft'—is intended to steer consumers toward authentic craft breweries, rather than other 'craft-like' or faux-craft brands that may not be independently owned. Now that we have provided some context and outlined what this book is proposing to achieve, we will discuss our various methodologies and modes of inquiry as we seek to understand the racialization of beer.

## Methodologies

In this book, we bring together a variety of data sources and utilize varying methodologies in order to grapple with the central questions that motivate our work: 'Why is (craft) beer so white?'; 'Why does it matter?'; and 'What is being done to change it?' Our approach is an interwoven combination of several sources: reading across the wide variety of writings on beer, brewing, and (when possible) the role of marginalized groups in those processes; canvassing contemporary and historical industry reports and data across the three-tiered distribution system; semi-structured interviews with brewers, beer sales representatives, industry folks, marketing specialists, bottle-shop owners, social media influencers, beer and brewing historians, brewery owners, museum curators and breweriana specialists, and festival organizers; and our own experiences as craft beer aficionados and our ethnographic engagement in bars, festivals, brewing competitions, bottle shops, and other craft beer spaces over the past decade.

First, we dug as deeply as we could to uncover literature that would help us to contextualize the role of race, racism, and racialization in the story of beer and brewing in the history of the US back to the earliest settler colonial endeavors in North America (16th century), as well as even further back if possible to engage with indigenous ingredients, processes, and meanings associated with brewing. Such a search clarified a few basic things for us—the results of which show up in this book in bits and pieces. One thing became clear: the story of race and beer is fundamental to this place we now call the USA but the story is deeply complex—more complex than one book will be able to uncover. Such a search takes one down a dizzying array of processes related to race/racism/beer/brewing, including but most certainly not limited to: ownership, labor, social movements, gender, migration, slavery, identity, urban development, agricultural production, technology, record keeping, war, architecture, capitalism, taxation, political campaigns, violence, embodiment, and so on. We aim for the contours here. Another thing that was clarified is that there is actually very little focus on race, racism, racial inequality, or even marginalized groups (for example, Africans in the American context, indigenous peoples, Latinos, or even women) by those who have taken beer as their central passion and substantive focus, whether historian, journalist, beer critic, and so on, who have written the 'canon' of what we know about beer. This is unfortunate but instructive. As the old adage goes: 'Until lions have their own historians, tales of the hunt will always be told from the perspective of the hunter'—and so it is here. A fundamentality about the whiteness of beer (and craft beer) is that the stories have been told by white people, for white people, to uphold whiteness. The result is the invisibility of the stories that highlight the initiatives of (as well as the experiences of) racialized minorities in the US reality of beer and brewing. Some stories are buried deep, and even after our research, we realize that there are *many* stories that remain buried. This is a beginning of sorts to uncover the sociological importance of beer and race. We hope that others will keep searching with us as there has been very little research linking beer with race and racism.

Second, although there are important histories of pre-Prohibition brewing industry realities that help contextualize our central research questions, there is no doubt that the three-tiered distribution ushered in by Prohibition and its aftermath is key to understanding the sociological relationships that animate the brewing industry; as such, we engage with this system directly throughout the book. The national industry organizations that represent each of the tiers—the Brewers Association for the brewers, the Beer Institute for the producers, and the National Beer Wholesalers Association (NBWA) for the distributors—and other such key organizations, provide publicly released data and news releases, as well as the craft beer industry with its data. It is both deeply disturbing and not surprising that most of these organizations have not gathered data on race (that is, 'diversity') until very recently—in the case of the Brewers Association, not until 2018! Other industry mailers, listservs, and social media feeds offer a variety of reports, commentaries, debates, and insights into the contemporary issues facing craft beer and its consumers; however, even then, there is very little to do with race, though there are droplets of data that trickle out from time to time. One can also glean information from the US Bureau of Labor Statistics, the Homebrewers Association, various state industry watchdogs, and prominent periodicals like *All About Beer*, *Draft Magazine*, *The Beer Connoisseur*, and so on. We utilize such sources and their data throughout in understanding the relationship between craft beer and race.

Third, we had conversations with a wide variety of key informants for this project. These individuals ran the gamut from top-level national figures in the industry, highly influential social media personalities, and pioneering brewers of color, to local-level marketing and sales representatives, taproom bartenders, and bottle shop owners—and everything in between. Many discussions were informal and took place across a wide variety of craft beer spaces as we were constantly taking notes for this project. In addition, we conducted 15 semi-structured interviews with brewers, beer sales representatives, industry folks, marketing specialists, bottle shop owners, social media influencers, beer and brewing historians, brewery owners, museum curators and breweriana specialists, and festival organizers. These interviews covered a lot of terrain in each and every case. Among other things, the basic interview protocol we used (see Appendix A) asked about their experiences in the industry, their 'origin story' with regard to beer and brewing, what they felt people looked for in a beer, their view of the history of beer in the US, their understanding of how one becomes a brewer, a representative, and a consumer, why there are so few minorities and women in the industry, and the future of beer. Of course, we covered *so much more ground* outside of these basic questions. These data are central to this book. In total, we have 907 minutes (15 hours and 7 minutes) of interview material, with the interviews lasting between 20 minutes and an hour and a half. Appendix B gives a breakdown of our respondents. The majority of our respondents are male (58.8 per cent) and are much more racially diverse than the industry at large: 52.9 per cent (nine) African-Americans, 29.4 per cent (five) white people, and 11.8 per cent (two) Latinx. The interviews were audio-recorded, transcribed by Otter.ai, and cleaned and coded by us.

During the transcription-cleaning process, we wrote analytic memos for each interview. These memos were coded for large themes across the interview data, which were instrumental in organizing the flow of the book. Each interview was then coded for sub-themes and all respondents were given pseudonyms to protect their identities. It is interesting to note that much of the most exciting aspects of diversity in the craft beer industry have been happening in the past few years—literally as we have been reading, researching, and interviewing people for this project. Much of the things that have been happening in terms of 'diversifying' the craft beer industry and its attendant culture have been occurring through creating and hiring key new positions in several important structural locations within the industry (for example, the diversity ambassador of the Brewers Association), the development and successes of key beer festivals and collaborations (for example, Fresh Fest in Pittsburgh), the significant engagements of broader audiences through podcasts and social media influencers (for example, Ale Sharpton, who is a black male), and so much more. Indeed, some of our respondents are fundamental parts of this fast-paced critique of the industry and proactive building of new spaces and new narratives about brewers, drinkers, and craft beer fans of color, as well as women. To protect the identities of our respondents in order to give them free space to share their thoughts and theories regarding our questions, and to not give more of a platform to one or more of our respondents, we use pseudonyms. Where published or recorded publicly available materials exist online, social media, and so on, we have felt free to use their real names and their words.

Finally, our own experience as craft beer aficionados, and as white males, and our engagement in bars, festivals, brewing competitions, bottle shops, and other craft beer spaces over the past decade, cannot but figure centrally in the field notes that we took, the interview questions and proddings that we engaged with in the interviews, the way in which we read the industry data, and the way in which we engaged with beer writings and scholarship. Our positionality and experience matters.

## Overview of the book

The remainder of *Beer and Racism: How Beer Became White, Why It Matters, and the Movements to Change It* will proceed across six more chapters. Chapter 2, 'Racism, Brewing, and Drinking in US History,' integrates an overview of the deep history of beer in the US context, largely from 1587 until the end of Prohibition due to the data sources at our disposal. Along the way, we illuminate and critique the 'origin stories' of beer, uncovering some stories that have been long buried and asking questions that have not been adequately asked up until now. This deep history reveals some mythological stories as well as the old narratives that have served to cover up a full knowledge of race, racism, and beer, many of which the new narratives being pushed by contemporary brewers, beer lovers, and industry folks of color, though few and far between, continue to fight.

Chapter 3 focuses our analytic attention on the post-Prohibition era up until craft beer arises as a response. 'The Making of the (White) Craft Beer Industry' focuses readers on the historical and contemporary (re)construction of the craft beer response, largely through a critical look at the relationality of the three-tier distribution system and its structural and cultural linkages to race, racism, and racial exclusion in the industry as homebrewing arose (again) and craft was emerging. Additionally, we examine the role of actors at each level of the three-tier system in order to fully understand how exposure to craft beer through industry employment, marketing, and consumption contributes to and is the product of the racialization of beer. Our respondents helped us see the three-tier distribution system in a whole new light as it plays out on the ground to make and keep the craft beer industry and culture white.

In an innovative sociological look at the industry, Chapter 4 uses our interview data as well as the history and scholarship of brewing to lay out the social structure of becoming a brewer, a beer representative/distributor, and a consumer—the three parts of the three-tiered distribution system. Focusing on the first (brewer/producer) and last (consumer) tiers, 'The Paths to Becoming a Craft Brewer and Craft Beer Consumer' illustrates historical and contemporary stories that show the various and all fundamentally racialized economic, social, cultural, and regional paths to becoming a part of the beer and craft beer industry as a producer, a distributor, and a consumer.

Chapter 5 tackles a central problem when trying to understand the relationships between the beer industry and communities of color historically and contemporarily in the US: the role of representation, marketing, and cultural appropriation in the industry. From the earliest of advertisements, through boycotts of racist big beer families like Coors, through the exploitative marketing in the case of Malt Liquor, to contemporary iconography and cultural appropriation designed to sell products (manifest), as well as to exclude (latent) and racially target those who do not belong (read: minorities and women), 'Exposure, Marketing, and Access: Malt Liquor and the Racialization of Taste' works through the complicated politics of racist representations and cultural appropriation.

Echoing a powerful quote from Infante's (2015) respondents—'I like the beer, but I hate the culture'—Chapter 6, 'Gentrification and the Making of Craft Beer White Spaces,' takes a contemporary look at the ways in which craft beer has reshaped spaces, places, and cultures in the image of white people, whiteness, and white supremacy. In doing so, we examine the role of gentrification and craft beer's position as a signifier of gentrified neighborhoods. We then argue that these spaces become new places, embedded with new meanings, and come to represent 'white spaces.' From the local microbrewery, to the grocery store that carries craft selections, to the brewpub that just went up in a neighborhood, through many spaces of craft beer, this chapter interrogates these spaces, drawing heavily from our respondents and the extant iconography and descriptions of such spaces to do so.

Chapter 7, '#WeAreCraftBeer: Contemporary Movements to Change the Whiteness of Craft Beer,' will review the primary findings and arguments of the book, as well as look at the contemporary movements by mostly brewers and consumers of color to change the whiteness of craft beer and its culture. There have been several significant movements, most taking place on social media through various hashtags (for example, #newnarritive, #somethingisbrewing, and so on), largely, if not solely, led by people of color to educate, experience, expose, and enlighten (for example, Ale Sharpton) in order to attack the central organizing principles of the whiteness of craft beer so as to imagine and create a new future for the industry. This chapter looks at the contours of these new narratives initiated by the consumer side of the industry.

# 2

# Racism, Brewing, and Drinking in US History

'I think the innovation behind those 19th-century beer makers is really unparalleled. These were some serious entrepreneurs. And that's what I think I'm the most proud to learn about and to read about. The disappointing part is that that is our country's history. That's the reality of it. In the 19th century, we had the same anti-immigrant sentiments that, sadly, we have today. We have a lot of poverty; there are different socio-economic aspects and social issues that we encounter. The fact that I couldn't just walk into a bar in 1890 devastates me, but it was a different time, of course. I think it's all just sort of congruent with other things that we see in history.' (Karina, Latinx, female, curator/insider)

'I can't really count the number of brewers who got in touch with me [after my talk], and said, "Oh, my gosh, I've never thought about this." That there might have been a history of brewing that doesn't look like what they see every day. And because I think for some of us, it's so evident. How do you not think about it? But I think a lot of people just don't.' (Patricia, black, female, industry insider)

## American (beer's) origin stories and the making of the American (beer)

The search for the origins of beer and brewing in what would become the US has been hampered by the realities of the racial, gendered, and classed inequalities that created the US in the first place. A look at the classics of US beer history (for example, Baron,1962; Downard, 1980), as well as more contemporary restatements of said creation myths (for example, Acitelli, 2013; Erickson, 1987; Hindy, 2014; Mittleman, 2008; Ogle, 2006), the influential writings of renowned beer traveler and writer Michael Jackson (for example, his three volume *World Guide to Beer*, 1977, 1991, and 1997), and the renowned work of Charlie Papazian, highlights a story that focuses on similar places, similar names, and similar processes, and makes similar arguments. Such books build on each other, though largely only by adding the stories of the next generation of white men, whose activities both continue the white paths laid down in a society designed to support such trajectories and, in the process, solidify the white mythology of beer and brewing, erasing the experiences of women, the poor, and racialized minorities. These books dot the prominent eras of the brewing industry and its growth: the era of big beer (for example, Baron, 1962); the homebrewing era (for example, Downard, 1980); early craft brewing (for example, Erickson, 1987); and the steep rise of craft beer (for example, Acitelli, 2013; Hindy, 2014; Mittleman, 2008; Ogle, 2006). Nearly all of the books cite previous books to continue the story. Consistently and incrementally, previous histories and accounts continue to tell the white story of beer in the US, which further solidifies the mythology, creates and legitimizes the actors within the imagined community, and, in the process, creates the echo chamber and the story that contemporary white craft beer lives by. Just as different societies around the globe have socially constructed the cosmologies, mythologies, and origin stories that serve to organize social institutions and individual and community life experiences (Berger and Luckmann, 1991 [1967]; Zerubavel, 1993), so too has US beer crafted (pun intended) its own. Looking across a wide swath of these US beer history books illuminates the basic origin story.

Jack Erickson (1987), perhaps somewhat tongue in cheek, begins his origin story in *Star Spangled Beer: A Guide to America's New Microbreweries and Brew Pubs* with cavemen (of course) in a damp cave, where clay pots of grain are stored from the fall harvest and are soaked with moisture. The caveman takes a sip. It is soothing, especially after long hunts and meals, and he feels a relaxed, pleasant feeling. Now, they could likely tolerate their tribesmen a bit more—life was more bearable. They began setting such pots aside more regularly and, before long, they were planting additional crops in the summer to brew this beverage in the fall. It is unclear where this takes place, but it is clear that the story has a particular audience in mind—men, a certain kind of masculinity, and whiteness, which research shows that invocations of Neanderthals, cavemen, and so on have as their unmarked center (Sterling, 2015). Never mind the various African, Mesopotamian, Egyptian (almost always whitewashed [but see Geller, 1993]), Nubian, and Moorish fermentation techniques and ingredients that ethno-archaeologists have described (Arthur, 2014) and worked on since the early 1950s (Braidwood et al, 1953), and that form the bedrock of brewing as we can even know it. While the realities of Chinese (McGovern et al, 2004), Indian, Aboriginal, and the fundamental, global indigeneity of brewing alcoholic beverages are not spoken of (Moseley et al, 2005; Piperno et al, 2009), the books will sometimes mention Noah's ark (again, coded in white, Judeo-Christian, patriarchal traditions). Actually, most do not dig too deep historically, and when they do, we get these sorts of superficial, dismissive, and whitewashed accounts that serve to render invisible the deep roots and branches of humanity's brewing tradition. In our canvassing of these books, most of the authors move quickly to 'Western civilizations' in Europe, and then take yet another leap to '[b]rewing was a well developed process by the time of the first English colonial settlements in America in the early 17th century' (Downard, 1980: 1). Yet, it is unfair to single out Erickson's (1987) origin story, for his is simply emblematic of the basic pattern. The commonly accepted, but historically inaccurate, story generally goes something like the following.

Early colonists arrived in the 'New World' on ships. The ships would drop these folks off with what supplies remained. Upon arrival, those who were dropped off were left without brewing equipment, or the taverns and public houses that they were accustomed to. In general, the transportation of beer was a problem and particularly difficult across the Atlantic. Those in Virginia advertised for brewers to be sent as soon as possible. This was a long, hard time—beer would have made it bearable. Along comes Lord Delaware, the governor of Virginia, arriving with supplies and more settlers—though the sailors had drunk all the beer. Egad! There is some talk of trade with Indians. Meanwhile, the Mayflower weighs anchor in 1620—pilgrims from the Netherlands, supported by London. And beer was brought. And beer was consumed. Thank goodness! There was a thanksgiving in 1621 and Samoset taught the pilgrims how to brew with corn. Good but not great. Those who continued to venture to the New World were urged to bring malted barley. John Winthrop, so the story goes, brought 10,000 gallons of beer in 1629. Eventually, the colonists established their own taverns as they attempted to recreate the Old World within the New. By 1640, most households made beer from bread with a bit of wild hops. Brewhouses are quickly established across New England.

Captain Sedgwick is perhaps America's first commercial brewer in Old Boston. People drank a lot of beer. There were concerns of widespread public drunkenness. Sprinkle in healthy doses of George Washington, Samuel Adams, Thomas Jefferson, Patrick Henry, and Benjamin Franklin. The moral of the story: beer is as fundamental to the US as apple pie.

When read from another perspective, such a mythology serves a collective (perhaps collectively drunken) delusion. Such a mythological tale seems to uphold a particular view of the context of 16th-, 17th-, 18th-, and perhaps even 19th-century 'American' society, along with a particular view of the role of beer, brewing, and drinking cultures within early America. Along with these kinds of beer narratives come cultural assumptions about who can (legitimately—according to such a mythology) drink beer, what counts as 'real' beer, the role of beer in social, economic, cultural, and political life in a society, and so on. Are these the stories that beer enthusiasts, brewers, and others live by? What are the consequences of such a whitewashed version of the story of US beer? Who is left out? Why? What is covered up by the deluge of whiteness and patriarchy in such a narrative? And why? What are the consequences for our understanding of history in general and beer history in particular? Or for our understanding of how cultural products, such as beer, get utilized by those in power and by those who are powerless in society? These and many other questions bounce around our reading of the extant beer histories. While this book cannot answer all of these questions and has other important goals, this mythological tale of the 'beginning of it all in the US' matters as it sets a narrative path that, while countered since the creation of such a myth, opens doors of the possible for some and closes it for others, and encourages some while discouraging others. Such a historical context, rooted as it appears to be in myth, is still with us as it dictates the terms upon which marginalized others can enter the space and the work that they must do to craft new narratives and chart the future.

Such a mythological tale overlooks many important facts. As the first African slaves landed in Virginia in 1619, hops and barley were both important components of their labor (Graves, 2019) from the earliest days of agricultural production by the colonists in the New World. Indeed, 'The records of Thomas Jefferson, and his wife, Marth, provide more details. An avid and highly regarded home brewer, Marth Wayles Skelton Jefferson bought hops from Monticello's slaves. She bought hops from neighbors' slaves. She bought hops from slaves in Williamsburg' (Graves, 2019). Meanwhile, Carney and Rosomoff (2009: 58) quote 17th-century Dutch slave trader Willem Bosman describing the area of Lower Guinea and Africans on the Gold Coast of the slave trade:

> Here is also a third Sort of *Milhio*, like the last [millet]. … Its Grain is reddish, and must continue in the Ground seven or eight Months before it is full ripe. This is not eaten, but mixed with the *Great Milhio*, to brew withal, the Negroes believing it strengthens the Beer. … The Negro Women are well skilled in brewing Beer. … All People here, the Slaves not excepted, drink only Beer.

This origin story also focuses almost myopically on the English story of beer, when there were numerous other settler colonial powers in what would eventually become the US as Dutch, French, and Spanish colonists established communities on the land. Most interestingly, the Dutch were here well before the English and cultivated and used hops much earlier, which they, in fact, sold to Virginia colonists as well as exported back to the Netherlands (Mittleman, 2008). However, the British took over New Amsterdam in 1664 and introduced their familiar styles of ales. While we are now fully aware of the central role that women played in the household and community brewing of beer and ciders, they have almost no role in the mythological story of beer and brewing, even though the Smithsonian's Theresa McCulla (*October*, 2018) has made clear that:

> To a certain extent … our collective memory of brewing history begins [with German immigrant lager]. But the original brewers in America were certainly indigenous people, and in our early history as colonies and as a nation, it was often women and enslaved people who were the brewers in the household. Brewing was very much a domestic chore, and there was nothing glamorous about it.

Also, it is curious that beer historians significantly overestimate the popularity of beer in the 16th, 17th, and 18th centuries, when it is obvious in colonial and early US histories that spirits, including gin but most notably rum, were much more popular and widely drank within families, public houses, and communities writ large. Importantly, although not critically analytically, Baron (1962) starts off his classic (and classically mythological) account as follows: 'To speak of the origins of brewing in America is to speak of the origins of the nation itself'—and, more informatively, slavery does not even appear in the index. Therefore, men, more specifically, propertied white men, wrote (and continue to write) these beer and brewing histories, and until they are not the only ones writing those histories, we will be subject to the delusionary cosmology and mythology of beer and brewing that upholds them as the true originators and heirs to beer. However, when you dehistoricize and 'make natural,' you create myth (Hebdige, 1979). Put another way, white men made America. America brews beer. Beer is white.

## From myth to reality in early America

How can such a mythological story scream so loud and paint such a one-sided story? And why? The silencing power of whiteness and the centering of its main constituents—white people, and particularly white men—in the American context did not happen overnight. However, it did happen through violence, exploitation, displacement, trauma, and the creation of social, cultural, economic, and political structures that served the interests of white men and the realities of the white settler colonial project that all the European projects centered themselves upon. This is the reality that beer in the American context has been filtered through—with real consequences. The realities for Native Americans, African slaves, Aztlans, and other minorities are important to consider. The social and cultural engagement with beer and liquor is an important part of the story of the use of racial and ethnic exploitation to maintain social boundaries between white people and all others, and men and all others, as well as an important component of the story of how beer became white, why it matters, and contemporary movements to change that.

The rich brewing traditions of Native American tribes throughout the US are rarely, if ever, mentioned (see La Barre, 1938). Even before the first settler colonialists landed on the shores of North America, it was home to millions of people and many, many indigenous groups, including the Iroquois and Algonquin (Northeast), Mogollon, Hohokam, and Anasazi ('Pueblo Indians') (Southwest), the Cherokees, Choctaws, Chickasaws, Creeks, and Seminoles (Southeast), the Pawnees, Omaha, and Cheyennes (Central), the Makah and Kwakiutl (Northwest), and the Shoshone, Ute, and Gosiute (West)—and this is only a fraction of the rich societies and cultures in America before the colonialists assailed. White people came under the auspices of imperialism and colonialism, seeing a *terra nullus* where 'no one lived,' usually under the motivation of the kingdom of God. Such a structure always represented a structure of domination that subjugated one group of people to another, marked groups as socially outcast and individuals of said groups as ontologically non-persons, and conquered these people in every possible way—beer was a part of that conquest. The colonies that developed within the Americas are best classified as settler colonies and the European elite who migrated to the settler colonies in the Americas were intent on settlement, the creation of a self-sustaining independent political/economic system, and the domination of both geography and indigenous populations (Coates et al, 2017). The first groups of colonizers, the Spanish and Portuguese, settled in the most densely populated areas. Later colonizing efforts by both the French, Dutch, and the British created settlements in the less densely populated areas primarily in North America and Canada, creating different contexts.

What these colonial enterprises brought with them would fundamentally alter the lives of those who fell under their violence. They brought perspectives on which people were citizens, which people were to provide labor, and which people had to pay taxes (and tribute). Black people, Native Americans, and others could be redeemed and baptized but they could still not mix with 'purebloods'—creating a permanent hierarchy based on race that developed early in the Spanish colonial situation in the Americas, was emplaced in the French, Dutch, and certainly British settler colonies, and was linked to social and economic inequalities that are still present in contemporary American society, its institutions (including beer), its attendant cultures, and its industry. The foundational and fundamental impact of the system of slavery in what would become the US cannot be overestimated—indeed, capitalism, American-style, exists because slavery did. As sociologist Matthew Desmond (2019) has recently written for the *New York Times*'s 1619 Project:

> What made the cotton economy boom in the United States, and not in all the other far-flung parts of the world with climates and soil suitable to the crop, was our nation's unflinching willingness to use violence on nonwhite people and to exert its will on seemingly endless supplies of land and labor. Given the choice between modernity and barbarism, prosperity and poverty, lawfulness and cruelty, democracy and totalitarianism, America chose all of the above.

Although we hear a lot about the desire for religious freedom and freedom from religious persecution as a motivation of colonists (mostly British), the reality is more naked and violent. Indeed, these settlements, these colonial arms of European countries, were motivated by the desire for land acquisition, empire building, and profit. Period. There was also the Christianization of the indigenous populations throughout the North and South American continents, as well as on the islands. The Spanish (largely on the islands and what would become Central and South America), followed by the French (largely the islands but also Louisiana), and ultimately paralleled by the Dutch and British would see the development of laws, ordinances, and codes that legislated the life, death, purchase, marriage, and religion of slaves, as well as the rights of masters over their slaves, that is, their property. Such 'black codes' came in many varieties across the colonies but ultimately dictated the every interaction, movement, and existential realities of slaves, as well as indigenous populations. Some of these codes are still on the books in some municipalities (see Loewen, 2018). The social structure of the plantation dictated the realities of black people (slave and free), as well as the lives of all minority individuals; as settlers moved across the nation, there were different kinds of social relations, and this would become important in the Midwest, West, Pacific Northwest, and Southwest.

From the beginning, especially in the British colonial system, full and total control of the enslaved population and exploitative relations with indigenous peoples were key to the Anglo-American slave-owning planter elite. Revolt, rebellion, and disorderly racialized peoples were always lurking as a perceived threat, and through constant legislation altering ways in which children's status would be determined (for example, through the mother), the members of the planter class responded by solidifying slavery into a racial caste system. In the process, whiteness was created with the terms of what Charles Mills (1997) has called the 'racial contract.' Quoting him here at length:

> One could say then, as a general rule, that white misunderstanding, misrepresentation, evasion, and self-deception on matters related to race are among the most pervasive mental phenomena of the past few hundred years, a cognitive and moral economy psychically required for conquest, colonization, and enslavement. And these phenomena are in no way accidental, but prescribed by the terms of the Racial Contract, which requires a certain schedule of structured blindnesses and opacities in order to establish and maintain the white polity. (Mills, 1997: 19)

Whiteness would be key to the building of the US as its central constituents (white people) would move across previously indigenous lands to all four corners of the country, establishing white structures, white laws, white practices, and white cultures and cultural products—like beer.

## 'Punk in drublic': tavern culture and the foundations of the whiteness of beer

As the white, mythological creation story of beer, brewing, and the social and cultural relations surrounding beer has rendered invisible the real story of beer in the US, we are only now beginning to excavate the truth—this book is but a part of that puzzle. Thus, although we are only just beginning to see scholarship that digs into the realities of indigenous brewing and drinking cultures, that investigates both free and enslaved Africans' relationship with beer and distilled spirits (both on and off the plantation), and that gets us to think through the ways in which race and racism impacted historical and contemporary realities of beer and beer culture, one interesting place to look at the early racial formation surrounding beer and its production and consumption is to look at a fundamental public institution in early America, and one that would be used as a model of place-making (and relation-making) as white people moved across the land: taverns and tavern culture. At this point, only the outlines of the picture are somewhat visible. In fact, reading the emergent histories of taverns and public (and private) drinking, engaging with the intense legislative actions regarding them, and peeking inside such drinking spaces at the activities and interactions that have been captured in the travel diaries, innkeeper logs, and personal letters of habitual inn-goers and early 'gentlemen's clubs' can help us start to meaningfully color within the lines of those outlines. In this section, we rely heavily on Sharon Salinger's (2004) unique and masterful history, *Taverns and Drinking in Early America.*

Taverns—also called ordinaries, inns, public houses, and so on—were ubiquitous in early colonial America. While they were scattered (and licensed strategically) throughout the colonies in order that no one be too far from one, and so that travelers (who were mostly white men) would run into them on prominent roads in the rural areas between towns, Salinger (2004: 4) importantly also notes that 'taverns and drinking in early modern Europe and England provide a guide to public culture, to the articulation of classes, and to the locus of political action.' In most colonial towns and villages, taverns were more plentiful than other kinds of public structures, like churches. Across several of the histories one can look at on the ratios between taverns and populations in the 17th and 18th centuries in both England and colonial America, the range is around one public house for every 200–400 inhabitants, though would get as low as one for every 400–600 by the late 19th century. In the 17th century, plantation owners were expected to provide lodging, food, and beverages for the traveler; the town and village tavern were for the local community, and rural area ordinaries largely followed the movements of labor and weather. Yet, the basic social functions of these entities were clear and have been articulated across both mythical and not-so-mythical histories of taverns: a place to bring the *people*, that is, the *public*, together. Of course, this 'public' was primarily designed for white, male sociability. This is generally true but also hides other realities. Early taverns were much more diverse in terms of class, race, and gender, though by the second half of the 18th century, men largely drank with other men from their own echelon of the socio-economic structure—elite with elite, laborer with laborer. By and large, the owners were white men—though, as time progressed, women would be licensed to operate a tavern, especially if they were widows. Despite the mythological rhetoric of the public house as for all of those of the community, for Salinger (2004), the tavern was fundamentally exclusionary in nature, much like it still is today in many cases.

The white elite men in the colonies, who owned the propaganda outlets such as newspapers and pamphleteering, were constantly concerned that public, collective drinking represented an ever-present threat to decent society and, more to the point, a potential threat to their power and control. The history of public houses and taverns, inns, and ordinaries is a history of such elites working to regulate, legislate, and oversee tavern cultures. Such tavern legislation was a key part in constructing the structure and meaning(s) of the relationship between the classes, sexes, and races—and thus always intended to ensure the class, gender, and racial order. Ordinances and laws, varying widely across the colonies and over time, dictated who could enter, how they must enter, who could sell what to whom, where, and so on—social policies for sure. When tavern access was defined legally, colonial authorities could limit it to particular groups within society—and they did. This was to be a particular public space: one for white men, and as time went along, white men of the same socio-economic status. This was a legislating of morality (a precursor to temperance and Prohibition), and a legislating of population control, being certainly designed to always make the most possible money off these transactions.

Salinger's analysis makes clear that such laws defined who constituted the public and reinforced the cultural assumptions about the place of dependent laborers and the separation of the races—personhood and law go hand in hand within the racial contract (Mills, 1997) as servants, slaves, apprentices, women, sailors, and so on needed the permission of their 'masters' to buy liquor, cider, and beer. Black people (both free and enslaved) were the objects of differential legislation across the colonies. For instance, in Philadelphia, William Penn saw no reason to deny Native Americans access to rum as long as they modeled their drinking behavior on that of the English (Salinger, 2004). Setting limits on the available credit of particular patrons also served to reinforce this effect—through alcohol and through taverns, the link between trust and whiteness, between honor and class, and between allegiance and gender, as well as who needed paternalistic protections (for example, Native Americans and women), would be established—mostly out of fear. It was 'understood that elite men knew how to drink; their tavern visits did not require monitoring' (Salinger, 2004: 123).

Therefore, taverns were largely white spaces, designed for white people to communicate with each other about politics and community affairs, receive news, and debate about this and that, all to support white male sociability, either as the oppressor or the oppressed. As pointed out clearly in Salinger's history, taverns were hubs of communication in many ways: they were the first post offices, would often have the local newspaper (often read aloud), and were the center for local gossip and news. However, these white spaces were also used in many places (for example, Boston) for the sale of slaves and servants (Salinger, 2004: 56), as well as places where the white working class, perhaps, but most certainly (based in fear) black people and Native Americans, might be fomenting rebellion. Throughout the legislative history of tavern laws, there is a clear indication that white elites had a distinct fear of revolutions, built in spaces, such as taverns, over alcohol, among black people (free and enslaved) and Native Americans, who all had significant reason to revolt. The white working class also perpetually held the possibility of fomenting rebellion, though white elites treated their gatherings very differently in the law than those of minority people. Early fraternal organizations and clubs, mostly (but not all) elite, utilized tavern space for their gatherings. The vast majority of these were white, early 'gentlemen's clubs,' but from the memoirs, innkeepers logs, and other diaries, historians are able to glimpse that there was much more happening than the white imagination would allow. Salinger discusses a fascinating story of the Geneva Club composed of free and enslaved New York City black people in the mid-1730s, which articulated as part of its aim a subversion of the class order by mocking the clubs of middling and elite white men. As Salinger (2004: 82) shows:

> The Geneva Club members performed a burlesque of members of the Freemasons. They mocked the supposed wisdom and learnedness of clubs by naming their organizations after an increasingly popular alcoholic drink. They proclaimed that rather than erudition and conversation, clubs were mostly about legitimating the regular gathering of white men for the primary purpose of drinking. Finally the Geneva Club critiqued the issue of privilege pointing out that by separating themselves from those whose status was beneath them and from women, the club men were creating the rules that would protect their positions of privilege within society.

The links between what occurred inside the tavern and outside the tavern were and are clear.

Given the aforementioned structure, there was actually much more interracial interaction than one might expect in these spaces. In order to make a buck (the production and trade of beer was lucrative), white tavern owners and operators would make it possible for the crossing of race, class, and gender lines (though they must keep an 'orderly—white, classy, male—society'). There is no doubt at all that despite the hypocrisy of the available documentation, for white men, getting completely wasted was the desired result of white male sociability, despite the window dressing of toasting, readings, and political debate. The mythological fiction that only Native Americans and others were prone to drunkenness and white people were not was a complete and utter sham. The message was 'We want your money, we want your music, we want your dancing, and we want your culture but we do not necessarily want you and your kind here'—a reality that is still with us today.

Such accessible history through available documentation also hides the private realities of beer itself, the brewing of beer, and cultural drinking practices. Women did drink, and at times to excess, but they consumed alcohol in private, rather than public settings (largely because they were not allowed). Salinger (2004: 129) tells a revealing story highlighting the fact that those few individuals who were prosecuted for drunkenness came from a particular stratum of society. She tells the story of Montonny's 'negro man' (from 1772) who was found guilty of drunkenness and sentenced to jail. He died the night he arrived to start his sentence after receiving the 'usual punishment in such cases … a plentiful does of warm water (three quarts) and salt enough to operate as an emetic; with a portion of lamp oil to act as a purge'; however, this punishment for a slave then never appeared in the records again, even though the contemporary accounts say it was 'usual,' indicating that such treatment of black slaves and, likely, Native Americans was consistent but hidden from public records.

In Philadelphia in the 18th century, for instance, despite laws to the contrary, tavern keepers enticed 'even negroes' to drink in their establishments. Hell Town harbored the city's 'underclasses' and was home to many of the city's transient mariners and a magnet to the apprentices, servants, and slaves when they gathered for their 'evening pleasure.' Black people and Native Americans were often inside taverns in early America—we just do not yet know much about it, though we should. Historical records inhibit our ability to understand or even *see* Native Americans inside the tavern as such activity often went unrecorded because selling to Native Americans was illegal. Salinger (2004: 239) makes this all clear:

> This lapse exposes the broad range of Euro-American hypocrisy. Colonists' representations of Indian drinking behavior and their expressed attitudes toward drinking reveal that the styles of drinking practiced by the two groups were not nearly as different as whites might have wished. And under self-serving circumstances, white colonists did join Indians to drink. Most indicative of Indians'; presence in taverns is that over time a substantial number of tavern keepers were indicted for serving alcohol to Indians.

Although the public culture was male (and white), it was perhaps more black, Native American, and female than we have been led to believe. Indeed, despite the tactics of whiteness to exclude them from the very beginning, those marginalized communities' engagement with beer and brewing may have been much more pronounced. The bottom line is as follows:

> Colonial authorities could not risk mixtures of classes and races, because this threatened to subvert racial and status hierarchies. It was in these disorderly houses that whites and blacks fomented rebellion and participated in the economic anarchy of illegal trade. … the legal culture of the tavern

> reinforced gender, racial, and status hierarchies within the colonies. (Salinger, 2004: 150)

All of this helps to problematize the mythological origin stories that articulate the public face of elite white men (and, to some extent, working-class white men too) as they owned the newspapers, ran the courts that provided licenses, and crafted laws. Local (white) officials would visit taverns for noise, smoke, and so on, and often found 'such establishments in defiance of good order because their clientele included both men and women, whites and blacks, free and unfree ... at the very least, the proprietors were in violation of the law that prohibited servants and slaves from being entertained without express permission from their masters' (Salinger, 2004: 50). This all also allows us to look at some stories of the experiences and initiatives of black, indigenous, and other marginalized communities as they attempted to bravely carve their own path. The spread of tavern culture is the spread of whiteness. Since the beginning of the US, taverns, drinking, and drinking culture have been but one way that social and cultural practices have been used to create white solidarity, white community, white identities, and whiteness. There have been some exceptions, though—ones that would be worthy of pursuing.

## Black tavern owners? The story of Toledo, Ohio

While we know a bit more about the operation of, licensing of, and even ownership of taverns, saloons, ordinaries, and public houses by women, there just simply is not enough research on the possibility that free black people or Native Americans ran such establishments. Yet, we do know that free black people, Native Americans, and emancipated Africans did, very rarely, own and operate businesses (Marable, 2015 [1983]), and derived some wealth from such entrepreneurial efforts. After emancipation, there were significant movements of black people from the South to the urban areas of the South and North in waves of migration. These largely followed the railroads to primary (New York, Chicago, Philadelphia, St. Louis, Denver, Detroit, Pittsburgh, and so on), secondary (Cleveland, Los Angeles, San Francisco, Oakland, and so on), and even tertiary (Buffalo, Milwaukee, Cincinnati, Toledo, and so on) destination cities—many of which would become what scholars would come to call 'chocolate cities' (Hunter and Robinson, 2018).

Across our canvassing of the scholarship on black ownership (specifically) of saloons, taverns, inns, tied houses, and public houses in the post-Revolutionary period and the free black population in the northern US, as well as looking at the primary, secondary, and tertiary destinations of black people after emancipation, while we can find evidence that black people frequented such places (see the previous section), we find almost no indication of them operating, receiving licenses for, or owning such establishments. One exciting study—a doctoral dissertation completed at the University of Toledo in 2004—currently represents a unique peek into one city's experience. Arnette Hawkins's (2004) dissertation, 'Raising our glass: a history of saloons in Toledo from 1880–1919,' begins to illuminate the black engagement with saloon operation and ownership, highlights the methodological challenges of researching such topics, and, taken together, encourages us that there may be so much more to be recovered in the story of race, racism, beer, and brewing.

During the time period under study (1880–1919), Hawkins (2004) shows that much like earlier moments in US history, the saloon remained a fundamental aspect of the daily lives of citizens of Toledo in general, and of neighborhoods, in particular, as was the case in many, many cities throughout the US. This was a period of immigration and urbanization, and Toledo was a manufacturing city. Like most US cities under Jim Crow, Toledo was fundamentally segregated into the German neighborhood, the black neighborhood, the Catholic neighborhood, and so on. Just like tavern culture more generally, during the late 19th and early 20th centuries, 'upon arriving in a city, a worker could approach the saloon as his point of entry into the social, economic, and political life of his new community' (Hawkins, 2004: 3), and there were saloons for each area of the city. Toledo is emblematic of other US cities at the time, with early saloons often in private homes and or linked to associated businesses (for example, hardware) in the neighborhoods where workers lived and near to the factories in which they worked. Hawkins describes the city's saloons as follows: being neighborhood based; numbering one for every 200–300 people; open six days a week between 5 am and 1 am; usually run by men (and widows); having early telephones; often being used as banks for the working class as well as post offices; and many providing a free lunch (the idea of a 'free lunch' came from saloons to mitigate the effects of alcohol throughout the work day).

Hawkins (2004: 11) shows that during a time of deep segregation in many occupations, 'the saloon trade was an occupation into which recent immigrants and African-Americans were accepted,' and because most saloons were neighborhood based, they were also mostly homogeneous in terms of race and ethnicity—'with commonality came comfort.' Right before her study period began, Toledo went from having five African-American families in 1880 to having a black population that continuously grew; indeed, between 1910 and 1920, the black population grew some 200 per cent. Across this time period, the vast majority of Toledo's black residents worked in domestic service positions, though some, but very few, owned hotels and restaurants. Like the neighborhoods, hotels, theatres, restaurants, and other public spaces were segregated, and this served as 'incentive for African American entrepreneurs to set up saloons or boarding saloons where others would be welcome' (Hawkins, 2004: 39). Hawkins (2004) discovered that African-American saloon owners were generally identified by codes such as an asterisk before the surname or the abbreviation 'col'd' in the city directories of the time. In 1868, John B. Tilton was the first African-American saloonkeeper listed in the city directory. He ran one of the almost 50 saloons that were listed in the 1868 directory. By 1869, there were four black-owned saloons: Tilton's as well as two boarding saloons (William Carter and the Mayos) and a billiard saloon (John H. Douglas), representing 3.45 per cent of all the saloons (116) at the time. Hawkins shows a consistency of black saloon ownership across the entire study period, with ebbs and flows of openings and closures; several would be turned into brothels run by women, often when the male owners would be arrested for a variety of things. From 1900 to 1913, Pearl Barber (male) was 'the highest profile African-American saloonkeeper during the period' and appeared in the struggle against Prohibition, while Josephine Lawson was identified by Hawkins (2004: 42) as the first female African-American saloonkeeper. Across the period from 1880 to 1908, the number of African-American saloons decreased and moved to a more concentrated and segregated black area of town that would be referred to by 1915 as 'the badlands.' Saloons and their keepers were often scapegoated, always political, and always suspect—a pattern that we will see throughout history and that underwrites the historic and contemporary whiteness of beer, beer spaces, and beer cultures.

Meanwhile, the brewing and malting industries, largely composed of white German immigrants, was the 11th largest employer in Toledo, and, according to Hawkins (2004: 58), 'unlike saloonkeepers, brewers were respected members of Toledo's population.' The German immigrants, and their structured relationships with saloons (via the tied house), represented an important chapter in the story of race and beer in the US, and, interestingly, Ohio was at the epicenter. Indeed, by 1907, the Ohio Supreme Court gave legal recognition to the existence of tied houses. Tied houses were saloons and taverns that were 'tied' to a particular brewery. Under this system, the saloon or tavern would be prohibited from serving beer from a producer that they were not 'tied' to. The spread of tied houses was one of the arguments used by the dry forces to press for complete prohibition rather than temperance. Saloons also became locations for unions and fraternal organizations: 'workers, unionized or otherwise, were the main beneficiaries of the saloon culture' (Hawkins 2004: 71). However, as beer became tightly connected to labor, that is, to working-class men, and due to the segregated nature of unions (Kelley, 2015) and fraternal organizations, these spaces became largely places for white men to gather.

While Hawkins's work is not able to fully articulate the black ownership, operation, and licensing of saloons throughout the time period of her study, she has done a great service to those of us interested in uncovering the stories that have been made invisible, lost, or covered up by the ever-present white drive of and writing of history. Imagine what there might be to tell if we traced the railroads and looked closely at Memphis, Atlanta, Philadelphia, and other 'chocolate cities,' where black institutions and black social, cultural, and economic life have thrived for generations. What if we looked at the role of beer, brewing, and the spaces of beer as woven into black, indigenous, and Latinx life knowing that it is there but just extraordinarily difficult to uncover? There is likely a lot more going on with race, racism, brewing, and beer throughout US history than the beer mythology laid out earlier in this chapter would lead us to believe. Indeed, in many ways, according to that mythology, the Pilgrims landed in 1620 and then the Germans arrived in the 1840s—skipping over a great deal and, indeed, though beyond the scope of this book (we leave it to historians who have the methodological tools to uncover these stories, experiences, and thick histories [see Lena, 2012]), creating a massive epistemological gulf from whence to understand the contemporary whiteness of beer, brewing, and beer consumption practices and cultures. Thus, the German immigrant story is certainly important but one that we will not fully rearticulate here as it has been stated over and over and over again at length across numerous books (see the mythology discussed earlier).

It is important to note that German immigrants, though European in origin, were not necessarily initially embraced by whiteness; rather, they were immigrants whose traditions were initially treated with social, cultural, political, and economic disdain and concern—as problematic for the white Anglo-Saxon protestant (WASP) settler colonials who built the country on white supremacist foundations grounded in WASP social structures. Although the ground to embrace them and their beer ways had already been laid for 200+ years, they were reviled and scapegoated, and their brewing traditions were used to bolster a nascent temperance movement and, ultimately, a movement to prohibit alcohol altogether; however, whiteness and white supremacy would wrap its arms around Germans, their beer, *and* the political power and profit arising from it. With Prohibition, the era of the saloon came to an end, but a new era was rising.

## Race, racism, white domination, temperance, and Prohibition

As we have seen throughout this chapter, there has always been a fundamental link between alcohol, morality, social control, gender, labor, religion, social class, citizenship, and race. The movement to encourage abstinence/moderation in drinking behaviors and establishments in public (and private) life—the temperance movement—drew on all of these registers as well. After generations of exploitative engagements between the white settler colonists and native populations, temperance was sought early on by the Maspee Indians in the 1820s. In fact, the idea of somehow legislating the engagement with alcohol between indigenous folks and white settler colonists was pursued by both groups since the beginning of their contact with each other, often initiated by native groups, though always exploited by white people for their own purposes. While the relationship between race, racism, and the broader temperance movement in the US is certainly significant, for our purposes, we will focus more on the long-term effects of the movement and how it has influenced beer consumption contemporarily (for a more in-depth overview of the history of the temperance movement, see Fahey 2015; Pegram, 1997). It is certainly a story about the maintenance of class boundaries, especially through labor (Who could work under the influence? Can one operate the heavy machinery demanded by the Industrial Revolution under the influence?). The movement was also fundamentally grounded in white, Protestant, religious traditions, where alcohol use was considered a sin (often hypocritically by the heavy drinking proponents of such religiosity) and had strong underpinnings of morality and social control—this also ultimately had North–South divisions in the US as many of the Northern proponents of temperance also supported abolitionism, while Southern states developed their own temperance groups that did not include the race and slavery question. It was also the era of eugenics and the building of the 'master race.' The story is also one about the building of the nation, who would be considered a citizen, and under what conditions, including those with social control in mind as the regulation of drinking behavior was often pointed squarely at minorities and immigrants. According to Shulman (2012: 200–1):

> To temperance advocates, beer was code for immigrant filth and sloth, unemployed men who abandon their women for the saloon. ... In the 1880s some temperance movement advocates would hand out pamphlets in 16 languages, by the 1890s the temperance organization in NYC [New York City] was advocating restricted immigration to stop the influx of 'the scum of the Old World.'

It is no accident that the significant push toward temperance gained quick speed in the years before the Civil War in the Northeastern and Midwestern states.

Prohibition, the 18th amendment, which would attempt the prohibition of the manufacturing, distribution, and sale of alcoholic beverages through the legislative and legal realm, also drew from these ever-present registers of anti-immigrant sentiment, especially against Germans but also, centrally, Catholics, during the turn of the century, through the First World War, and beyond: 'Drinking became invisible, as it was no longer necessary to frequent the saloons that had become more often restricted to the inner city and industrialized areas in the twentieth century' (Hawkins, 2004: 144). There were significant racist, nativist, and state- (and empire-)building fuel that stoked the flames of one of the largest constitutional overreaches in US history. This important part of the story is told magnificently by Harvard historian Lisa McGirr (2015) in her brilliant book *The War on Alcohol: Prohibition and the Rise of the American State*—which should be slightly retitled from our read to, perhaps, *The War on Alcohol: Prohibition and the Securing of the White Supremacist Eugenicist American State/Empire*. Her analysis lays bare the centrality of anti-immigrant hostility, hate, and violence that drove the move from temperance, through anti-saloon, to Prohibition itself in the US. It seemed that the entire system of white supremacy was seen as fundamentally threatened by mass immigration at the turn of the century:

> With more than a million men and women coming to the United States in 1907 alone, anti-liquor crusaders railed against a 'foreign invasion of undeveloped races.' The boisterous drinking culture of the ubiquitous working-class

> saloon, dominated by immigrant men, seemed to make manifest the dangers mass immigration posed to a white native Protestant American way of life. (McGirr, 2019)

In her incisive analysis, McGirr shows that the federal government's thinly staffed and weak agents who were to work to close the trade in alcohol simply could not accomplish what they set out to do in the larger markets like Chicago, New York, Seattle, and so on, and would end up going after immigrants despite the fact that they were much less likely to violate the law. (Sound familiar to the 17th, 18th, and 19th centuries, and even today?) McGirr even shows how Prohibition and its reach were responsible for the rebirth of the Ku Klux Klan:

> As enforcement failures multiplied, anti-liquor crusaders found a powerful new ally in the so-called second Ku Klux Klan. Established in 1915 by William Simmons in Atlanta, the organization snowballed after 1920 in the Midwest and West. Its savvy promoters, Elizabeth Tyler and Edward Young Clarke, former fund-raisers for the Anti-Saloon League, drew in a bumper crop of new recruits with their anti-Catholic, anti-immigrant, white supremacist message. (McGirr, 2019)

Thus, we have alcohol, racism, xenophobia, and religious intolerance all coming together to bolster American white supremacy. This was also a period of 'reconstruction,' Jim Crow, lynchings, racial segregation, racist violence, eugenics, discrimination, and the reclaiming of the white racial state—which emerging world leaders like Hitler were taking cues from (Whitman, 2017).

One must also understand that it was in the run-up to and through Prohibition that we see the making of the great white beer baron families: Schlitz in the 1850s in Milwaukee, Pabst in the 1860s in Milwaukee, Anheuser in the 1860s/70s in St. Louis, Busch in the 1870s/80s in St. Louis, and Coors in the 1870s in Golden, Colorado—all German white immigrants. Their successes were no doubt a reason for the social, cultural, religious, and legislative pushback from the old monied white power structures throughout the country. These beer baron families became fully immersed in whiteness after Prohibition and served as the new model for the whiteness, and racism, of beer and the brewing industry as the next wave of post-war immigrants and African-Americans would face distinct discrimination and exclusion from the industry by these larger producers. Midwestern German brewers, who lacked the luxury of a giant local market (for example, New York City, Chicago, and so on), were seeking to expand their distribution, and as soon as bottling technology and refrigerated railroad cars were more common, these producers were able to distribute their products in a more regional footprint, rather than a somewhat restrictive local footprint. Additionally, Prohibition accelerated the expansion of existing networks of depots and warehouses, salesmen, and agents, who were tasked with distributing beer throughout a particular region. Given the ever-increasing reach of these growing brewery empires, the political power of these white beer families cannot be underestimated. Indeed, there are some scholars who show the clear links between these families and white supremacist groups (Bellant, 1991).

During Prohibition, the US brewing industry came to a complete stop: no beer was legally produced or consumed during this 13-year period. Prohibition brought on the rapid closing of hundreds of regional and local breweries around the country. Many breweries closed their doors, never to be reopened. A few breweries managed to stave off the effects of Prohibition by outsourcing their equipment to other industries. While Prohibition was devastating to most breweries, a handful of larger producers were able to weather the storm. When the saloon doors closed, the buildings reopened as 'pool halls, soda shops, restaurants, candy stores, soft drink parlors, and speakeasies, the saloon as a major social, political and economic institution was closed for good' (Hawkins, 2004: 154). The bars, cocktail lounges, and nightclubs that opened after Prohibition was repealed in 1933 bore little resemblance to the old-time saloon. Ultimately, one key reason why Prohibition was finally repealed in 1933 was because the political economy of white supremacy took too much of a battering as its control over a productive economy was significantly undermined by Prohibition: too many profits were lost; too much control of the industries was lost; there was too much illegal production, distribution, and sale of alcohol outside of the control of the established white owning class; and there was too much problematic private consumption affecting the laboring population. Brewers such as Anheuser-Busch, Schlitz, Pabst, and a handful of others reopened their breweries to virtually no competition. In turn, this helped pave the way for the monopolization of the US brewing industry. In the years following the repeal of Prohibition, these white, male, brewers would come to dominate the industry and help to define what 'American beer' would become.

# 3

# The Making of the (White) Craft Beer Industry

Without a full accounting of history, we are likely to repeat it. Understanding how beer became racialized helps us to grapple with the continuities of its whiteness and the maintenance of racist practices within the beer industry writ large. Prior to Prohibition, the US brewing industry consisted of large regional breweries and small local breweries, and before that, a deeply rooted tavern system and related cultures. At the historical peak of brewing in the US in 1887, there were 2,011 breweries; at the beginning of Prohibition in 1920, the number stood at 1,179 (Brewers Association, 2018a). These breweries largely used recipes and techniques brought over by white European immigrants. Some of the more popular styles were pale German lagers and pilsners. These would come to define what beer was in the US. Upon ratification of the 18th Amendment, the production of alcohol came to a screeching halt. Breweries were forced to close their doors and hope that 'the great experiment' would come to a timely end. That day came on December 5, 1933.

After the repeal of Prohibition, many breweries remained closed—for some, the damage done during Prohibition was too great to overcome. Other breweries were able to reopen and continue their operations under a new structure: the three-tier distribution system. Under this system, beer passes through three-tiers—the brewer, a wholesale distributor, and a retailer—before it reaches the consumer. Following the repeal of Prohibition, several firms, including Pabst, Anheuser-Busch, Coors, and a few others, were able to use their considerable wealth to acquire smaller local and regional breweries. The period following the repeal of Prohibition in 1933 and up through the 1970s—a period of acquisition and consolidation, the death of old regional breweries, and the capitalist myopia of the bottom line—had great effects on beer itself but also further solidified the racialized structure of the industry that existed prior to Prohibition.

As it relates to the history of craft beer in the US, the consolidation and acquisition of breweries, which began prior to Prohibition and intensified in the years following its repeal, led to high levels of industry concentration and very little innovation. Larger producers such as Anheuser-Busch, Miller and Coors, who would become known as the 'Big Three,' all produced a pale German lager that would become lighter, less bitter, and even less traditionally German, which remains popular to this day. The lack of innovation that is a latent function of high industry concentration homogenized US beer. One result is that the industry saw an increase in imported beer, being purchased from international producers and sold in the US or another country. According to Tremblay and Tremblay (2009: 12), 'imported brands are far from homogeneous ... many of the brands from Canada and Mexico are similar to regular domestic beer, while most brands from England and Ireland are more like domestic specialty (craft beer).' Many imported brands are 'darker, more bitter in flavor, and higher in alcohol and calories than regular domestic beer' (Tremblay and Tremblay, 2009: 107). McGovern (1980: 4) notes that 'the majority of imports have what most domestic beers do not; pure ingredients, complex flavor, smooth body, and robust aroma.' It was the dawn of the 'pale American adjunct lager.' To better understand how this affected craft beer and further racialized the beer industry, it is important to provide some context as there were several other factors at play.

Hicks (1979: 2), contends that 'the gradual swing by Americans to imported beers has probably been a delayed reaction triggered by many things.' First, Hicks (1979: 2) suggests that 'the disappearance of countless small breweries' has led to fewer options for the consumer. American beer was becoming increasingly more uniform and the economic prosperity of (white) Americans in the 1960s led to an increase in demand for higher-status products (Silberberg, 1985). Hicks (1979) points to international travel as another factor contributing to the rise of imported beer. American tourists (largely white) helped spark a change in taste by sampling beers from all over Europe during their travels. Additionally, as Hicks (1979: 3) notes, the 'vast number of G.I.s who spent months or years abroad drinking the native brews of many lands' further aided in the shift in taste. Upon returning home, tourists and soldiers alike found that most American producers of darker and more traditional beers had gone out of business and left the door open for foreign brewers to 'fill this void, as they already produced quality brands of darker beer for consumption in their homelands in large enough quantities to realize scale efficiency' (Tremblay and Tremblay, 2009: 107). Additionally, imports 'came in a variety of styles and sold for a premium price, fulfilling the new desires of US beer consumers,' which limited the growth of craft and domestic specialty brands (Tremblay and Tremblay, 2009: 114). During this time, we saw a solidification of (white) tastes amid a continuing divergence of racialized experience.

Not all Americans were benefitting from the post-war prosperity. Black people were still living under oppressive and racist Jim Crow laws and segregation in almost every aspect of life. The Civil Rights movement was gaining momentum in black communities; however, meanwhile, middle- and upper-class white people were spending money on high-status goods. Given this context, black people were not afforded the opportunity to travel (especially internationally), did not possess the necessary disposable income to afford high-status or imported goods, and, in many cases, would not have been allowed to consume beer in segregated white spaces, including the continuing white imaginary (and reality) that was beer. This lack of exposure to new and different beer styles and flavors, along with racist marketing campaigns, systematically excluded black people from participating in this more elite type of consumption.

Second, and perhaps most importantly, the homogenization of American beer led people to begin to create beer themselves. The hobby of homebrewing, which was not legalized until 1978 with the passage of H.R. 1337, was becoming more and more popular, particularly on the coasts and largely among white people. The legalization of homebrewing opened the door to the exchange of information and knowledge. Homebrew clubs, such as the Maltose Falcons, were able to meet in public rather than behind a veil of secrecy or a garage door. The Maltose Falcons, who are still active today, were founded in suburban Los Angeles by Merlin Elhardt, a war veteran and PhD candidate at UCLA (Ogle, 2006). Homebrew clubs were composed of individuals with disposable income, basic knowledge of chemistry and other science-related fields, and a lot of free time. The DIY nature of homebrewing requires a base level of knowledge or access to knowledge about brewing, certain pieces of specialty equipment or the know-how and materials to construct the equipment, and considerable space, time, and effort.

Many homebrewers did not receive formal training, but learned from word of mouth. Bodies of knowledge were transferred to budding homebrewers through ritualized cultural practices such as 'brew days' and other homebrew club events, which would be energized and captured by books like Charlie Papazian's (2014) *Complete Joy of Homebrewing*. Homebrew clubs connect homebrewers to a network of like-minded and similarly socially located individuals; homebrewers are (and largely remain) white, middle-class, educated males. This is a trend that is mirrored in the craft beer market today. Social capital is one of the most important resources in homebrewing. This further evidences how the historical context and socio-political and racial climate of the 1960s and 1970s created manifest and latent barriers that prevented black people from not only consuming beer, but also, just as importantly, gaining the knowledge, social capital, and economic resources to produce beer. This is also supported by the lack of minority-owned breweries and minority brewers, as well as minority-owned businesses in general, during this time.

The importance of, and emphasis on, homebrewing in our analysis cannot be understated. Historical accounts of the craft beer movement show that the earliest craft brewers started out as homebrewers. Some of the more notable names are: Jack McAuliffe, founder of New Albion Brewing, one of the first craft breweries to open its doors; Jim Koch, a white brewer of Samuel Adams Boston Lager and founder of the Boston Beer Company; and Ken Grossman, white brewer and founder of the Sierra Nevada Brewing Company. In the case of Jim Koch and Ken Grossman, their breweries would become the high-water mark for all later breweries. Both are still in operation and currently top craft producers. These breweries also pioneered new styles that would come to define early craft beer, particularly Ken Grossman and the innovative use of hops in Sierra Nevada Pale Ale. Following the models of Koch and Grossman, homebrewers began to open up breweries—the start of the craft beer movement was beginning, though all were white men. Aspiring homebrewers who possessed the necessary capital began to open breweries on the coasts. Access to these resources and networks most certainly follow similar racialized patterns as industry access. As our interview data demonstrate, homebrewing is one of the most common pathways to becoming a brewer, though a path that is largely available to white men.

As we have begun to illuminate in Chapter 2, the history of beer and brewing in the US has been racialized, and is, in fact, racist—distributing opportunities and creating spaces and cultures centered in whiteness and white supremacy in the beer industry. As this chapter seeks to demonstrate, the craft beer industry emerged as a direct response to the homogenization and consolidation of the US brewing industry. While imported beers exposed middle-class white people to new flavors, it was the access to these beers, whether via international travel or through availability in retail markets, that helped to usher in the rise of craft beer. This change in tastes was further manifested by the rise of homebrewing and its attendant cultures. The social capital and knowledge gained through homebrew clubs empowered many of the first craft brewers to open their own breweries. However, the history of craft beer is most certainly and centrally white. It is both a product and response to the larger US brewing industry, and most certainly reflects the same structures of racism and racialization.

The lack of access to knowledge through social capital, the lack of disposable income and prosperity, and the lack of equality overall for black people and other minorities in the US created racialized structures that can be seen in the brewing industry, as well as other industries, in the US. While we will further engage with social capital, exposure to craft beer, and the various pathways toward craft consumption and production, it is first imperative to examine the structure of the brewing industry itself. The craft industry appears as an alternative product to domestic beer; however, the structure of its industry closely mirrors that of its larger counterpart. In this chapter, we discuss how the structure of the US brewing industry, in particular, the distribution system known as the three-tier system, has created opportunities for white people through industry hiring practices, the marketing of beer, and exposure to craft beer. In doing so, the industry has systematically created obstacles that have prevented minorities from gaining access to jobs in the food and beverage industry that are a primary pathway into the brewing industry.

## Post-Prohibition

The structure of the US brewing industry changed dramatically after the repeal of Prohibition. Prior to 1920, there were over 1,000 breweries in operation; in 1935, there were 766 breweries producing in the US (Brewers Association, 2018a). This number would steadily decline over the next two decades, dropping to 188 in 1960. The decline in the number of breweries allowed several large firms to establish oligopolistic control over the industry, meaning that a few firms effectively control the majority of the production. This is similar to the recording industry. Peterson (1990) suggests that in oligopolistic industries, large firms dominate the market; however, these large firms cannot effectively control the entire market. This allows smaller firms to serve smaller portions of the market. For example, smaller record labels in rural and suburban areas were able to serve the population who were not reached by the broadcast signals of larger firms. In terms of the beer industry, large domestic producers are also unable to control an entire area or region and, as Chapman (2015) argues, this created an opportunity for craft breweries to fill the void in the market.

Industry concentration is expressed as three- and/or four-firm concentration ratios. Concentration ratios are used by economists to determine the degree to which a particular industry is oligopolistic. These ratios are a measure of the total market share of a given number of firms. Typically, they are expressed as four-firm concentration ratios. As Tremblay and Tremblay (2009: 43) note, 'the concentration ratio measures the market share of the four largest firms in the industry, giving equal weight to the share of each of the four largest firms and no weight to the shares of other firms.' Four-firm concentration ratios can range from 0 to 1 and economists suggest that a high concentration ratio indicates that an industry is oligopolistic. The effects of such a structure are important to understand when thinking about industry reach and impact.

Tremblay and Tremblay (2009: 44) report that during this period, the US brewing industry's four-firm concentration ratio increased from just below 0.20 to 0.95. This suggests that the concentration and oligopolistic control of the four major firms—Anheuser-Busch (now known as AB-InBev), Miller and Coors (who formed a joint venture in 2008 but still produce independent brands, now under the umbrella of South African Breweries), and Pabst Brewing Company—has increased drastically over the last 50 years. Scherer and Ross (1990) and Shepherd (1967) contend that 'once CR exceeds 40 percent, the level of effective competition diminishes and an industry can be classified as an oligopoly' (Tremblay and Tremblay, 2009: 45). As Tremblay and Tremblay (2009: 45) note, the US 'brewing industry has been oligopolistic since 1968' if we use this measure of concentration. Mergers and acquisitions are still taking place. The 'big three' have merged and are now acquiring smaller craft brands. Currently, the domestic market share is 68.9 per cent of the total market, which is still considered to be oligopolistic (Brewers Association, 2019a).

The main factors contributing to high concentration ratios are mergers and acquisitions. Mergers and acquisitions can take two forms: vertical and horizontal. Vertical mergers and acquisitions involve the merging of firms that exist at separate phases of the production process. For example, if Anheuser-Busch were to merge or acquire a company that produces aluminum cans, they will have vertically acquired the said company. Vertical mergers allow larger firms to control more aspects of production because more of the raw materials and resources are in-house, which therefore lowers the costs of production. During both vertical and horizontal mergers, labor and employees are also acquired. The available contemporary industry data on labor statistics in the brewing industry do not yet report race or ethnicity figures (though, as of the time of writing, we understand that the Brewers Association is slated to release such data). Going back to research from the 1970s gives us insight into this particular period. As Alexis (1970: 55) notes: 'the history of black employment in the United States is one of limited job opportunities and low pay,' 'systematic job discrimination,' and segregation from white workers. Alexis (1970: 55) asserts that, 'historically, black employment has been concentrated in the service, unskilled, and semiskilled labor categories.' Furthermore, 'opportunities in clerical, managerial, skilled labor, and professional occupations have been very limited. World War II did much to improve the situation. But there is evidence of continuing job discrimination based on race in manufacturing, distribution, and unionized trades' (Alexis, 1970: 56).

Large breweries operate much like a factory. Jobs in the industry are skilled labor positions for which black people were systematically discriminated against in hiring practices. Additionally, they lacked the skills to work in these positions, and when hired, they often performed lower-skilled and lower-paid labor. According to Sugrue (1996: 108), 'the brewing industry's hiring arrangements allowed employers to pass responsibility for nondiscriminatory hiring to the union [Brewery Workers Union], and the union to avoid charges of discrimination by reiterating its policy of relying on the references of union members.' Sugrue (1996: 108) also attributes 'union recalcitrance' as ensuring that 'blacks remained grossly underrepresented in brewing jobs.' The Brewery Workers Union, which operated as the primary hiring agent for beer manufacturers, 'was responsible for excluding blacks from production and driver-sales jobs' (Sugrue, 1996: 107). Local breweries were to report job vacancies to the union, who filled the jobs through referrals from friends and family members. Housing segregation also played a role: 'because few blacks lived near whites, they had few opportunities to develop the relationships that would provide them access to jobs' (Sugrue, 1996: 107).

A horizontal merger is a form of consolidation that occurs between two firms who operate in the same space, produce similar products, and are often in competition with each other. Many of these acquisitions and mergers are the result of a smaller firm's inability to compete in the market. Rather than closing their facilities, they consolidate with other breweries. Greer (1998: 32), reports that there were 'more than 600 horizontal mergers and acquisitions of facilities and/or brands in the US brewing industry since 1950.' Further, Tremblay and Tremblay (2009: 187) contend that 'evidence indicates that most of the brewers that exited the industry during this time did so by combining with another beer producer'—a further concentration of white ownership and whiteness that saw little regional boundaries.

According to Tremblay and Tremblay (2009: 187), 'for several brewers, the acquisition of another firm's brands, plants, and equipment became an important means of expansion.' Most of these breweries were classified as regional breweries, meaning that they distributed in a very limited geographic region. By acquiring these smaller regional firms, large firms were able to reach new markets through increased distribution and a wider variety of brands. White industry insider Patrick Baker (1983: 17) laments that 'with the closing of breweries, the drinker lost regional character in his beer and a choice in styles.' Another function of these regional acquisitions is that it allowed macro-producing breweries 'to ship long distances, and gain maximum benefit from their advertising, they standardized their beers, eliminating styles and regional tastes'; what resulted was 'a plastic beer, very efficient and economical to produce, but lacking in character. Hence the void being filled by imports and the real beer microbreweries' (Baker, 1983: 14). As more and more regional breweries were closing, the level of competition in the brewing industry was also decreasing. Larger firms bought the facilities of small breweries and began producing their own brand of beer, rather than what the original regional brewery was producing. The result was a more industrialized, delocalized, and more homogenized beer that was quickly coming to dominate the public perception of what beer should taste like and who should make, have access to, and drink it.

As Warner (2010: 34) notes:

> the lager introduced by German immigrants was called the Bavarian style … that Bavarian style had caught on in the US because of its comparative lightness. American brewers began experimenting to try and replicate the style with domestic ingredients and it was found that a very acceptable version could be created with the use of white corn and rice as adjuncts—and sold for a premium price.

This adaptation of a traditional European style would become known as the adjunct lager. Perhaps the most famous of these adjunct brews is Budweiser (Warner, 2010). Prior to Prohibition and its repeal in 1933, regional brewers produced distinct flavors and styles that reflected the culture and heritage of a region, particularly the culture of the immigrant population who brought brewing techniques with them, which was undoubtedly a 'white' brewing heritage. Upon acquisition, these breweries began to produce the same pale adjunct lagers that their parent companies were producing. This halted innovation across the industry and further homogenized the tastes of American beer drinkers. This style of beer would come to define 'American beer' and Americans' taste in beer. However, as this book seeks to shed light on, that was a very racialized process.

One must ask the question: 'Is it beer for all Americans?' While the style socially and culturally constructed and defined American tastes, in many ways, it also constructed and described Americans themselves. Beer became the status symbol for white working-class males in that it evokes the image of a blue-collar worker enjoying his leisure time—something ubiquitous and pervasive in advertising, television programs (recall the image of Archie Bunker in his chair), and sporting events (for example, alcohol sponsorships and sales at sporting events). Nickles (2002: 582) notes that 'an increasing number of these blue-collar workers now had middle-class pocketbooks that allowed them to live in suburban "mass produced domestic comfort" and participate in the white identity defined by that racially homogeneous environment.' Furthermore, an ethos that Nickles (2002: 582–3) refers to as 'more is better' came to define the tastes of the working class through status symbols like 'big cars and shiny refrigerators.' As Davis et al (1941) explain, status symbols have been systematically denied to black people, particularly in the South under Jim Crow but also in the North. They further contend that black people and other minorities who earn disposable income were still not allowed to participate in activities that serve as social and economic status symbols for white people of similar economic standing (Davis et al, 1941)—the question still remains.

Advertising during this time reflected the 'more is better' ethos and depicted white working-class men unwinding after a hard day of work with an ice-cold beer. It is important to dissect this image through the lens of race and racism. Images of white men sitting on their couch and watching television, or at their kitchen table reading the newspaper, or grabbing a cold beer from the refrigerator are inherently racialized. This can all be encompassed in the classic Budweiser slogan, 'America, this Bud's for you,' which implies not only that *all* Americans like Budweiser, but also that Budweiser was produced for them. This slogan is both inclusionary of the white working-class male—as if to suggest: 'You worked hard today. You earned this beer, and we made it just for you'—and exclusionary in that black people were not included in advertising, nor did they have the same access to beer as white people.

The view that this represents the 'American male' is at minimum problematic, and indeed racist. Beer ads such as these assume that a beer drinker owns a television set, owns a refrigerator, or even has free time to sit and relax. This may have been the reality for white Americans but black people were not benefitting from the economic prosperity of the time. According to one look at the consumer experiences of black people in the 1960s/70s (Alexis, 1970: 56), due to the fact that they were not employed in high-paying jobs, 'the fact that unemployment rates among blacks average twice the national level in good times and bad, and the fact of greater sensitivity of black employment to economic downturns and more lagged response to expansion, there is good reason to expect differences in black consumption behavior.' Due to the restrictions of Jim Crow laws, black people were limited in their consumption of certain goods and forms of recreation (Alexis, 1970). Furthermore, looking back during the Jim Crow 1930s, according to Edwards (1936: 155), 'on the average, the Negro common and semi-skilled labor family probably does not spend more than one or two percent of annual income for house furnishings and equipment, whereas the low income urban white family budget will usually yield in the vicinity of 4 per cent for this purpose.' Household consumption and expenditures on things such as appliances, particularly refrigerators, could also represent one factor in the disparity in black beer consumption.

The refrigerator plays a vital role in the history of beer post-Prohibition and changed the way that Americans consumed beer forever. Prior to in-home refrigeration, beer had to be consumed at bars or saloons. Along with the advent of the aluminum can, beer suddenly became portable. As beer is a perishable product, it must be refrigerated to maintain its freshness and quality. Refrigerators, and many other newly invented household appliances, were rather expensive and not accessible to lower-income families. Additionally, as McNeil and Letschert (2005) note, the refrigerator is also a major consumer of household energy and electricity. While Nickles (2002: 582) notes that during the postwar period of economic prosperity, 'ownership of mechanical refrigerators increased from 44 percent to about 90 percent of American households,' those figures do not reflect the racial disparity in homeownership, particularly in the South, or the income gap between white and black workers. Black people in the South and other low-income areas may not have been able to afford a refrigerator; therefore, they could not store beer to drink in the home. Under Jim

Crow, black people were not allowed in bars or saloons, and due to labor discrimination and having lower income than white people of similar social standing, they lacked the disposable income and leisure time to have a beer at a bar. Beer was never intended for black people. Beer was, and still is, for white people.

As discussed previously, the homogenization of beer led some to start homebrewing and others to seek more robust flavors from imported beer. Homebrewing and the taste for imported beer were much less accessible for black people. The disposable income and knowledge to travel, or to brew, was simply something the black people did not have access to. While the homogenization of beer most certainly made it more inexpensive and accessible, black people were not actively targeted through advertising. When black people were advertised to, the ads were often racist and classist. It also helped usher in the craft beer movement as a response, alternative product, and entirely new industry. As Tremblay and Tremblay (2009: 14) suggest, the emergence of the micro- and craft beer movements are interesting because 'these small brewers have returned to the brewing practices of Europe, a strategy that has proven successful and changed the behavior of many mass producers.'

During the time of increasing industry concentration between the mid-1960s and early 1980s, the microbrewery and craft beer movement began. Peterson (1990) notes that when an industry becomes highly oligopolistic, an alternative industry structure may emerge. In this structure, several smaller firms begin producing a distinctly different product that fulfills the needs of a niche market. In essence, the rapidly changing structure of the US brewing industry created a set of circumstances that allowed craft beer to emerge as a new alternative to mainstream industrial lagers. The craft and microbrew movement emerged as an alternative to this and produced a different product, using more traditional means of production. Consolidation and market concentration have no doubt affected the type of beer produced, and in the late 1970s, many new players were ready to get their feet wet in a newly formed market, the regional-specialty, or more commonly known craft, market. Hence, we can view craft beer as an alternative product, rather than one in direct competition with macro-produced lagers.

## Three-tier distribution and the consolidation of power

The repeal of Prohibition accelerated the homogenization of American beer, and the concentration of the US brewing industry, but this was not the only consequence. When the 21st Amendment was passed, it also ushered in a new system of taxation and distribution of alcohol, one that reflected and exacerbated the already-entrenched racialized structure of the brewing industry. It is a story of the various ways in which each tier has been, and continues to be, racialized through hiring practices, marketing, and exposure to beer. The three-tier distribution system, which is still in place today, gave individual states the right to regulate and tax the production and consumption of alcoholic beverages. According to the NBWA (2019a)—a trade association founded in 1938 that represents the interests of the over 3,000 independent distributors in the US—'the three-tier distribution system provides the infrastructure, capital and personnel small brewers need to reach a wide network of retailers.' This system was intended to prevent alcohol from being sold directly to consumers, to prevent breweries from establishing monopolies, and to help states more effectively tax alcohol. The three tiers are: the producer (for example, Anheuser-Busch and Sierra Nevada), the distributor (for example, Silver Eagle Distributors and Constellation), and the retailer (that is, traditionally, white men).

Producers of alcoholic beverages represent the first tier. Under this system, brewers are prohibited from selling directly to consumers. There are special circumstances and licenses that apply to breweries and brewpubs but these regulations vary by state. Some states allow breweries and brewpubs to sell directly to the consumer but these are often privately owned. In order for a producer to get their product to market, it must first change hands and enter into the second tier—distribution. Distribution is handled by firms known as wholesalers. Since the inception of the three-tier system, wholesale distributors handled the marketing and selling of beer. These firms operate within a given territory (most often confined to one state) and are usually licensed to sell only a limited number of brands. Additionally, no two distributors may sell the same brands in the same territory (though different wholesalers may sell the same brand across different territories). For example, a distributor has the rights to sell Bell's, Stone, and Lagunitas, three prominent craft brands. Another distributor in the area may have the right to sell Founder's and Uinta. This leads to competition among wholesalers over which brands are sold at a given retailer. Some states operate under the franchise model. According to Matt, the term 'franchise state':

> 'means that the right to sell certain breweries', any brewery's products, the rights are actually owned by the distributor,

> which can be bought and sold or traded by the distributors, but not by the breweries or the retailers. So the retailers have to buy for whoever for they distribute, whoever has the franchise rights.' (Matt, white, male, sales rep)

(For a more detailed description of franchise laws by state, see Brewers Association, 2015.) As Malkin and Hanke (2018) note:

> Beginning largely in the 1970s, franchise laws were established in various states to protect local businesses. The intent was to combat unequal bargaining power of the big brands—which was then more prevalent—and to prevent large producers from dominating small distributors by abruptly taking their business elsewhere, which would likely result in a complete shutdown of the distributor. This led many wholesalers to consolidate and merge, and as a result of this consolidation, distributors are not at the mercy of big brands anymore.

One producer in Georgia described the relationship between producer and distributor as 'like a prenup,' saying: 'franchise states are like a marriage you can never get out of' (Malkin and Hanke, 2018). Such agreements also solidified racialized relations within the industry, with white people protecting white people.

Essentially, once a brewer enters into a franchise agreement, they have little say in the selling of their product. The Brewers Association (2015) further describes these relationships as protectionist and unfair, stating that:

> A majority of the states have enacted full-fledged beer franchise laws. Although it is not hard to detect a whiff of protectionism in these enactments, their stated purpose is to correct the perceived imbalance in bargaining power between brewers (who are presumed to be big and rich) and wholesalers (who are presumed to be small and local).

As Malkin and Hanke (2018) contend, 'in some franchise states, like Georgia, it is nearly impossible for a supplier to switch distributors.' According to the Brewers Association (2015: 1), brewers and a brewery 'should become familiar with the state laws that regulate brewer–wholesaler relationships. Such "beer franchise laws" frequently dictate many terms of a brewer–wholesaler "agreement," trumping contrary terms in any contract.' This model gives tremendous power to the wholesale distributor, making it the most influential tier in the three-tier system. Distributors effectively operate as gatekeepers, or middlemen between the consumer and the producer (Chapman, 2015).

According to the NBWA (2019b), distribution personnel include 'not only employees that handle warehousing, transporting and delivering all types of beer to local retailers, but also sales and merchandising professionals who help promote each label of beer they sell.' Thus, the task of marketing a particular brand (that is, placing advertising material in stores and stocking the shelves) is left up to the distributor. Wholesale distributors are the people who set up the in-store displays, drive the beer trucks, and pitch the beer to retailers; they handle the marketing and advertising, and many other services. While the three-tier system was designed so that distributors have no control over the production of beer, they actually have a great deal of control over the actual point of sale of alcoholic beverages. As Reid (1997: 12) asserts: 'while distribution may not be the most romantic aspect of the brewing industry, wholesalers are crucial in providing consumers with the widest selection of the finest possible beer.' This can create competition for tap space and shelf space in local retailers, which would most certainly vary by region. A restaurant or bar may have 12 taps that are then allocated to specific distributors. This leads to competition between distribution firms, and also effectively gives the distributor control of what products are available in a given market and who the products are marketed to. As Hartfiel (1991: 47) notes: 'depending on which distributor gets a hold of a product, a beer can be introduced to major market centers like Chicago, New York, and Los Angeles.' If a bar or retailer has limited shelf and tap space, that space becomes more valuable. When working with several distributors, retailers have a choice of who to work with. Ultimately, this relationship between retailer and wholesaler hurts the producer and consumer as it limits the available options for purchase and the amount of actual beer sold.

When selling to a retailer, distributors must take into account the geographic location of their market and the demographics of the area; given these racialized reasons, some beers may sell better than others in certain areas. According to our interviews with several distributors, distributors in larger cities may have more brands on display where the level of income is much higher, whereas in more rural areas, they may limit their brand displays. The same is true of whether or not a distributor chooses to sell craft brands, and how many of those brands to sell in a given area with certain demographics. Our respondents agreed that the decision to place craft brands in a retail store is based on whether or not that product will sell. Given that craft beer is more expensive than regular beer, the socio-economic status of the consumer is taken into consideration. Let us cut to the chase.

The craft beer market is majority white, college-educated males. Craft beer consumption among women is on the rise, with some studies showing women now drinking more craft beer than wine (Chapman et al, 2018; Darwin, 2018; Klonoski, 2013). Despite this increase in consumption, the craft beer market remains overwhelmingly white and male. Black people and Latinx individuals make up less than 15 per cent of the total craft beer market (Brewers Association, 2018b). Given the gender and racial differences in craft beer consumption, distributors—which, according to Patricia (black, female, industry insider), are overwhelmingly white men—are tasked with marketing specific brands and styles of beer grounded in their perceptions of the tastes of women and minority groups. While there are not yet significant studies examining the taste preferences of black, Latinx, and other racialized minorities in terms of craft beer, Chapman et al (2018) and Darwin (2018) contend that women are often marketed alcohol through sexist imagery, pink labels, and the perception that women prefer softer, more feminine, flavors such as fruity flavors and more wine-like beers. Part of the issue is that, as Chapman et al (2018) assert, beer itself is perceived to have an inherent gender; also, as we have seen here, beer is perceived to have an inherent race. As a result, women report being offered certain styles of beer that are perceived to be more 'feminine' and less robust than styles such as stouts or IPAs. Most of the distinction between masculine and feminine beers is related to the style of beer. According to data on craft consumers from the Brewers Association (2018b), 'from 2015–2018, 81 percent of new craft drinkers were white, and 19 percent came from minority groups.' Chief economist for the Brewers Association Bart Watson points out that:

> Given that only 68.7 percent of the 21+ US population is non-Hispanic white, that's not progress. Minority craft drinkers are growing, but only because the total population of craft drinkers is growing, not because craft drinkers are getting more diverse along racial lines—as we saw, the gender trends are more positive. (Brewers Association, 2018b)

Another factor is that craft beer is simply not marketed to black and other minority groups. In reality, black tastes have been shaped by racist and classist marketing campaigns, an example of which being the malt liquor advertisements of the 1970s and 1980s—issues that are centrally important to grapple with in order to understand the whiteness of beer.

While there are perceived differences in taste by gender, there are also perceived racial differences in preference. For instance, Matt, a white male distributor in a large mid-Atlantic region, recalls his experiences: "I've noticed with people of color—just in my region [a well-educated, predominantly white college town] as well as the larger city center up the road, another major market—I have noticed that women and men of color usually stick to beer and malt liquor." As discussed previously, the black community has a long history with malt liquor and the marketing of stronger, lesser-quality beers. Part of the issue is that craft beers and other brands are simply not marketed to people of color. We point to several reasons for this but begin our analysis with the role of the distributor in the marketing of craft beer, and the lack of minorities in these positions.

The final tier of the system is the retailer and the taproom writ large. Under this system, a consumer can only purchase alcoholic beverages from a retail shop, bar, or restaurant. The cost of beer is greatly affected as it passes through each tier. At each stage, the beer is taxed and marked up; therefore, by the time a consumer purchases beer in a retail store or taproom, it has effectively been taxed and marked up twice. In effect, the three-tier system creates hurdles that end up costing the consumer more and limiting available options. There are a few exceptions. Small breweries and brewpubs are able to bypass the three-tier system, though not without some cost and special licensing. These small (or micro-) producers are allowed to operate both as producer and retailer. They are able to do so by sacrificing their out-of-state distribution rights. In order for a brewery to be sold out of state—extending its brand and market potential—it must pass through the distribution system. Hartfiel (1991: 47) notes that 'depending on which distributor gets a hold of the product, a beer can be introduced to major market centers like Chicago, New York, and Los Angeles, yet meet the definition of a regional brewery.' Many microbreweries still retain only regional distribution; however, as the industry grows in size, more and more breweries are distributing more widely. According to the NBWA (2019b), 'because independent beer distributors help get new brands to market, consumers benefit by having the choice between the largest international brands and the smallest local brews all on the same store shelf, restaurant list and bar tap.' However, under this system, the distributors can essentially control where a certain product is sold with little say from the brewer. This limits the options available to consumers and also drives up costs. Retailers form relationships with distributors and this can also affect the brands that are sold in a bar or shop.

## Wholesale distributors: the (white) face of the three-tier system

What may appear as myriad choices is actually a calculated and thoughtful curation of select brands placed by the distributor. These calculations are based on what products they feel will sell the most, and limited by the marketing budget that each distributor is allocated. If a distributor feels that a certain brand or style will sell better than another, and a retailer asks for a certain type of product, they may focus more energy on marketing that particular brand. As the NBWA (2019b) notes: 'distributors deliver customized inventory based on the requirements of each individual retailer in their local market.' For instance, if a distributor is in an area such as the college town that Matt described, they may be more inclined to stock more expensive craft brands. College towns are populated by educated adults of legal drinking age, and make an excellent place to sell craft beer. We also know from industry data (*Mintel*, 2012) that 59 per cent of craft beer drinkers live in suburban areas, while only 15 per cent live in rural areas. Additionally, 26 per cent of craft consumers earn less than US$49,000 in annual income (*Mintel*, 2012). Knowing more about who the consumer is, we must also look at who the distributor is.

According to the NBWA (2019b), there are more than 3,000 independent beer distribution facilities that 'operate in every state and congressional district across the United States,' and 'they provide 141,000 solid jobs with good benefits to people who live in their communities.' The NBWA does not report statistics on the race or ethnic background of its members; however, it should be noted that on the official website of the organization (see: www.nbwa.org) the promotional slideshow titled 'Faces of the American Beer Distribution Industry' featured a paucity of people of color, and only two women of color (NBWA, 2019b). Most of the images of these individuals showed them working in a warehouse or driving a truck (NBWA, 2019b). While no official statistics are available, based on interviews with distributors and other industry insiders, Patricia (black, female, industry insider) jokingly suggests that distributors "reproduce asexually … there's like a million of them; they've all come from spores," and that they are all "like pigeons on a line, like, they're very much the same dude." Distribution jobs are fairly highly sought after. Matt (white, male, sales rep) notes that "these jobs are few and far between, they're desirable, and they're hard to get." Patricia suggests that this is partly due to the prestige of working in the industry: "the reps are a tight social group. … I think, to some degree, there's a lot of people who are in that industry because they are looking for the social capital of saying they work in the beer industry, not necessarily because they care that much about the beer."

Patricia contends that the price of craft beer is a major determining factor in what someone chooses to drink, along with the strength and 'buzz' generated by the beverage:

> 'Some people are only going to drink the cheap strong stuff because they want to get a good buzz. They can't afford it [craft beer]. Another example is college kids. They're not poor, but some of them have limited funds, and that's why you see them walking out of the Food Lion with a suitcase [24 beers] of Natty [Natural Light]. They're not impoverished or anything, but they want to get as many beers as they can for US$12.99.' (Patricia, black, female, industry insider)

This point is crucial to understanding why particular brands are marketed in certain areas. Consumers with limited disposable income often try to find a balance between enjoyment and the intoxicating effects of an alcoholic beverage. What Patricia is suggesting is that to some consumers, the desired effect of intoxication is more important than the enjoyment of the beverage itself. This 'quantity over quality' relationship can also be seen in lower socio-economic areas where malt liquor is prevalent. Areas of affluence such as college towns, urban town centers, and metropolitan areas with high-paying jobs have populations with more disposable income than more rural areas. These areas, and other gentrified areas, are populated by predominantly white, middle-class and college-educated families and single adults. Distributors in these areas understand the demographics and market their products accordingly. However, distributors are also in a position to reach out to untapped (no pun intended) markets.

When asked about how to market craft beer to minorities, Matt (white, male) admits that his view is from the perspective of a white man: "I'm not saying all of my observations are 100 per cent accurate, you know, but I've got my own biases, just like anyone else." He continues saying: "we haven't really seen much about the industry trying to figure out how to market across racial barriers." While it may come as no surprise that the industry is not coordinating massive efforts to reach black consumers and other minority groups, the perception of black and other minority drinkers is problematic and in line with the marketing strategies deployed in the 1960s. The perception is that black consumers cannot afford craft beer; therefore, to market to them would be a waste of time and resources. This is echoed by Matt, who says:

> 'Because white people are basically marketing to white women and white men, that's the majority of it. I am a white man, and my wife is a white woman and we [white people] have a disproportionately better socio-economic status than other white couples across the state and across the country. So, what's the point of marketing a bunch of craft beer to a bunch of people that, by the very nature of their disproportionate underprivileged-ness, can't afford to buy it?' (Matt, white, male, sales rep)

The view that black people cannot afford a particular product highlights the profit-driven motives of distributors, who often work on commission. At the end of the day, their job is to sell as much beer as possible. In order to do that, in their view, they must market effectively and efficiently to their primary constituency—white men.

So, how could distributors affect the structure and create change in the industry? As our interview participants contend, exposure to craft beer is crucial to developing a taste for it. For example, as Kevin, a black brewer and brewery owner, suggests:

> 'Everything comes back to exposure for me. But I like to differentiate between what I would call corporate-level marketing and ad exposure, and geographic exposure. I'll explain the difference. I think the biggest barrier to black and brown people being more avid consumers [of craft beer] on a national level, or their biggest challenge, is that, in the past, there has either been an intentional decision not to market to certain communities or it was an intentional write-off.'

This means that craft beer needs to be in places where minorities live, work, and drink. Craft beer needs to be available in corner stores, gas stations, and restaurants in these areas. That task falls to the distributor. Yet, simply having beer available for purchase is not enough. The price of craft beer prohibits people of lower socio-economic status from purchasing it. Consumers may see a 12-pack of domestic beer with a price of US$9.99 and a six-pack of craft beer with a price of US$15.99. To the non-craft drinker, the decision becomes strictly one of economics and disposable income. If someone has never tasted craft beer before, they are much less likely to spend almost twice as much for half as many beers. One of the tasks that the industry faces is simple: get racial and ethnic minorities to try beer. There are several existing marketing tactics that distributors employ to expose people to craft beer; these could be utilized in efforts to bring minority drinkers into the market.

It is not uncommon for distributors to host 'tap takeovers,' where all the taps at a bar will be devoted to a single brewery or style of beer. They can also host free tastings at retail shops and grocery stores. In our interviews with prominent social media influencers, one in particular recounted several times that he took six-packs of craft beer into neighborhood barber shops to get people to try it. On a much larger scale, there have been social media campaigns, and even entire beer festivals, dedicated to black brewers and exposing black people to craft beer.

By providing access to craft beer in these ways, distributors and influencers could bridge the gap between minority drinkers and white drinkers, as well as diversify the brewing industry at large. This also includes hiring black and minority people to positions within the industry. When it all boils down, the distributor is making a business decision. If the job of the distributor is to sell as much beer as possible, why would they not try to reach out to new markets? Is the cost of marketing in these areas too expensive when weighed against the potential profits? Or, is there a deeper issue? Matt again suggests that the income gap is a major contributing factor: "I think that if you see the socio-economic gap between people of color and white people shrink, you definitely see more, you know, marketing and ad dollars." He also defends the lack of marketing as a business decision. The following is an exchange between David and Matt:

DB (interviewer): 'So, it's a business decision?'

Matt (white, male, sales rep): 'Going into [discussing] race, it's a business decision. Do you [a distributor] want to spend a bunch of money to promote Bell's Two Hearted Ale [popular nationally distributed IPA] in the "hood," where everybody's drinking Colt 45? It's just not smart. You can call it racist, you can call it whatever you want, but the bottom line is it's just not responsible. Everyone's [distributors have]

> got a marketing budget, and it's not a responsible use of those ad dollars. I think when we see that gap shrink, we'll see a lot more ads for craft beer targeted at people of color.'

This admission says quite a bit. When we unpack this, there are two key issues. One is the perceptions of black people held by distributors, who are largely white men, that they do not have a taste for 'good' beer, and nor can they afford it. Second, there is the view that all marketing decisions come down to simple economics and profitability. Minorities are not viewed as a viable market by distributors; they are seen as a waste of time and money. While this view is steeped in racism, it also exposes a deeper issue within the industry. Such profit-motivated marketing strategies of distributors actually perpetuate and solidify stereotypes of minority drinkers. Since distributors are in control of what products come to market, their perceptions of minority drinkers is crucial to understanding why black people and other racialized minorities do not drink craft beer.

The suggestion that there are deep structural issues that limit the spending power and economic impact of minorities is certainly nothing new; however, when considering the relative low cost of beer, the targeted marketing of the craft industry, and the industry's growth, it would seem that the industry could attempt to rectify the problem. One suggestion may be to employ more people of color as distributors. Having a black person market craft beer to black people could remove the racist perception of the industry. In fact, it could change perceptions at an industry level. Many of our respondents commented that having black people in these positions would make craft beer more approachable, more representative of them, and more understanding of the structural issues facing black people and other people of color, both historically and contemporaneously. In the next section, we examine the pathways to employment in the distributing networks.

## Pathways into the industry

The structure of the three-tier distribution system, as well as the latent functions of the distribution model, have greatly affected the marketing of craft beer to, and consumption of craft beer by, minorities. From an industry perspective, most positions in the industry, at all three tiers, are filled by white men. Craft brewers are overwhelmingly white men. Concerning the other two tiers of the distribution system and how they affect minority craft beer consumption, we point to two key ways.

First, there are very few minorities that are employed as wholesale distributors. At the time of writing this book, there were no data available on the demographics of distributors. However, through our interviews, we heard the same sentiments echoed time and time again: "these dudes all look the same." Indeed, of the three distributors we interviewed, all of them were white and only one was female. While certainly not a representative sample of the entire industry, our sample does reflect trends in employment and anecdotal data from our interviewees. Having a position in the industry provides exposure to craft beer. As previously discussed, Patricia (black, female, industry insider) noted that many of the distributors that she had encountered were not even into craft beer, but were more business-minded. This is certainly not generalizable to all distributors, but it is one of many pathways into the industry. Indeed, Matt and Scott, another white male distributor in the same region, stand in stark contrast to this. Both self-proclaimed craft beer lovers who worked in the food and beverage industry, they were exposed to craft beer from a retail perspective first. According to our respondents, the most common pathway to becoming a distributor is through the food and beverage industry.

While black people certainly do work in the food and beverage industry, they do so in less visible positions such as cooks or dishwashers. Jack, a black male general manager for a large craft brewery, described how he worked his way up through the restaurant industry before becoming employed by the brewery. However, this is a much rarer occurrence for black people. As the group Restaurant Opportunity Centers United (ROC, 2015: 1) notes: 'women and workers of color are largely concentrated in the lowest paying segments and sections of the restaurant industry.' These lower-tiered jobs are often in the back of the house, where customer interaction is minimal (ROC, 2015). This creates an unequal opportunity structure that benefits white males and provides them with greater opportunities to increase social capital. Additionally, the ROC (2015: 3) asserts that there are patterns of discrimination and racial segregation in the restaurant industry, which further solidifies racialized barriers to opportunity. This is evidenced by a 2013–15 study conducted by the ROC (2015: 4), which reports that tier-one positions (management, bartender, beer or wine specialist, and so on) are 64 per cent white and only 9 per cent black. In fact, according to the same study, black people make up only 11 per cent of the restaurant workforce across all tiers and positions (ROC, 2015). This is disturbing considering that one of the most common pathways to becoming a distributor is working in the restaurant industry.

Layla, a white female distributor, recalled her journey through the industry: "I worked my way up from server to bartender, to front of house manager, and from there, you know, this is a big community, you kind of connect with a lot of people, you get to know everyone." These positions were all tier-one positions, which the ROC (2015) suggests are highly racialized and discriminatory. Furthermore, just as Patricia (black, female, industry insider) suggests, the industry is very much about who you know and the amount of social capital you possess. The food and beverage industry, particularly the higher-end craft beer or wine bars, have a distinctly white clientele and employment base. So, why do restaurants and bars not employ black people and other minorities? The ROC (2015) outlines several real and perceived barriers that prevent employers from hiring minorities: barriers that workers themselves face; and barriers for customers. Employers face the real barrier that there is a lack of a candidate pool (ROC, 2015: 5). This means that there are simply not many black people and minorities applying for these jobs. There is also implicit bias of employers to hire white workers, which dovetails with the barriers of customers' own implicit bias, and the real barrier that they may have a 'lack of experience with servers of color and racial anxiety' (ROC, 2015: 5). Given that most craft beer consumers are white, there could be evidence that the implicit bias of employers and customers alike has an effect on the hiring of black workers in breweries. Black workers reported the 'lack of training, social networks, transportation' as real barriers to their employment (ROC, 2015: 5). By not employing minorities in these positions, further barriers that prevent minorities from being exposed to craft beer are created. Simply put, one must be around craft beer to develop a taste for it.

Through exposure in the food and beverage industry, individuals develop a passion for craft beer. In the case of our interviewees, this exposure and passion drove them to pursue a career in the industry. However, as Matt (white, male, sales rep) suggested, industry jobs are lucrative, limited, and difficult to obtain. All three distributors that we interviewed noted that their opportunity, or entry into the industry, came from the connections that they made in the food and beverage industry. Both Matt and Layla recalled how their positions in the restaurant industry led them into distribution:

> 'I used to drink with the rep from a company that was supplying craft beer to the restaurant I was working at. And when he decided to leave the state, he asked if I would like to take over his job and he recommended me [to his

employer], and that's how I got my first sales-level job in distribution. … I did that [work as distributor] for three years and then when my portfolio was acquired by a larger company, I was laid off from my sales job and brought into the new company on a more administrative basis, a more brand-focused position.' (Matt, white, male, sales rep)

'Managing [an Italian restaurant with a large craft beer selection and adjacent craft beer retail shop] was one of the best things I have done. And that led to my connections into [a large wholesale distribution company]. I was trying to get out from behind the bar; I was looking for something more sustainable … so it was one of those things where I learned how to write a résumé because I never had to do that before. You get all your jobs [in the restaurant industry] over shots at the bar and the people you know, and word of mouth. And, ultimately, that [experience and social capital] led me down this road. I applied, interviewed, and beat out the rest of the competition. … I've known my boss for a decade. I don't want to say that he very much made it clear: "You're on your own applying, but I am just giving you a heads-up, this position is open and I think you would be a great fit."' (Layla, white, female, sales rep)

These interviews demonstrate the fact that social capital is key to working in the industry, particularly higher-level positions such as distributors. As Sugrue (1996: 107) suggests, historically, 'the main cause of discrimination in the brewing industry was the importance of personal connections in hiring decisions.' This is crucial as our interviews with social media influencers and brewers contend that having minorities working in the industry is key to exposing minorities to craft beer. If minorities are not employed in the positions that control the marketing and distributing of craft beer, they are much less likely to be exposed. Many of our respondents said that if black people are going to develop tastes for craft beer, they need to know that they are represented in the industry, and they need to feel welcome in these spaces. There need to be black brewers, distributors, and retailers that can make the culture more inclusive. This is increasingly difficult to achieve when the employee pool is white and the employee recruitment process happens in white spaces, and when job offers are given through under-the-table recommendations.

The structure of the three-tier distribution system perpetuates racial stereotypes through marketing and product selection and placement. It also denies opportunities to minorities through under-the-table job offers and its reliance on social capital as a form of job qualification. In order to work as a distributor, one must be in the food and beverage industry, know people in the distribution network, and, on some levels, be white. The power that these individuals possess as both gatekeepers and marketers allows them to abide by and reinforce racial stereotypes. They limit the exposure to craft beer, which is the single most important factor in developing a taste for it. Additionally, the perceptions of black drinkers and their socio-economic status is a lens through which distributors view potential profits. To say that distributors themselves are all racist is certainly not the case. However, to say that the distribution network and marketing strategies are not steeped in racism is a gross misstatement of fact. Black people need to be employed in the industry in order to expose black drinkers to craft beer and to market products from the perspective of shared identity, rather than the racialized and stereotypical view that is so commonly held among distributors. Simply put, black people are not valued as employees, or as a viable market for generating profit. In fact, they are seen as a waste of time.

# 4

# The Paths to Becoming a Craft Brewer and Craft Beer Consumer

## Getting crafty

Given the historical realities that have built the current structure of the craft beer industry in the US, we today see a structure that is itself racialized, gendered, and exclusionary. The systematic erasure of black and brown practices of brewing and drinking in early America; the creation and solidification of pubs and taverns, and the subsequent establishment and legal consecration of such spaces as 'white' establishments; the construction and solidification of the three-tiered distribution system that defined the oligopolistic beer structure that launched the big beer families; and all the way through the signing of the Homebrewers Act in 1978—all these things have contributed to and solidified this structure. It is worth interrogating how it is that individuals have gotten and contemporarily get into the positions within the three-tiered system itself. The structure itself is one thing; the bodies within that structure are another, having the potential to either challenge the structural realities and/or to build the culture and symbolic violence that continues to actively exclude people of color:

> 'The people that I've seen here in the Chicagoland starting breweries, came either from a background of working for a larger brewery that became a macro, or are owned by a macro-brewery. They [brewery owners] are, largely speaking, young, white millennials. A lot of them come from the art world, where, for better or worse … they know

> that that's not something they could make money off [selling works of art], but they got into the brewing industry. You don't see a lot of different ethnicities … or other differences in the scene here.' (Juan, Latinx, male, brewer/owner)

In order to grapple with this, we asked our respondents several key questions that will help us to uncover the process connected to becoming a craft brewer and becoming a craft beer consumer, the two poles of the three-tiered distribution system—leaving out the fundamental structure of the middle-tier of distributors, who fundamentally connect the producer and the consumer (Withers, 2017) but in highly racialized, classed, and gendered ways. Their responses not only solidify what the industry has already known, and perhaps encouraged, but also illuminate the racial-organizational, structural, and cultural aspects that etch the paths more fully for some, and deny those in spades for others.

## Becoming a craft brewer in the US or following the white brick road

> 'I do think that as the industry continues to mature over the next five to ten years, when you ask the question, "How do you become a brewer?," there will be a very clear answer.' (Kevin, black, male, brewer/owner)

Liking beer is probably a good start to wanting to become a brewer. However, as we have seen and will see even more clearly, being a fan of beer in general, or craft beer in particular, is obviously not a historical given, and because of that fact, it is certainly not a contemporary given either. It seems to depend quite fundamentally on one's position within the racialized, gendered, and classed social structure in the US. Yet, for a moment, let us say that one has an inkling to look into what it might take to become a brewer in the US. One might do a basic search on, say, 'how to become a brewer' in order to gain some insight into the process. Scrolling past the paid advertisements, this is indeed revealing of the possible paths that one might need to begin walking down in their quest to become a brewer, in no particular order: seek formal educational credentials from universities (for example, UC-Davis) or traditional brewing schools (for example, Siebel in Chicago); volunteer at your local brewery (keg washing and the like); homebrew and enter brewing competitions with your beer; learn chemistry and biology;

network with local brewers; work your way up through long hours lifting heavy things (that is, as one site suggests, be sure to work out 30 mins/day); and do a lot of soul searching. Our research and discussions with folks in the industry, including brewers, indicate that this is a good list as regards what it highlights; however, such a list of 'do's' leaves out the social, cultural, and economic realities. In fact, more telling, we think, is that of the first 12 results in this Google search, the images (if they had images, which most did) were *all* white men (or disembodied white hands), with different lengths of beard growth, in brewing action. Even those with artist renderings were of white, male, brewers. The only woman present was admiring the brewing prowess of the white male in the image. One can create the list; however, creating the reality that makes brewing in the US as something for more than a small fraction of the population is quite another story.

Therefore, Kevin's previous quote indicates an unclear answer to the questions of how to become a brewer—but perhaps it is because the answer is out of reach of so many that the industry needs to 'mature' more fully. Juan, one of the male, Latinx brewers that we interviewed for this project, covers the bases:

> 'One of our other good friends said, "Oh, yeah, I homebrew," and I got really interested. He works for [a chemical lab], so he's a scientist. My passion for brewing started with science. So, I went to his house one day and brewed with him. And, he had three books open and was takin' all kinds of measurements, checking the pH, the sugar content on the wort, and measuring the beer that was already being produced in a carboy. I looked at it [homebrewing] as an opportunity for a hobby. I'm not really into sports, and I like to do things with my hands a lot. So woodworking was another one of my hobbies. My wife bought me a homebrew kit. That first year, I probably spent about US$2,000 on equipment and brewed almost every other week. Going back to that friend who introduced me to brewing, at the time, he said, "I'll usually only brew two or three times a year." I brewed over 20 times that year and got really interested in the whole process. I learned a lot from listening to podcasts, reading books on the subject, and reading the science behind malting and hops and water chemistry, which gave birth to some of our recipes here.' (Juan, Latinx, male, brewer/owner)

Everything is here in this story of the path to brewing—networks, homebrewing, interest and knowledge in science, free time and hobby development, disposable income (and lots of it), education, and so on. Yet, given the socio-economic reality in the US, even in the 21st century, what if this is a story that is not at all in reach of everyone? More to the point, what if this story highlights paths that are available to white people, men, and those from the middle to upper echelons of the class structure? In the year 2019, Juan is what is referred to as a 'unicorn,' that is, a rarity in the industry, but the US has always loved the rare story—that which masks the more general reality for the vast majority. Or, it could be as simple as Tony, a social media influencer and organizer, and Scott, a distributor, put it:

> 'You have to want to alter your reality. You have to like flavor, and you have to want to tinker around with some things and figure something out. So, if you have those three fundamentals, then you have what it takes to be a brewer. That's how people get into it.' (Tony, black, male, influencer/organizer)
>
> 'You're a nerd that likes beer.' (Scott, white, male, sales rep)

There seems to be an agreed-upon path to becoming a brewer. In fact, according to a career-finder website, Joyner (2016) outlines five basic steps to becoming a brewmaster. In order, these steps are: educate yourself, get social, attend a professional brewing school/course, and put that degree to use (Joyner, 2016). As noted, Joyner (2016) suggests that the first step is to educate yourself: 'any brewmaster will tell you that the first step to becoming a Master Brewer is to do research on your own, and set up your own homebrewing project.' Another crucial part of this education is heavily investing in equipment, trying and tasting a wide variety of beer styles, and experimenting in your home. After you have mastered the art of homebrewing, and taken some educational courses in brewing (not required, but highly suggested by Master Brewers), it is time to 'get social,' which is all about 'getting your name out there, networking, and gaining more and more experience in the world of beer and brewing. Enhance your local people' (Joyner, 2016). Now that you have an established a name and have connected with other brewing professionals, you should attend a professional brewing school. Of course, 'attending a professional brewing school or university affiliated brewing program will only aid you in achieving your dream faster' and the aspiring Master Brewer has no time to waste; after all of that hard work, schooling, training, networking, and effort, it is time to 'put that degree to use … you are a learned brewer now' (Joyner, 2016). In the final step, while still highly optimistic about how this pathway to brewing would certainly help *anyone* to become a Master Brewer, Joyner (2016) offers this last piece of advice with a nonchalant realism: 'if you have to start at a lower level position than you'd like, it's okay, just breathe. Remember that you're surrounded by delicious beer, and not working in a 24/7 call center anymore.' The last line here seems to suggest that becoming a Master Brewer is not only a lengthy, and presumably expensive, process, but one that is more fulfilling, satisfying, and ultimately enjoyable than a low-skilled call center job. While this career-finder website offers a simple pathway to brewing, it should be noted that neither the Brewers Association nor Master Brewers Association of the Americas offer any such guides or tutorials. You are simply left to find the pathway on your own.

However, are these maps, blueprints, pathways, and so on ones that all brewers follow? Or *can* follow? One of the key things that our respondents made clear to us, and that makes perfect sense, is that one of the keys to becoming a brewer is, well, exposure to beer and knowing 'good beer.' Obviously, this is a fundamental starting point for anyone in the three-tiered distribution system that shapes the craft beer industry—but especially for brewers. One must first become a discerning consumer of craft beer in order to have a seed of interest in brewing the concoction. We will see, though, that this most basic component—exposure to beer/becoming a consumer—is not equally available to all for a wide variety of structural, cultural, and economic realities. Due to the wide variety of barriers facing racialized minorities at the gate of this industry, that is, exposure/consumption, there are a series of significant contemporary moves afoot to make a dent in this structure.

## *Homebrewing: the first (white) step*

Aside from the all-critical exposure factor, when asked 'How does one become a brewer in the US?,' a majority of our respondents placed homebrewing front and center. Our data indicate several aspects to this: purchasing or being gifted a homebrewing kit; access to a homebrew supply store (somewhat mitigated now due to the internet); joining a homebrew club and/or brewing with friends; and developing beer social networks comprised of sharing information, recipes, and so on.

While homebrewing has been around since the beginning of the settler colonial situation in the US (and, of course, well before that in indigenous communities), homebrew kits come in many different varieties and have been commercially available for quite some time, with the most popular iteration of these being the product appropriately called 'Mr. Beer,' a kit that started to be marketed in 1993. Celebrating its 25th anniversary in 2018, the company highlighted the centrality of its kit (ranging from US$44.95 to US$129.95 today) by stating online: 'today numerous breweries across the United States are headed by brewmasters who started with a Mr. Beer Kit' (Mr. Beer, 2018). Black brewer Kevin tells his origin story, which includes a brewing kit, a book, and some unexpected money from his father:

> 'I think I'd gotten around US$100 from my dad to replace some tires or something on my car because I was broke. I thanked him for the money and told him that I was going to use it to buy a homebrew kit. That was like eight years ago. And that's how I got started. I bought the book, *How To Brew*, I bought a homebrew kit, read the first chapter of the book, and I thought, "Oh, yeah. I like this. I'm all about this." And that's how it started. I started mostly working with other people's recipes and trying to recreate certain beers and whatnot.' (Kevin, black, male, brewer/owner)

For some, the homebrew kit was not what got them hooked on brewing, but it was still what started them down that path. This is the case for brewer Albert:

> 'I went down to Charlotte, where my friends lived, and my roommate had just bought a homebrew kit. He doesn't have very much common sense. So, obviously, I wanted to help him brew. I said, "Let's do it." I'd always wanted to try and brew and tried it once before with a Mr. Beer kit and my buddy. But that didn't get me hooked. Not like to the level where I was brewing a five gallon batch and then putting it in bottles. After my first five gallon batch, I literally said to my friends that week, "This is what I'm going to do."' (Albert, white, male, brewer)

There is a cultural image of the lone, often white, often male, middle-aged homebrewer, brewing some gallons of his own brew, on the weekend, perhaps in his basement. However, such an image masks the importance of the social networks and access to brewing communities that both sustain and encourage the lone homebrewer.

After the passage of the Homebrewers Act of 1978, what were likely pre-Prohibition disparate social networks of homebrewers were now given legal stamps of approval and formalized homebrew clubs became more prominent in the late 1970s and early 1980s. While we know very little about the demographic make-up of these early clubs, we can extrapolate that they were almost all-white and all-male given the socio-economic locations of the first wave of craft beer barons. Whether homebrew clubs or, 'guilds,' or just friendship networks, the role of social networks is key for our respondents in understanding the paths to becoming a brewer. Latinx, male, brewer Juan discusses finding community:

> 'Through the homebrew club, I found several homebrewers that lived a few blocks away from me. I had been here [neighborhood] for three years without knowing that they existed. So, I started entering competitions and sharing my beer with the homebrew club. I started to become someone with a little bit of a clout in the community. I don't like to toot my own horn, but that was exactly what was happening. I started thinking more and thought I'd love to maybe do this professionally, someday.' (Juan, Latinx, male, brewer/owner)

He had found a community that had been homebrewing, connected through a homebrew club; they competed with one another in competitions (another important part of the path to becoming a brewer), and the possibility that he could do it professionally entered his mind. If one can break into such majority-white and majority-male (and heterosexual and middle- to upper-class) spaces (a very tall order), that community can provide just the social push one needs:

> 'And just like that, it was starting to happen more and more. And it became telling that this beer [Kevin's homebrewed beer] is good enough. And it was the nod from a small brewery that gave us the opportunity to brew on their system. We actually had a little, like, launch party for that beer. That party was insane and the place was packed. We sold a lot of beer in a very short amount of time. And I think I registered the company literally the next week.' (Kevin, black, male, brewer/owner)

Black and brown folks in the industry have important bird's-eye views that those interested in craft beer, and the role of homebrewing, social networks, and the like in the industry, should listen to:

> 'Craft beer and homebrewing in traditionally white communities is typically something family oriented. You learn [to drink craft beer and/or how to homebrew] from your father, your mother, your uncle, your aunt, or your cousin. If you went to college, there may have been some kids buying homebrewing kits, and they learned from that experience. But then, as you transition to that next level and try to open a brewery, you have to ask yourself, "Do you have craft beer in your community, and do you recognize craft beer when you see it?"' (Corey, black, male, influencer/organizer)

Therefore, homebrewing is a significant step along the path to becoming a craft brewer, which is a key position in the industry itself. Earlier this year, for the first time that we are aware, the American Homebrewers Association (AHA) released a brief look into the characteristics of homebrewers. It is interesting to consider what the AHA chose to release publicly on their website. According to the AHA (2019), in 2017 (the most recent data available): there were 1.1 million homebrewers in the US, and 40 per cent of them had started in the past year (that is, 2016/17); the average age of homebrewers is 42 (52 per cent of homebrewers are in the 30–49 range); 85 per cent of them are married or in a domestic partnership; 68 per cent have a college degree or 'some form of higher education' (it is unclear what this means); 68 per cent have annual incomes of US$75,000 or more; they range across the 50 states of the US; and they produced 1.1 million barrels of beer in 2017 (which was about 1 per cent of total US production). Curator Betsy thinks the following about these data:

> 'I think the American Homebrewers Association claims that upwards of 90 per cent of professional brewers began as homebrewers. That's their statistics. But what is important about that is you don't want to underestimate the importance of people who become homebrewers or professional brewers. They [aspiring homebrewers] are encouraged to start brewing and they understand that they can brew because they see people who look like themselves, or come from similar backgrounds or groups. They see these

> other people are brewers.' (Betsy, white, female, curator/historian)

What do these publicly facing data say to potential homebrewers, let alone potential brewers down the road?

There are several important things to point out about this publicly facing information. First, the AHA chose not to report the gender or racial demographic distribution of homebrewers from their survey. While it is unclear why the organization chose not to include this information, one can surmise that it is because the numbers would have shown the amazing *lack* of diversity in this key training ground of the industry, that is, homebrewing. Our best guess is that some 85 per cent or more are men, and some 90 per cent or more are white. Second, given the information that they *did* provide the public, one only has to scratch the surface of those socio-economic numbers to reveal the whiteness correlates. In 2016/17, out of all adults above 25 years old in the US, some 39 per cent of them had some kind of college degree; however, for white people, that number was closer to 43 per cent, while for black people, it was 29 per cent, for Latinxs, it was 21 per cent, for Asians, it was 61 per cent, and so on. Aside from Asians, white people are much more likely to have a college degree (NCES, 2019; US Census Bureau, 2017), and 68 per cent of homebrewers had one—the math indicates a path more likely for white people and Asians (though we find very little Asian engagement in the brewing industry historically and contemporarily). Minority women are more likely than minority men to have college degrees. Furthermore, looking at income makes this even more striking. The median income in the US in 2017 was US$61,372, meaning that 50 per cent of Americans made at or above that amount that year; an income of US$75,000 puts you in the 78th percentile (US Census Bureau, 2018). Of course, these values vary significantly by race and ethnicity, as well as gender: white people have much more income and wealth than minorities; and men have more income and wealth than women. What this means is that while only 22 per cent of Americans in 2017 made at or above US$75,000, *68 per cent of homebrewers made at least that much!* Clearly, homebrewing is not a possibility for all. Despite this, several of our respondents are hopeful about the clearly low number of minorities who may now be homebrewing, including Tony: "Statistically speaking, there's more homebrewers than there are brewery owners. I would confidently say that there are more black people brewing at home than are brewing at breweries" (Tony, black, male, influencer/organizer). Moreover, as Patricia states, "Again, this is a resource- and capital-intensive hobby.

You need equipment, you need space to brew, and you need access to a homebrew store. Those facts eliminate a large portion of the population by virtue of geography or access" (Patricia, black, female, industry insider). Not only is this part of the path inaccessible to many, but there is also now a whole industry popping up to provide a system of credentials necessary to enter the industry.

### *Education and interests: the credentialing and ideology of brewing*

While homebrewing is probably *the* key element in beginning the walk down the path of becoming a craft brewer in the US, we were very interested to learn from our respondents that the industry has embedded within its social and cultural logics a particularly potent set of ideological starting points and that these are being solidified, perhaps, by an ever-increasing credentialing system. As we have seen in this book thus far, there are several streams that define brewing in the US, which do not always flow the same direction. On the one hand, brewing has always been about the chemical reactions that constitute the process (for example, yeast strains consume sugars to create alcohol); on the other hand, brewing was part of household labor. One stream flows in the direction of the passing down of oral folk knowledge, while the other stream creates brewing institutes and schools in order to 'discipline' those knowledges. While one could go, the point is an important one: there are currents of the people (Who is that?) and there are currents of the industry (Who benefits?).

Several of our respondents did acknowledge that one is more likely to be interested in becoming a brewer if one has also always had an interest in science, in technology, and, specifically, in chemistry and biology. Juan definitely felt this way:

> 'I can actually apply all of the above processes [chemistry and biology], procedures, and measurements to brewing. What's interesting about brewing is that you don't need any of that [background in hard science]. You can be a great brewer, I believe, by just being a great cook, or by having a good palate and an understanding for the ingredients. That's how brewers were back in the day, right? They were good note takers. But if you do have a knack for chemistry and biology, you can certainly make your products better, repeatable and consistent. And that's where it hit the spot for me.' (Juan, Latinx, male, brewer/owner)

They also recognize the increasing importance of receiving credentials from brew classes and brew schools, and/or even earning a brewing degree at traditional or emerging programs at universities and colleges around the US. Black brewer and one-day hopeful owner of a bricks-and-mortar brewery Kevin discusses this at length:

> 'I think a lot of people take different paths. But what I'm finding, even from a conversation I had yesterday, is that the industry is becoming so established that the path toward becoming a brewer is starting to become more structured, if that makes sense. Now, people have access to programs and certifications, and degrees [in fermentation science and brewing]. I was at a small brewery in Rockville. I was talking with the owner because we're working on a collaboration, and a guy walks into the bar. He was a big bearded guy, and he said, "I'm really interested in picking up brewery experience." And the first thing he does is slap down a very professional résumé. I don't know how often that happens in breweries, but just hit me. I started peeking at this guy's résumé. It was a legitimate beer résumé. And I thought that was very exciting and very interesting.' (Kevin, black, male, brewer/owner)

The idea of a 'legitimate beer résumé' is becoming a part of the vernacular of the beer culture in the US. Just a cursory glance at a variety of online breweries looking for brewers, sites that specialize in finding jobs for folks (Brewbound, Indeed, and so on), and even links to exemplar or example 'brewer résumés' make this clear. These résumés have previous brewer experience (for example, 'independently performed and monitored brewhouse and cellaring operations,' 'created recipes and evaluated ingredients for series,' 'autonomously produced two 20-barrel batches daily according to company, collaborative, and independent recipes'), intern experience (for example, 'learned and performed brewing and cellaring duties on 15-, 50-, and 150-barrel systems,' 'cleaned lines and washed kegs according to industry standards'), and some have relevant experiences like chemistry labs, creating patents for equipment, judging for homebrew competitions (for example, 'for stylistic and palatal creativity'), and, of course, the right education (for example, 'UC Davis Master Brewers Program,' 'Bachelor's of Science in Chemistry,' and so on)—all indicative of an 'epistemology of homebrewing' (Rodgers and Taves, 2017).

The fact is that brewing schools have been around since 1872 (Siebel in Chicago) and they have always produced brewers for the industry. However, there are now an increasing number of contemporary brewing schools and institutes to lay alongside the historic ones (like the National Brewers Academy, Consulting Bureau, Hantkes Brewers School and Laboratories, Wallerstein Laboratories, Carl Nowak's Chemical Laboratories, and so on). This specific educational inequality and the extant inequalities at every level of education, which is fundamentally organized by race, class, and gender, make this factor almost insurmountable for minorities in the US.

### *Apprentices, volunteers, and restaurant workers (Oh my!)*

While having interests and having those interests legitimated by a credentialing institution like a trade school or university program constitute an emerging set of bricks overlaid on the white brick road of brewing in the US, there is a centuries-old social structure seemingly built into the process as well: apprenticeship. Many of our respondents discussed this path to becoming a brewer. Black social media influencer and craft beer connoisseur Marcus discusses the path to brewing:

> 'They [aspiring brewers] will go get a homebrewer kit—which is usually the story with any successful brewer, they will buy a kit first—or they jump in and start an apprenticeship with someone who knows how to brew. It's no different from people who are aspiring to become chefs. What are you going to do [to become a chef], you have to start cooking. How do you do that? Are you going to learn from a chef and work side by side with that person, or learn from an expert chef? You're going to watch them, and then you're going to try and cook like them. Then you can start to come up with your own interpretations on whatever it is that you're preparing.' (Marcus, black, male, influencer)

Therefore, apprenticing appears to be a significant next step, of sorts, on the path to becoming a brewer in the US craft beer industry, and it appears that there can be formal as well as more informal ways of getting into apprenticeships.

We were told that one way in which many folks gain their first entry into the process is by volunteering their time at a local brewery (of course, one needs to be available). Recognizing that "every homebrewer wants to hang out in a real brewery," Latinx brewer and successful brewery owner Juan lays out this process:

> 'Sometimes, individuals that want to get into the industry will ask me, "Can I come visit you guys and, and help you out?" And then when they come [to volunteer], they see that our intention is to get things done the best possible way, and that's not necessarily the environment they are expecting. At the end of the day, I need my employees to go home and not stay until 10 pm. So we [volunteers and Juan] clash a little bit on the purpose of their visit. Someone wants to come in [and] talk about brewing over a beer, but I'm there to work. What I do notice is that the smaller the brewery is—especially a very busy small brewery like us—is that we have to watch ourselves and try to not to be jerks. Sometimes, when people come to visit—because we're so busy, we're so focused on the day's work, and there's only so many of us multitasking like crazy—that we have to pause and say, "This is my customer, my ambassador, let's give him two minutes."' (Juan, Latinx, male, brewer/owner)

Juan goes on to discuss turning that volunteering into actually working at a brewers, starting at the bottom, with the (slim) potential to work one's way up:

> 'Working at a brewery would be my first step towards working in the industry. That would be my first recommendation. Work at a brewery for at least six months, if not longer. You're going to move up from lower-skilled tasks—most likely keg washing, moving sacks of grain, and helping with basic steps in the brewing process, all this hard sweat work—to, probably much later, watching a brew and cleaning tanks. But I feel it's so important because it gives people—and we've seen many people pass through the brewery here—an idea of what the day-to-day operations are and what the challenges are. And they will learn a lot.' (Juan, Latinx, male, brewer/owner)

Volunteering one's time has a complicated relationship with the matrix of oppression in the US (Musick et al, 2000). For many, time is money. Time to work is time to get paid.

Several of our respondents also discussed the importance of hanging out in and/or working in the restaurant industry in your local area. Ida's discussion exemplifies the potential of this somewhat spontaneous process:

> 'It [working in the brewing industry] boils down to who you know. One of my good friends works at one of the larger Asheville breweries, and he had no brewery experience, no high school diploma, nothing. But he happened to be eating pizza at this large Asheville brewery and one of his friends worked there as a brewer. He said he was looking for a job. So, he started putting O-rings on kegs. And then went through school and got a full scholarship at AB tech, and then did his internship at the brewery. And now he's the lead brewer of specialty brews.' (Ida, black, female, brewer/owner)

Later, we will discuss at length the social *fact* of racial, class, and gender discrimination in the restaurant industry (Benner, 2015). However, for now, readers should note the ways in which racism, sexism, and classism are woven into the structure of the restaurant industry (Benner, 2015), whether it is in who works back or front of the house, who gets paid more, and why these differences vary by race and gender.

Therefore, apprenticeships, volunteering, and hanging out in the local bar/restaurant industry represent possible paths to becoming a brewer, lines of the brewer résumé, and important experiences to have. Yet, our respondents, especially those in our sample who are *not* white and who are not at the center of the typical brewer position in the social structure, have important critical perspectives on the realities behind this for people of color and women. Patricia has a unique bird's-eye view of the industry from her industry vantage point, which highlights the role of social networks:

> 'I meet very few brewers who don't know other brewers. And although there's not a formal apprenticeship structure, we almost have the equivalent to a social apprenticeship structure in the US. And I think that's one of the reasons why diversification can be so difficult. It's as if getting hired depends upon someone's existing social networks. It's really tough for someone who has none, connections to break into the industry.' (Patricia, black, female, industry insider)

This highlights the importance of apprenticing, for sure, but it also complicates this, pointing out that our fundamentally segregated social networks (as discussed earlier), especially by class, race, and gender, likely prevent cross-class, cross-race, and cross-gender apprenticeships from ever occurring in the first place—especially when "there are no black local brewers" (Tony, black, male, influencer/organizer) where you live as a person of color. Tony lays out the reality in communities across the contemporary US craft beer scene:

> 'There weren't any apprenticeships like the ones that white folks are privy to. We [Tony's community] weren't privy to those things. If we wanted to do something, we had to figure it out on our own. … So, the aspiration to be a part of that industry was viewed by us as more of a product of privilege. The schooling is a huge factor as well. What it takes to understand how to be a brewer. A lot of brewers are chemists, biologists, and engineers. They have free time to tinker around in their basement. They have disposable income to spend on homebrew kits, malt and grains, things of that nature. It's hard in the black community, when you don't have any free time. When you do have free time, you're typically not dinking around in your basement with expensive things that may not taste good after you're done. It's a risk. So, when you look at these barriers, you see that they start to pile up.' (Tony, black, male, influencer/organizer)

Of course, the racialized networks that prevent these from the get-go also present a structural impediment to even getting off the ground:

> 'I realized quickly upon moving to Asheville that there were millions of dollars being poured into the brewing industry, and the brewing industry was really the backbone of the community. However, there were virtually no black and brown faces in the industry. So, I applied for all of the open brewery positions I saw available, and received not one position, not even as a janitor, which was frustrating.' (Ida, black, female, brewer/owner)

Finally, we have not even begun to touch on the social-structural dynamics that influence the move from a brewer (with all of its constraints and barriers for minorities) to an *owner* of a bricks-and-mortar brewery. While our respondents did discuss this at length, it represents both an entirely separate and lengthy engagement with the realities of funding and financing—where to get it, how to get it, the social networks involved, and the complex process of getting loans—that is ultimately grounded in the racism, sexism, and classism that is foundational and embedded in the US banking industry. Ultimately, there is (and always has been) a barrier for racialized minorities to enter this position with the industry. Tony brings it home, articulating a common sentiment across our respondents:

> 'It's not like a bunch of people all of a sudden were, like, "We like craft brewing. Let's homebrew now." The homebrew club that I am involved with held an event. All of the homebrewers looked to be 40 years old. That's 40 years of homebrewing experience, and they were all white men. There were a couple of women but they were mostly white dudes. Those are traditions that have been going on for longer than I've been alive. I just came to the understanding that homebrew was a "thing" five years ago. So, when I look at why it's [homebrewing is] dominated by whites, it is because America as a whole, and every other industry in America, is white dominated. And, in order to be successful as a black man, you have to go through a lot of different shit and go outside of your comfort zone in order to do so. And that's not typically rewarded.' (Tony, black, male, influencer/organizer)

The brewing tradition is white; as such, the brewing industry is white. It is structured by white social networks. It has always been this way. It also leads to a really difficult situation: "you know, if you don't drink craft beer, and you don't see craft beer, and you don't realize that craft beer needs forklift drivers, you're not going to Brew Down for that job" (Patricia, black, female, industry insider).

## Becoming a craft beer consumer in the US

As we have seen, quite clearly, becoming a brewer in the US is based on several social-structural phenomena—from homebrewing to volunteering at local breweries, from early interest in chemistry and science to obtaining formal credentials, among others—rooted in the fundamental workings of social networks (who you know, information sharing, and so on), which all end up working to structure women and people of color *out* of the brewing of beer, either for personal or professional reasons. We also saw that one of the key elements in even beginning to walk down the white brick road of brewing in the US is to actually consume its primary product—beer. Today, more importantly, one also needs to have a discerning taste with regard to craft beer and its associated cultures. In other words, the gate that one first needs to open in order to even attempt to tread down the white brick road of the industry is to drink (craft) beer, and, preferably, love and know how to select, talk about, and engage with craft beer culture. In other words, one has to be a consumer.

We asked all of our respondents to tell us their own origin stories as to how they each became a (craft) beer consumer. We found several key structures that raise the probability that one will engage with craft beer and its attendant cultures: being embedded in social networks of beer, homebrewing, and drinking craft beer; having experience of college; having access to a beer scene, bottle shops, and craft beer distribution channels; and affordability. All of these help us to uncover a broader and more nuanced story of how craft beer consumers are fermented in the contemporary social, economic, and cultural vat of the US. The story often goes sharply against the grain of the mythos about beer for all.

## *The social networks of craft beer*

The role of social networks is, again, critical for engagement with beer in general, and craft beer in particular. Familial networks, friendship networks, and networks established through the worlds of work, education, and leisure, among others, represent key social locations where craft beer as a possibility is often initially raised, and where information about the whats, wheres, whos, and even whys of craft beer can be shared among those in the network. For many growing up in a family where homebrewing was a part of daily life, this planted the early seeds of exposure to beer, craft beer, and its attendant possibilities. Betsy discusses her earliest memories when asked how she got into craft beer and its histories:

> 'I grew up with a dad who was a homebrewer and started homebrewing in the early 1980s—which I now appreciate was pretty early in the swing of things for American homebrewers, at least of our recent era. I remember growing up, when I was seven or eight, he would have me

> and my sister help him cap bottles on days when it was a bottling day. I also remember being very unhappy when he brewed because I felt like the aromas were very strong and unpleasant. So, I would run outside into the backyard, or cover my face with a bandana in the back room. I remember the bottle-capping device that he would use in our kitchen, and how he would store his homebrewed beer in our garage, which would periodically explode in the heat during the summer.' (Betsy, white, female, curator/historian)

Here, Betsy remembers the everyday practices in her childhood home: the sights, the sounds, the equipment, brewing, bottling, and the storing of her father's homebrew. This is akin to what French sociologist Pierre Bourdieu would call a 'habitus': those consistent, ongoing, everyday practices, inculcations, and socialization(s) that make individuals have what he calls 'cultural capital' (Bourdieu, 1984). Our data point to the importance of what one could call a 'craft beer habitus,' for Betsy, birthed in the social structure of her home and upbringing.

Others discussed being a part of social networks of beer that would inevitably link them to craft beer through friends, friends of friends, and even friends of friends of friends—networks can often work like that, through what sociologists call the 'strength of weak ties' (Granovetter, 1977), allowing information about job opportunities, as well as craft beer, to move from one network to another through dyadic relationships that link one network to another. Often, one is at an event of that friend of a friend, as in the following example: "I was at a friend's wedding, and the father of the bride gave each guest a bottle of his homemade IPA with a cute little label on each bottle. And I thought, 'This is cool'" (Juan, Latinx, male, brewer/owner). Here, brewer and owner Juan shows the power of these networks, where an introduction to the possibilities of homebrewing and craft beer can be shared at events like weddings, graduations, and so on—making an impact on this young Latinx man, who would take it further than most Latinx folks can ever dream of. In fact, at another part of the interview, he also ruminates that had it not been for such networks, it may not have happened:

> 'The more I talked to people in the industry and to brewers, I noticed they were drinking beers they had acquired from another brewer, or someone who owned a brewery, or worked for a particular brewery. I noticed they were somehow connected to the "thing" that they were drinking.

> Whereas in our community, we were never really connected to any of the booze coming into our neighborhood.' (Juan, Latinx, male, brewer/owner)

Connections. Social connections. Not just being marketed to from outside, but linking to what people are making within their communities. Social networks connecting networks, repeat exposure, and the socio-logics of such engagement can make the difference between becoming a craft beer drinker or not.

We also had several people discuss with us that, for them, working in the restaurant industry and/or simply hanging out in local restaurants, bars, and so on, becoming regulars, and having discussions with the wait staff, bartenders, and the owners can nurture the possibility of craft beer engagement. This can be seen in beer sales representative Scott's experience, which was quite common:

> 'That [Scott's taste for craft beer] was 100 per cent a product of working in restaurants. I wasn't really into beer when I started working in restaurants. I had to work my way from Bud Light, to Yuengling, to Sam Adams, and developed a taste for more malty beer styles. And then that developed into a taste for the hoppier beers and due to my employment, I was in a position to explore that.' (Scott, white, male, sales rep)

The experience of working in and around the restaurant industry can provide a structural space where it is possible to have more options available, a cultural space in which to understand and talk about one's product options, and a social space where the sharing of and encouragement of those options can provide a gateway from light beer to a hazy IPA.

Of course, as we have already covered, since we know that social networks are fundamentally segregated—whether we are talking about neighborhoods within cities (Arcaya et al, 2018), friendship networks (Munn, 2017), workplace environments (Stainback and Tomaskovic-Devey, 2012), educational environments (Byrd, 2017), leisure settings (Arai and Kivel, 2009), and even restaurants, bars, and community spaces like parks (Wolch et al, 2005)—even the role of social networks in creating the craft beer consumer is likely to actually reinforce the whiteness of craft beer and its spaces and cultures. Juan is fully aware of this reality and acknowledges that this is why there is a need to fundamentally think outside the box:

> 'There are barriers of opportunity that prevent people from getting into homebrewing, or having the knowledge that homebrewing is a thing. Meeting other people that brew, talking to successful brewers, and asking how to get along in the hobby are all things that you can introduce to someone through a festival, a panel discussion, a pop-up tasting, and so on.' (Tony, black, male, influencer/organizer)

We will see that this kind of set of approaches—taking it to the people who the networks actively exclude—is an important component of the movements to change the whiteness of craft beer in the US.

## *College = craft beer*

We have already seen the fundamental importance of a particular position within the socio-economic status for becoming a brewer in the US—very high incomes and college educated—and we also know that this is much more available to white people in the US. It turns out that college also represents a particularly important experience for developing a taste for craft beer as the vast majority of our respondents discussed college as a gateway for being introduced to, trying, and becoming a craft beer consumer. This was particularly true of our respondents of color, whose families did not homebrew, whose communities did not have brewers that looked like themselves, and whose access to craft beer scenes while growing up was off their radar. Social media influencer and black craft beer lover Tony reminisces about his experience:

> 'I had a couple of Sierra Nevadas in college. Like, it was, like, fancy beer that I could never really afford. So, like, you know, if I was meeting with somebody that had the ability to spend more than US$5 on a meal. I would maybe have a Sierra Nevada, and I thought it was fancy. I didn't really know much about it. I just thought it tasted good. My, my palate was still kind of attuned to Natty Ice and things of that nature. So, I really wasn't into it. But afterwards, Blue Moon came about … and this bar had these dollar nights where Blue Moon was only US$1. And the beer had an orange slice in it. I thought it was like orange juice. I had no idea that that was what beer actually tastes like. So, that was what I thought of as craft beer at the time.' (Tony, black, male, influencer/organizer)

Blue Moon came across in quite a few of the interviews as a game-changer for many people—that and Sierra Nevada. Beer historian and curator Karina thinks back on her college days and beer as well:

> 'I drank crappy beer in college. The reason I got into craft beer at all, and really started appreciating beer, is because I went to a bar where my friend was bartending and she said, "Hey, we got this new beer, give it a try." These were the days of me drinking like Keystone Light and stuff, right? So, she hands me this beer and I was like, "Holy, Jesus!," this actually tastes like something, and I love the taste of it. And I thought, "Wow, I'll totally finish this beer." And in fact, I asked for another one. And that beer was Sierra Nevada Pale Ale. Just like everyone's first beer story is Sierra Nevada Pale Ale. That [taste for craft beer] happened because my friend said, "Here, try this beer."' (Karina, Latinx, female, curator/insider)

Again, networks and friends, in particular, college networks and friends, worked to open up a social space where craft beer could have more potential to walk in. This can then really open up worlds, as expressed again by Juan:

> 'My roommates at the time got into it [craft beer] and they said, "Well, how about we each just buy a case a week. And we'll just trade-off." So, that's how I started to drink craft beer regularly, this deal I made with my roommates over the summertime to buy a different case every week.' (Juan, Latinx, male, brewer/owner)

In so many ways, college is important for understanding why craft beer is so white and why it matters. In a social-structural sense, for most, going to college often literally takes you out of your local neighborhood and your local social network. Therefore, although the college experience for most people of color is one of being around a bunch of affluent white students, which comes with its own significant set of problems (Byrd, 2017), we find that it is also *because* of a college experience that many racial and ethnic minorities are exposed to craft beer *because* college exposes them to white networks—networks that, as we have seen, are more likely to have engaged with craft beer and its attendant practices and cultures.

### *Access to craft beer scenes and craft beer selections*

Just like with the path to homebrewing, one has significantly limited probability of becoming a craft beer consumer if one: (1) is not in or around a craft beer scene (with taphouses, breweries, brewpubs, bottle shops, bottle shares, and so on); or (2) lives where craft beer is not distributed to one's neighborhood through corner grocery stores, gas stations, and other locales where one might purchase beer. Even though the American Brewers Association states that the vast majority of Americans are within ten miles of a brewery, the bottom line is that craft beer scenes are *not* evenly distributed and the distribution of craft beer is *not* equal—both functions of the racialized three-tier distribution system connecting producers to consumers. Being surrounded by a craft beer scene—like Boulder, Colorado, affectionately called the 'Napa Valley of Beer,' where there are over 300 breweries and 'more beer per capita than anywhere else in the country'—will certainly help introduce one to craft beer (Neuman, 2019). Consider Juan's story:

> 'It wasn't until I met my wife in Boulder that we started going out to different places. And I still remember the two beers that I fell in love with and decided, "Wow, I really like this stuff." One was from Southern Sun in Boulder. They have two locations there. And one of their beers was called On A Corner, which is an Amber Ale, and I still remember their growlers weren't growlers, it was just a 32-ounce mason jar you could go and pick up. And by the time I got home, it was leaking because of the pressure. And the other beer was, "1554" From New Belgium; it was a darker ale. I would buy a case of those two beers whenever I found it.' (Juan, Latinx, male, brewer/owner)

In some places, the 'scene' is much harder to come by, let alone find, as Tony relates:

> 'A friend of mine was telling me about this space that was kind of on the down low, where you could get growlers filled. I said, "What's a growler?" And my friend replied, "It's a jug of beer that you fill up with beer." But the place was only open during certain hours, and you had to know when they were open. It sounded like some kind of secret knock system, or some shit like that. It was super clandestine

> and weird. But that was the first time I was aware that there was a craft beer scene here.' (Tony, black, male, influencer/organizer)

Therefore, knowledge of, access to, and engagement with a craft beer scene, no matter how large or small (though size does matter here), is also a critical step in becoming a craft beer drinker, and maybe even a connoisseur.

Such accessibility and availability is simply much less likely for black and brown communities in the US. There is still a significant divide, some might say, a gulf, between white people's access to craft beer and everyone else's, and between the middle- and upper-class strongholds and everyone else. While we will deal with this more fundamentally in later chapters, consider the reality expressed by Marcus:

> 'When it comes to beer, you'll see great beer selections only in white-dominated towns. Towns that are majority white, or affluent, and they have a lot of restaurants and bars with lots of beers. And all these places feel like they are mostly white. Whereas in black clubs, they basically have bullshit beer most of the time. I'm not trying to call out people, but it'll be mass-distributed beer. It's just not what a beer advocate would hold his pinky up when he's sipping a glass or when she's sipping a glass. So, a lot of that is exposure.' (Marcus, black, male, influencer)

Exposure in the US is racialized and classed. As Kevin further states:

> 'And that's how it kind of feeds into the next piece. You run into people in places that are championing homebrewing, and experience the joy of homebrewing and the pride associated with the hobby. So, when you get down to the city and local level, geographically because of who the consumers are, you find that these breweries and these homebrew shops are not located in places where predominantly you have black and brown people. So, even on a day-to-day basis, you're not running into anyone or anything that looks anything like craft beer in most cases. And so, I think that's the biggest barrier. It's not that someone's putting up a wall to say, "Hey, you can't come here." And that's been our big challenge early on. We're very intentional about bringing our beer to certain spaces that

> maybe you won't normally see a lot of African-Americans.' (Kevin, black, male, brewer/owner)

The industry knows that accessibility and availability is unequal but they misread the problem. There has been some work by cultural geographers (Patterson and Hoalst-Pullen, 2014) and others (Chapman et al, 2017) that identifies the problem, though more work is needed. As mentioned earlier, according to the Brewers Association, almost all Americans now live within ten miles of a brewery (Hindy, 2014); however, this does not take into account the racist and classist, as well as sexist and heteronormative, reality of historical and contemporary craft beer in the US.

*Affordability of craft beer as a barrier: 'It's much cheaper than weed!'*

Craft beer is much cheaper than weed but significantly more expensive than the mass-distributed beers. As such, the affordability of craft beer is often given as an indicator of why some people will never have significant exposure to craft beer and its many varieties. Often, it just comes down to pure, personal economics: "Craft beer is more expensive, and white people, in general, have more disposable money. Also, we [craft beer industry] don't build craft beer bars or breweries in low-income areas, until really after they've been gentrified" (Scott, white, male, sales rep). Recognizing this, some brewers who have a background of being excluded try to remedy this through tastings, though the reality still exists:

> 'I think it's expensive, right? We do tastings all the time. And once in a while, we hear things like, "Oh, this is great, but I'm just gonna buy some Heineken because I can buy a 12 pack for US$12 bucks. Instead of a four pack for US$12 bucks." And so I think it's a little bit on the, you know, kind of how certain groups and it, you know, you have to, I have to try really hard not to sort of put, you know, make certain associations with ethnical groups because I don't think that's, that belongs, but, you know, kind of goes together with, with a social, economic, you know, like, so if, if I'd say, like, if we have a, a group of Latinos in our area that, that are largely working in the food industry making seven bucks an hour, they're not going to be able to spend money on, on what they would like to, they mean, they love to, but they probably can't.' (Juan, Latinx, male, brewer/owner)

There is no doubt that a 750 ml bottle of American wild ale from Bruery Terreux is more expensive than a Corona Extra. In fact, by the ounce, it can be two to four times as much. As such, in the end, affordability is a key factor in whether or not one *can* become a craft beer consumer. Furthermore, the relationship across the three-tiered distribution system reverberates throughout the entire system:

> 'I think it mostly stems from the lack of diversity in the consumer market. Which is why there's such a lack of diversity in the supplier and wholesaler market as well.' (Scott, white, male, sales rep)

> 'You just have to go back to the idea that, whether we like it or not, we're still segregated, everything is still segregated. Laws change, things change, but people don't fucking change. Everyone wants to live in separate neighborhoods. White guys come in, and we gentrify a black neighborhood. And then they put a couple of breweries in the neighborhood. I feel like our worlds are so different because of the racism that exists in America.' (Albert, white, male, brewer)

While there are numerous other factors that our respondents articulated, this one is significant. Joe Satran (2014) of the *Huffington Post* lays out the reasons why a six-pack of craft beer costs, on average, twice (or more) of a comparable amount of Bud Light due to the distribution of costs embedded in the process: 31 per cent retailer's margin; 21 per cent distributor's margin; 13 per cent packaging; 8 per cent brewer's margin; 7 per cent sales tax; 6 per cent shipping; 5 per cent malt; 4 per cent hops; 2 per cent loss; 1 per cent yeast; 1 per cent labor; 1 per cent federal tax; and 1 per cent state tax. However, he does not engage at all with the correlate structures here. We have already learned (and will learn more later in the book) that the locations that retail craft beer are most likely raced (read: white) and classed, that distributors rarely go into other race markets and 'sell whiteness' (Withers, 2017), that marketing/packaging has a deeply problematic history, and that brewers are predominantly from white networks and higher up in the socio-economic hierarchy.

## Certain feet were made for walking

> 'I don't know. I don't understand. I don't know why. I don't know. I have no idea. Maybe at one point, it'll cross race

> barriers. But I just have no idea why it hasn't. I've never even met a black guy that was really interested in craft beer.' (Albert, white, male, brewer)

Albert is a white brewer, his response is, by and large, characteristic of the white people in the industry that we talked to; there is a sort of 'that's just the way it is' attitude toward the whiteness of craft beer. There is a sense across our research that there is some privilege-blindness going on here. Since craft beer and its correlate spaces, places, cultures, and ideologies, as well as its images, identities, and realities, are white and male, its primary practitioners, that is, white men, cannot see the forest for the trees. More realistically, they are rendered invisible and unmarked because the social structure and cultural playground that they engage with (here, craft beer) is white—they are the center, the norm, the moral weight. Almost all of the respondents of color in our interviews mention barriers and the lack of resources repeatedly, with evidential articulation to back it up—based on experience. *None* of our white male respondents do.

The importance of, and emphasis on, homebrewing in our analysis cannot be understated. Historical accounts of the craft beer movement show that the earliest craft brewers started out as homebrewers (Hindy, 2014). Many of the first craft beer gurus were first homebrewers, with many inspired by *The Complete Joy of Homebrewing* by Charlie Papazian (2014). Some of the more notable names are: Jack McAuliffe, founder of New Albion Brewing, one of the first craft breweries to open its doors; Jim Koch, brewer of Samuel Adams Boston Lager and founder of the Boston Beer Company; and Ken Grossman, brewer and founder of Sierra Nevada Brewing Company. In the case of Jim Koch and Ken Grossman, their breweries would become the high-water mark for all later breweries. Both are still in operation and currently top craft producers. All are white and all walked down and reinforced the white brick road. Indeed, Tony considers his city—a large 'chocolate city' in Hunter and Robinson's parlance—and shakes his head: "there are no black local brewers." By and large, this has been and continues to be a striking fact in the US. When asked about whether there are any black or brown histories of brewing in the US and/or owning and operating a brewery, the only name that comes up is Theodore Mack and the story of People's Brewery in Oshkosh, Wisconsin, in the late 1960s and early 1970s (for the full story, see Harry, 2019). As Tony continues:

> 'I wanted to go out and get a loan back in the 70s, or 80s, or whatever, there was redlining. If I wanted to open a brewery, I couldn't, I couldn't own a brewery in certain neighborhoods. And if I did open it up, would I be run out of the town? I would be working my ass off if I opened it in the black community because the black community didn't have the funds to support that at the time; we were all disenfranchised.' (Tony, black, male, influencer/organizer)

Meanwhile, long-time social media beer influencer Marcus brings his years of engagement with the whiteness of craft beer together in articulating the four E's relevant to the possibility of minority community engagement with craft beer: education, experience, exposure, enlightenment (Marcus, black, male, influencer).

In Chapter 5, we will address how issues of exposure are structural in nature. Key to this discussion is providing a more robust and critical engagement with the second tier of distribution—the wholesale distributor. In doing so, we will highlight the ways in which alcohol has been marketed to black people and other minorities, while also examining the role of the distributor and the relationship to the consumer. Additionally, we will demonstrate how marketing strategies and targeted ads have shaped the cultural tastes of black consumers and further excluded them from craft beer consumption, as well as how craft beer has co-opted black cultural symbols to promote beer.

5

# Exposure, Marketing, and Access: Malt Liquor and the Racialization of Taste

## Industry representation

We have seen that exposure to beer, access to jobs in the beer and restaurant industries, access to a craft beer scene, and homebrewing, all undergirded by the fundamental power of social networks, are the most common pathways to becoming a brewer and a consumer. These social structures are classed, gendered, and raced, leading to a fundamental lack of diversity. We want to look more closely at how the lack of diversity and representation in the industry has led to the systematic exclusion of black people from beer consumption. One way to do this is to focus on the use of racially targeted marketing to sell cheaper products of lesser quality to communities of color; malt liquor is a critical case. Another way is to interrogate the ways in which the contemporary craft beer industry has appropriated black culture and iconography to sell beer to white people.

The issue of representation, both socially and culturally, is of key importance in looking at the marketing of beer. According to our interview data, the issue of representation—at all levels of production, distribution, and consumption—is a major barrier in preventing black, other minority, and female participation in craft beer and its cultures. Given this reality, it is not surprising at all that most significant efforts to diversify the beer industry have mostly been led by consumers. As Patricia contends:

> 'When you look at the landscape of people who are pushing such efforts, in terms of trying to racially diversify, those efforts are coming from folks who are largely on the consumer side. They say to themselves, "I am a huge fan of the industry, and I don't see myself represented in it." Or, "I tried to get into this industry and there wasn't space for me to find my way in."' (Patricia, black, female, industry insider)

This lack of diversity mirrors the structure of other industries as well. A point that Tony questions, asking:

> 'Why aren't there more black people in the industry? A large part of it is representation. The beer industry was yet another industry where there were very few of us. It was almost as if, at this point, we just kind of accepted it. If you actually wanted to diversify the people that you're around, hire more [diverse] people.' (Tony, black, male, influencer/organizer)

In the US context of beer and brewing, Latinx, Asian, indigenous, and other racialized minorities, and certainly African-Americans, as attested to by Patricia and Tony (both African-Americans with significant experience in the industry), have faced consistent exclusionary representational structures.

We have now heard the voices of many of our respondents clearly saying that seeing people who look like you brewing, selling, or consuming craft beer fundamentally matters as an issue of representation in terms of the various pathways by which one becomes an industry employee, a brewer, and a craft enthusiast. We are going to take a deeper look into these structures of representation in this chapter, particularly homing in on the ways in which the industry has shaped the tastes of black consumers through racially targeted advertising, and the latent effects on contemporary patterns of black and minority beer consumption. Additionally, more contemporarily, as a result of such manipulation, it is also important to look at how black culture has been (and continues to be) appropriated by craft breweries to market craft beer to white consumers. Both trends have stunted widespread efforts to make the craft beer industry more diverse, though such efforts have gained momentum in very recent years, in large part due to the efforts of social media influencers. Our focus here remains on how the beer industry has maintained its whiteness through marketing and targeted advertising, as well as cultural appropriation.

## Bourdieu and Brettanomyces: cultural tastes and social location

Beer is a cultural product that has been historically linked to particular social structures and practices serving to solidify whiteness and white sociability. It has also been produced by an industry undergirded by a structure that has been exclusionary in its hiring practices and marketing strategies. Cultural objects like beer are distributed within cultural hierarchies arranged by processes of 'taste.' According to Pierre Bourdieu (1984), these processes involve the exchange of cultural capital and processes of distinction that are closely linked to social class. So, what is cultural taste? Broadly defined, 'cultural taste' is our 'manifested preferences,' 'the practical affirmation of an inevitable difference,' and the process by which we make distinctions between and across cultural goods (Bourdieu, 1984: 56–7), such as movies, music, books, and so much more, including beer. Taste is a social process that turns cultural objects into symbols and signs that when used (consumed) by individuals, places them in a meaningful way within the sociocultural order of things. Cultural taste is an important process, especially as it relates to social class and, as we shall see, how it neglects to engage with the organizing structures of race and racism. Thus, as opposed to the physiological act of tasting a beer (for example, bitter, sour, malty, and so on), Bourdieu is identifying processes of social and cultural taste whereby actors show preference and distinction in making decisions about cultural products, as well as ways of *organizing* and *classifying* shared understanding of cultural goods based on social or class position through what he calls 'the habitus' (Bourdieu, 1977; Fiske, 1992). As we will see, it is highly possible that the structures of representation in the beer industry have, for generations, created such processes of taste and habits of beer production, distribution, and consumption, which have etched strong (and largely unconscious) grooves into the everyday engagement with beer that have enduring hierarchical effects.

In addition to the processes of taste, there may indeed be a social structure to the American 'habits' of brewing, distributing, selling, and consuming beer: a beer 'habitus.' Bourdieu (1977) constructed the concept of the habitus to describe the knowledge that we possess, our expectations for behaviors, and the ability to improvise and interpret social interactions and consumption practices. It may be useful to see the beer habitus as a combination of the habitat (for example, your local taphouse), the habitant (for example, beer lover), the process of habitation (for example, ordering, consuming, discussing within a life of beer), and habits (for example, the routines of beer) (Fiske, 1992). The habitus is a construction of and, at the same time, a reflection of an individual's social environment and the ways in which one has been socialized to negotiate one's environment and interact with others. Taken together, there are likely beer habituses that serve to order and classify the social world through processes of taste. What is more, given the structural and class differences between white people and minorities, one could therefore reasonably argue that there are white and black habituses—racialized means of understanding the social world, socialization, social environment, cultural capital, habits, and tastes (Perry, 2012). These habituses reflect the racial stratification in the larger social structure. Beer would not be immune to such fundamental social processes.

Social class is deeply entangled with racism; therefore, in order to understand cultural taste and habitus fully, one must also understand the ways in which racism can inform the habitus. Bourdieu does not address racism as a social structure that influences taste processes and habituses. However, Horvat (2003: 2) does note that 'in Bourdieu's formulation, every aspect of an individual's social condition, including race and ethnicity, contributes to class membership and the development of the habitus. The habitus is generated by the social conditions of lived experience including race, ethnicity, geographical location, and gender.' The ways in which someone interacts with others and their consumption practices are the products of their social class position, particularly as it relates to the available cultural capital and socialization of groups in the same social space. In order to understand the differences between social spaces, one must look at the structural order and its intersections with race, class, and gender. The differential access and distribution of wealth, particularly across racial lines, most certainly affects the trajectories and patterns of consumption, and ultimately the inter- and intra-racial processes of cultural taste. Therefore, we must include a discussion of racism in shaping these tastes and as an organizing principle in terms of practices of consumption, as well as the perception of those practices by other consumers.

Indeed, as Bourdieu (1984: 170) suggests, tastes are guided by the habitus, which 'organizes practices and the perception of practices.' In terms of social structure, the habitus is therefore, 'at one and the same time, a position in the social and historical trajectory through it … the tastes and dispositions that are formed in and by those practices' (Fiske, 1992: 155). Essentially, the habitus *informs* our decision-making in terms of our consumption, and *is informed by* one's social location and the cultural capital available through education and socialization—it is *the ways in which* and *how* we consume. The habitus exists in a social space with two dimensions: spatial and temporal. The spatial dimension is a 'dynamic relationship among the major determining forces in our social order—economic class, education, culture'—which materializes itself in the form of 'behavior, tastes, and dispositions'; therefore, given the racial structure in the US, those who are positioned differentially 'embody and enact those forces differently' (Fiske, 1992: 163). If we understand the spatial dimension to be a relationship between class, education, and culture, we must also acknowledge the differential access to and unequal distribution of resources across racial lines. Fiske (1992) posits that one's tastes and consumption behaviors reflect the enactment and embodiment of one's social location.

The temporal dimension suggests that the social space is a product of history and socialization, and is therefore subject to change. This means that tastes and behaviors can change but only when one's social location has changed and one has gained access to new forms of cultural capital, as well as when new means and modes of socialization that reflect and guide these changes in status positions are employed. However, it also means that due to the structural weight of history, socialization, and learning about the who, how, why, when, and where of beer production, distribution, and consumption, existing structures like the ones analyzed here, that is, the beer industry, create habituses. We learn the habituses of brewing and beer, as well as the cultural processes of inclusion and exclusion connected to beer as a cultural and social object. However, Bourdieu's work implies that we misrecognize that these processes are etched in our socialization and practices, and therefore take for granted what we think we know. Thus, the reproduction of inequality continues, both through systematic exclusions (and inclusions), for instance, in the beer industry, and, equally powerfully, through the guise of what we think are individual 'tastes' and 'preferences.'

To fully understand cultural tastes, one must understand taste as a reflection of position within the social structure, not only in terms of the available products to consume, but also in terms of the knowledge and cultural capital needed to draw a distinction between different goods. Concerning beer, then, social location, in particular race and social class but also gender and region, among other positionalities, should also be viewed in relation to power—particularly the ways in which those in power influence and coerce the interests and tastes of subordinate social positions through hegemonic control. For example, through hegemonic control, the white beer industry has systematically excluded black people and other minorities through hiring practices and limited exposure and access to higher-end products such as craft beer, and also engaged in racist and targeted marketing to influence the tastes of all social groups, including black people and minority groups, in the service of domination. Therefore, class differences in socialization and income are made manifest in the goods that one consumes. The beer industry has had a heavy hand in constructing the social structures that reproduce themselves through the boundaries of a 'beer habitus,' as well as in cultural construction through controlling the images and processes of taste and distinction within everyday engagement with beer. Representation—both seeing oneself in the industry and how the industry sees you—has (and continues to be) foundational in understanding the whiteness of beer.

## Cultural consumption: you are what they let you drink

Following the work of Weber (1978 [1968]), many sociologists of culture believe that some forms of cultural consumption serve as status markers. Bryson (2002: 108) posits that 'by restricting access to resources, social status can be translated into market position and political status.' In terms of the beer industry, this is evidenced by the lack of industry jobs occupied by black people, as well as the restrictions on interactions imposed by Jim Crow laws and segregation. This process is the result of two interrelated types of exclusion: social exclusion and symbolic exclusion. Social exclusion is the 'process of social selection that is based on a previously determined set of cultural criteria and is exercised by people with high levels of income and prestige' (Bryson, 2002: 108; see also Bourdieu and Passeron, 1977). Social exclusion, or, in the Weberian sense, social closure, refers to the monopolization of resources and inclusion as social intercourse (Weber, 1978 [1968]). Individuals in positions of power are able to manipulate the availability of and access to resources, such as industry jobs, social capital, education, and so on. Such monopolization manifests itself in the form of the social exclusion of groups from interactions centered around a particular mode of consumption, in this case, drinking beer.

The second type of exclusion is symbolic exclusion. According to Bryson (2002: 109), 'whereas social exclusion refers to the monopolization of human interactions, symbolic exclusion depicts the subjective process that orders those social interactions—taste.' Symbolic exclusion can be understood to mean the exclusion, or, more accurately, the prohibition, of a group from not only consuming a particular good, but also acquiring the necessary cultural capital to 'value' the good. These types of exclusion are assumed to work similarly to the terms 'prejudice and discrimination' in that they are employed by actors in positions of power in efforts to further demarcate lines of social and cultural distinction between groups (Bryson, 2002: 109). In other words, while symbolic exclusion highlights the social differences between groups, it must also be seen as the coordinated and intentional actions on the part of powerful individuals (cultural tastemakers)—and an entire industry structure (the three-tier distribution system) in the case of beer—to exclude a social group from 'meaningful' consumption. As such, the social and symbolic exclusion of black people and minorities from the beer industry and culture is a form of physical segregation in terms of the exclusion from particular spaces of consumption, and a form of cultural segregation in terms of controlling and limiting the dissemination of social and cultural capital.

By limiting, or prohibiting, the accumulation of cultural capital through access to education, exposure to various goods, and social exclusion, subjugated groups are unable to evaluate, or even begin to 'appreciate,' a particular good within a particular social and cultural field, such as beer. The process by which consumers classify and evaluate their consumption choices is what Bourdieu (1984) refers to as 'distinction.' This process of classification and evaluation reflects an individual's cultural tastes, as well as their class position. Therefore, as a classificatory system, taste is directly related to the social position of an actor and that actor's potential in the socially and culturally constructed market. As such, one's market potential should be viewed through the lens of power, and seen as an interpretation of perceived value, both economically and culturally. Power, then, becomes a major factor in the exchange of economic and cultural capital. In terms of the beer industry, the three-tier distribution system represents a power structure that reflects, and, in many cases, perpetuates, racial and class stereotypes. These stereotypes affect not only hiring practices in the industry, but also what goods are marketed to whom, where, under what conditions, and how. We have already seen that distributors and marketing agents hold stereotypical views of consumers of color and their spaces. Such perceptions shape their strategies when marketing a particular product, as well as their decision to sell a particular product in a given area.

In many ways, taste 'functions as a sort of social orientation, a "sense of one's place," guiding the occupants of a given place in social space towards the social positions adjusted to their properties, and towards the practices or goods which befit the occupants of that position' (Bourdieu, 1984: 466). Who, then, determines what goods befit a particular group, and what is their degree of power relative to the production of cultural goods? This view suggests that certain goods are 'best fit' or 'not intended' for certain audiences or consumers. While this notion does seem to fit with discussions of high or low cultural goods—most often in terms of being able to afford a particular good—it is simply not sufficient to view these differences in consumption strictly in terms of social class. This view discounts the structural and institutionalized racism that has kept black people and other minority groups from the same opportunities for social mobility afforded to white people. In the story of American beer, race and racism must be brought to the forefront of this theoretical discussion regarding taste, habitus, and distinction in order to understand the historical, present, and future (possible) reproduction of the whiteness of beer.

Key to our discussion here is the process by which tastes are formed, how those tastes reflect a socially and culturally constructed marginalized position, and the ways in which black people and others have been excluded from participation in beer consumption and its cultural practices. As we saw earlier, access to the requisite social capital needed to gain entry into the industry has been granted along strict racial lines. This has prevented black people from experiencing beer, and from acquiring certain cultural capital with which to draw distinction between marginal, lesser-quality products and higher-quality, craft products. Additionally, as we argue later, symbolic exclusion has been manifested in the form of these lesser-quality products, particularly malt liquor, as well as through the use of targeted advertising that encourages emulation and conspicuous consumption on the part of black consumers. While we have already made clear that the foundations of this story occurred hundreds of years ago, a very important chapter of the story is much more recent. We now turn to the story of malt liquor.

## Malt liquor

> Since its creation, malt liquor's fortunes have been entangled with America's sorest social bugbears, from race, to class, to poverty, to whether or not capitalism ought to give a shit about any of those things. (Infante, 2016)

With its inception in 1952, malt liquor was first produced by second-tier producers. In line with this model, lower-tier producers, with less advertising capacity and influence, were some of the first to produce and market malt liquor. According to Robertson (1984: 35) malt liquor has no 'legal or accepted definition'; today, there are myriad legal definitions, varying widely by state and largely related to alcohol by volume (ABV) percentage. Metropolis Brewing pioneered the style in 1952 with the introduction of Champale (Tremblay and Tremblay, 2009). Malt liquor is still made with the traditional brewing ingredients (hops, water, yeast, and malt) and maintains a similar flavor profile to the pale adjunct lager produced by the larger domestic producers but is characterized by a higher ABV than regular or light beer. Typically, most brands of malt liquor have an ABV in the range between 4.5 per cent (which is closer to standard 'regular' beer) and 8.5 per cent. This makes malt liquor about 20 per cent stronger than normal beer. Although not its original vessel, malt liquor as we know it is typically packaged in a large-format, 40 oz bottle. Commonly referred to as 'forties,' they are generally less expensive than other beverages, with some 40 oz bottles being sold as low as US$0.99, and are also typically not packaged in resealable bottles, which, according to Collins et al (2007: 138), provides 'the implicit message that it is intended to be consumed in one sitting.' Essentially, malt liquor provided more bang for your buck. Marketing strategies and distributors seized on the larger-format bottles and higher ABV to attract lower-class, and particularly minority, individuals. As Hacker (1987: 12–13) contend, malt liquor provided many undereducated and unemployed young black men with a 'potent and relatively inexpensive means to escape a depressing reality.'

Malt liquor was not immediately popular when it debuted in the mid-1950s. It was not until the 1960s, when the domestic beer market was in a relative decline, that malt liquor became more popular. As Infante (2016) points out, 'malt liquor was intended to provide the boost the industry needed in the face of falling per-capita beer consumption and increasing competition from spirits and wine, and malt liquor marketers bent over backward to ingratiate themselves with the white middle class.' The original target market for malt liquor was the white middle class. It may be argued that malt liquor was never intended for black people or lower-class individuals; however, these individuals would consume the overwhelming majority of malt liquor during the 1970s–90s. Malt liquor advertisements were targeted toward white middle-class sensibilities. The brand names themselves evoked white middle-class culture and consumerism. Some of the more popular brands were Country Club and Champale.

Country Club was marketed as being an alternative to 'regular' beer and as a 'new party brew!,' to be shared at an upscale party with friends (Goetz Brewing Company, 1955a, 1955b). Goetz, the makers of Country Club, used slogans like 'so smooth—so different' and 'looks inviting ... tastes exciting' to appeal to the perceived more refined tastes of middle-class white people (Goetz Brewing Company, 1955a, 1955b). Their ads featured Rockwellian images of white middle-class adults enjoying a backyard cookout, or gathering in the living room around a fireplace. These ads also commonly featured a female hand with painted fingernails pouring the beverage into a wine-style glass, carrying a tray of glasses, and serving the beverage to party guests. Ads such as these also implicitly depict leisure time and middle-class consumption as rendered in the minds of the tastemakers of the time. In each of the ads, males are wearing suits with ties and women are wearing dresses with painted nails and lipstick. Such ads are intended to get the consumer to associate the beverage with a higher social class.

Brands such as Champale used slogans like, 'it certainly isn't the same old thing to drink' and 'the beautiful way to celebrate nothing' to entice middle-class white people to try something new (Iroquois Brands, 1970). The name 'Champale' itself, as well as the ads for the beverage, compared the drink to champagne while highlighting its lower cost. One representative ad suggests that Champale is 'the alcoholic beverage that looks, tastes and sparkles like champagne. But costs just pennies more than beer. And that's a perfect combination for unimportant occasions' (Iroquois Brands, 1970)—a phenomenon that recently experienced a renaissance of sorts in the whiteness of craft beer via 'brut' beers. Another such ad described Champale as 'the ultimate experience' while depicting a white couple (in the foreground) and a black couple (in the background) on a beach in evening wear enjoying Champale from a champagne glass (Iroquois Brands, 1979). The ad reads: 'when the time is right and the mood is light, go with your feelings. ... Champale tastes like a light bubbly wine. Champagne quality without the champagne price' (Iroquois Brands, 1979). Brands such as Country Club and Champale attempted to provide an upper-class experience (that is, drinking champagne with friends or while celebrating an occasion) but on a working-class budget. Concerning cultural processes of taste discussed earlier, malt liquor was marketed not to the bourgeoisie, but to the white middle class through their aspirations for the tastes of luxury and practices associated with the bourgeoisie. Yet, despite the attempts to brand malt liquor as refined and upscale, the beverage was not selling well with its intended white market. However, there was a growing popularity in black neighborhoods. Marketing experts from the time suggested that the 'upper-class packaging may have been a contributing factor to its appeal to black customers' (Infante, 2016). Veblen (2017) describes this as conspicuous consumption. According to Trigg (2001: 99), Veblen's theory suggests that 'individuals emulate the consumption patterns of other individuals situated at higher points in the hierarchy.' In effect, black people may have consumed more malt liquor because it was perceived to be a higher-class consumer product, showing that the black market was not monolithic and also wanted to emulate the tastes of upper-class (white) people, as well as because it was less expensive and had a stronger alcohol content than regular beer. As Hacker (1987: 12–13) note, market surveys of the time revealed a preference for malt liquor as a 'power brew,' which often contained 20 per cent more alcohol than regular beer.

Once a new market demographic was identified in the 1970s, the strategy changed. National Brewing in Baltimore gambled that perhaps people were buying malt liquor because of its perceived higher strength and ABV, rather than its upscale appearance (Infante, 2016). Olde English 800 also saw an increase in sales, particularly on the West Coast, where alcohol content restrictions were more relaxed than the East Coast (Infante, 2016). One of the first malt liquors to be marketed in terms of its strength was Colt 45, whose name was a reference both to Baltimore Colts running back Jerry Hill, who wore the number 45, and to the powerful handgun (Infante, 2016)—a handgun that also had strong symbolism regarding racist violence in the US.

Marc Lacey (1992) of the *Los Angeles Times* reported that 'malt liquor ... has become the drink of choice among many in the inner city ... it is heavily discounted in black and Latino neighborhoods nationwide, and promotions coyly—and sometimes not so coyly—plug its potency.' According to a *Harvard Business School Case* study, 'one third of consumers in the malt liquor category had household incomes of less than $15,000 per year, while 75 percent had household incomes of less than $35,000' (Schille and Geyser, 1991: 3). Chick Powell, a marketing expert who worked for several large brewers, described the phenomenon as follows: 'when you get a marketing guy in there who sees it's a disproportionately black business, it *becomes* a black business' (Infante, 2016: emphasis in original). These marketers were the tastemakers/cultural intermediaries serving as proxies for imagining the black community, with both short- and long-term consequences. A shift in advertising and marketing strategies was in the works—a shift toward much more targeted advertising. Corey contends that these targeted ads shaped the tastes of black beer drinkers:

> 'It all starts with exposure. If you look at the difference between traditional communities of color and the white community, beer exposure is quite different. In the black and brown community, specifically in the middle to low

> incomes, there's target advertising, with malt liquor, with cheap, poorly made mass-produced beers.' (Corey, black, male, influencer/organizer)

Tastes distinguish between the social and economic classes. In the decades of the 1950s and 1960s, tastemakers and cultural intermediaries were attempting to market an inferior and more potent beer product (malt liquor) to the white middle class, attempting to link it to a lifestyle of refinement and distance from necessity. It did not take in the white community. The sights were therefore redirected at the black community, where similar processes were in play, as well as the structural constraints distributed by a racist society, where there were limited beer options and economic ability. Through all of this, as well as advertising, the beer industry created a 'preference' for malt liquor.

## Advertising malt liquor in the 1970s and 1980s

Throughout the 1970s, malt liquor was being marketed more aggressively and almost exclusively to black people. Over the next 25 years, malt liquor saw a slow but steady increase in market share from 2.4 per cent in 1970 to 4.7 per cent in 1995, which is the most market share that the beverage has ever commanded (Tremblay and Tremblay, 2009: 138–9). While malt liquor reached its peak market share in the mid-1990s, it was ushered in by the bold advertising strategies and market campaigns of the 1980s. As Hacker (1987: 13–14) contend, in addition to highlighting the 'cheap high' of malt liquor, advertising campaigns were tailored to specifically target black males and their sensibilities. Schille and Geyser (1991: 3) note that during the 1980s, 'advertisements for the products typically featured virile black males and symbols of sexual prowess.' One ad for the brand Midnight Dragon 'featured a black woman dressed in red, garters showing, straddling a chair and sipping a 40 through a straw,' with a caption that read: 'I could SUCK! On this all night' (Rodell, 2013). As Weems (1998: 110) states: 'the makers of malt liquor sought to reach a primarily young black male constituency with allusions to sexual conquest and the alcoholic "kick" of the products.' Hyper-sexualization and catering to the masculinity of the urban drinker were successful strategies. Malt liquor production and consumption increased during the 1980s due, in large part, to the more targeted marketing strategies.

In order to extend the appeal of malt liquor, and to avoid marketing based solely on the higher alcohol content, malt liquor producers began to hire celebrity pitchmen to market their products. One of the most successful ads of this nature was produced by Colt 45. Jim Dale, a pitchman for Colt 45, reflected on the ad campaign: 'we said, "[malt liquor has] become an urban product. We're gonna find a really cool guy for that market, but someone who has great crossover appeal … someone who's well known, but not so well known that people look at him and say, 'oh he is [basically] white'"' (Infante, 2016). Enter Billy Dee Williams. Fresh from his success in the *Star Wars* franchise, in 1986, Williams became the perfect spokesman for Colt 45. As Dale points out, Williams's 'blackness was important' but due to his fame as Lando Calrissian, he also could still appeal to white people (Infante, 2016). The makers of Colt 45 sought to utilize the suave image of Williams to implicitly suggest to black men that Colt 45 would help them increase their sexual encounters with women (Hacker, 1987). Ads featured Williams appearing with attractive women and the now infamous tagline: 'the power of Colt 45, it works every time' (Hacker, 1987: 14). Williams was not the first black celebrity to market malt liquor; however, he was certainly one of the most effective, likely because this campaign retained some of the upward mobility and aspirational dimensions that had attracted much earlier black consumers of malt liquor. Meanwhile, the beer industry and its ad executives, marketing directors, and distributors remained white.

Schlitz, Colt 45, and King Cobra also called upon black celebrities such as Rufus Thomas, The Commodores, Richard Roundtree, Fred Williamson, and Redd Foxx to appeal to the consumers (Infante, 2016). Former athletes, musicians, and actors were natural salespeople as they were seen as more relatable to their black audience. Prominent figures in the black community were seen as adding an air of authenticity to malt liquor, in a sense, legitimizing it as a 'premium' beverage despite its lower cost and lower-quality ingredients. Ads featuring these celebrities relied on funky backing tracks, images of bulls barging through walls, and taglines such as 'don't let the smooth taste fool you' to tout the strength of the beverage. Lacey (1992) and Allen-Taylor (1997) provide further evidence of the targeted marketing in a brochure sent to retailers by Pabst Brewing, the makers of Olde English 800, which states that the top-selling brew appeals to minorities because of its 'smooth, mellow taste brewed for relatively high alcohol content (important to the ethnic market!).' These ad campaigns continued throughout the late 1970s and 1980s, and as a result, the production of brands such as Colt 45 grew from 1.79 million barrels to 2 million barrels, a figure that out-produced its rival Schlitz (Infante, 2016).

## Hip-Hop and malt liquor

Throughout the 1970s and 1980s, malt liquor had primarily been associated with an older black population (Quinn, 2004: 3). As Quinn (2004: 3) notes: 'with the arrival and increasing ascendency of Hip-Hop, a consumer-driven product realignment occurred. Rap groups Run DMC and NWA started to brandish and "name check" malt liquor in publicity material and on records.' According to Scott (2015), 'two things have always attracted young and poor urban kids to malt liquor, price and potency. ... These are also the reasons why forties have often been celebrated by Hip-Hop stars.' One of the pioneers of using Hip-Hop stars to advertise malt liquor was St. Ides. Much like Colt 45 changed the malt liquor ad game, St. Ides was pioneering in its use of Hip-Hop stars to market malt liquor in the late 1980s. The McKenzie River Corporation launched St. Ides malt liquor in 1986. Originally, the producer employed famed 1960s' soul group The Four Tops to market their new high-strength malt liquor (Quinn, 2004). Marketers sought to create a new marketing strategy that focused more on the burgeoning Hip-Hop culture, which also subsequently meant targeting the younger African-American market. Eithne Quinn notes that, 'back then, part of the excitement within the Hip-Hop subculture, as it still was at that time, was the dawning realization of the potential for Hip-Hop marketization ... many artists, from poor backgrounds as they often were, didn't see this as selling out' (quoted in Coward, 2015).

As Coward (2015) notes: 'what made St. Ides different was that it's one of the earliest examples—if not the earliest—of a brand with no inherent ties to Hip-Hop completely building its identity around the genre, entrusting the culture's tastemakers with its messaging.' Essentially, St. Ides let the target consumer also do the marketing for them. One of the ways in which McKenzie River achieved this was by giving up creative control to an up-and-coming producer by the name of DJ Pooh (Mark Jordan) (Quinn, 2004). At the time, DJ Pooh was an underground producer and writer who had worked with some of 'gangsta' rap's earliest stars. Ice Cube, of NWA fame, became a pitchman for St. Ides in 1993. In perhaps one of the most famous ads, Ice Cube raps the verse: 'get your girl in the mood quicker / get your jimmy thicker / with St. Ides malt liquor.' These types of ads highlighted the perceived 'side-effects of consuming malt liquor in 40oz quantities' (Infante, 2016). This sent another message to African-American youth in addition to those linking the product with socio-economic success: 'drink malt liquor and you will have a successful sex life.'

Similar to the ads of the 1970s and 1980s, these ads featured rhythmic backbeats and catchy hooks that served as taglines for the brands. As Aaron Paxton Arnold, a brand management consultant, notes: 'as a kid, you're walking around, singing these songs and basically endorsing these liquor and spirit products … you don't know what it is, but you know that it's cool because it sounds good' (Coward, 2015). African-American youth began to see Hip-Hop stars as their idols and therefore wanted to be like them. This meant consuming malt liquor. The ads were working. As reported by the *Los Angeles Times* (Lacey, 1992) sales of malt liquor had increased by 15 per cent from 1990 to 1991. Infante (2016) notes that the increase was due to the 'rap-aligned' brands such as St. Ides and Olde English, which featured popular Hip-Hop stars as pitchmen and prominent placement in lyrics of the day. Although malt liquor never held more than a 4.7 per cent share of the overall beer market, it was hugely popular with African-Americans. According to census data from the 1990s, African-American drinkers comprised about 12 per cent of the population but consumed around 28 per cent of the nation's malt liquor (Infante, 2016). In terms of the mainstream audience, Quinn (2004) contends that the ads provided an authentic look into the aesthetic and culture of Hip-Hop, providing the mainstream with a glimpse of what Hip-Hop culture 'was all about.' As Serrano (2015) suggests, the connection between rappers (who were predominantly black men), the disadvantaged neighborhoods where rap was most popular, and malt liquor was undeniable. In addition to the catchy hooks of Hip-Hop music and gangsta rap, another iconic image of malt liquor was being rapped about and consumed in mass quantities—the 40 oz bottle.

## Forty ounce culture

According to Pete Brusyo, a blogger and collector of 40 oz bottles, 'the first beer to be sold in that specific bottle was called A-1, and the oldest known bottle is from 1961. But it wasn't until the 80s that the 40 became common' (Rodell, 2013). 'Forties,' as they are commonly referred to, are most often sold in liquor and convenience stores, and, as Jones-Webb et al (2008: 160) note, are 'commonly sold chilled and wrapped in brown paper bags for immediate consumption,' and 'rap lyrics and movie scripts encourage "chugging" the bottles before they get warm.' Although it is not clear why the brewers started using 40 oz bottles, in an interview with the *New York Times*, a Miller Brewing Company spokesperson claimed that it was a matter of 'retailer and consumer convenience,' and that store owners preferred forties because they took up less shelf space (Marriott, 1993).

Once the 'forty' had been established as the preferred vessel of consumption for urban minority drinkers, it was only a matter of time before it entered the lexicon of another disproportionately black market: Hip-Hop (Infante, 2016). According to Quinn (2004: 3), 'forty-ounce bottles ("40s") of malt liquor became iconic accessories of gangsta rap, homologous with the focal concerns, activities and collective self-image of the working-class subculture from which the music sprang.' The Forties came to symbolize, in the words of Hall and Jefferson (1993: 56), 'objects in which [the subcultural members] could see their central values held and reflected.' Further, forties came to symbolize the values of gangsta rap and working-class black communities. Much in line with the view of subcultural artifacts as manifestations of resistance to mainstream values, as promulgated by the Birmingham Centre for Contemporary Cultural Studies (Hall and Jefferson, 1993), Quinn (2004: 3) notes that 'the brew boasts a sweeter taste, and in so doing declares a rejection of finesse: it stands, just as gangsta rap does, in opposition to respectable or acquired bourgeois tastes.' As George (2001) contends, malt liquor came to reflect a certain 'ghettocentricity.' 'Ghettocentric' is a term used to describe the identity and values of poor, working-class, urban, marginalized communities (George, 2001). Quinn (2004: 3) suggests that ghettocentricity further reflects a culture and system of values that 'Increasingly pervaded black youth culture in the 1980s and 1990s ... [and] provided an expressive response to the deindustrialization, right wing policies, and market liberalization that had been draining away productive resources from America's urban centers since the 1970s.' From a subcultural perspective (Hall and Jefferson, 1993), malt liquor came to represent a solution to the social problems faced by black youth. In essence, '40oz culture,' in the words of Quinn (2004: 4), 'was a response or symbolic solution, as it were, to the problems posed by economic disadvantage and social isolation.' Malt liquor became a source of objectified subcultural capital (Thornton, 1995). J. Nikol Beckham, Diversity Ambassador for the Brewers Association, notes that 'the 40 has this particular nod to masculine excess ... it says, "this is a lot, and I need a lot"' (quoted in Infante, 2016). However, malt liquor's popularity in the black community would not last forever.

## The decline of malt liquor

Former St. Ides marketer Chick Powell recalls that the industry 'took a pretty down-and-dirty road to be able to get some business quickly ... they kinda cast [themselves] like a "ghetto" brand, and that set some people off' (quoted in Infante, 2016). Other rap artists, like Chuck D of Public Enemy, were upset at the fact that a high-alcohol beverage was being targeted at the black community (Coward, 2015). In fact, Chuck D actually wrote a song called 'One Million Bottle Bags,' which he described in an interview with *Melody Maker* as follows:

> [The song is] about the malt liquor problem in black America. Malt liquor has twice as much alcohol content and twice as many residues, that's to say, waste products from regular beer. It's fucked up beer, with more alcohol. Instead of making people laid back, it makes them hostile. And it leads to a lot of black on black violence in America. They have massive campaigns for this shit that are targeted at the black community. Malt liquors are made by the major brewers in this country. When they put their regular beers through filters, all the excess bullshit they push to the black community. And it's been killing motherfuckers for the longest period. (Quoted in Scott, 2015)

As Rodell (2013) notes: 'many African-American scholars saw malt liquor as specifically targeting black youth, or as being used to control and keep down people of color.'

The New York Attorney General's Office even filed suit against St. Ides for allegedly targeting underage minority children in their ads (Coward, 2015). According to Exavier Pope, an attorney who specializes in intellectual and entertainment property issues, 'there isn't any legal precedent explicitly banning an ad campaign like this—one that is targeted at a particular community in a way that some in the community perceive to be harmful' (quoted in Coward, 2015). TJ Crawford, an activist as well as an editor for the African-American lifestyle magazine *Rolling Out*, lamented: 'do I think Ice Cube telling people to get tested for AIDS is a good thing? Yeah, it would help, but that positive message wasn't promoted the same in comparison to the economic message of "Buy Malt Liquor"' (quoted in Coward, 2015). The US Surgeon General, Antonia Novello, even chimed in, saying: 'the ads have youth believing that instead of getting up early, exercising, going to school, playing a sport or learning to be a team player, all they have to do to fit in is learn to drink the right alcoholic beverage' (quoted in Hilt, 1991).

Branding and marketing has long been an issue for the alcoholic beverage industry. According to the Beer Institute (2011: 1), 'in the United States, beer is a product category with broad cultural acceptance and a history of memorable and distinctive advertising that because of its humor and creativity, has long been a favorite among American adult consumers.' Tremblay and Tremblay (2009: 210) note that several of the top producers had been 'accused of using offensive brand names and promoting high-alcohol products in minority communities.' As Jones-Webb et al (2008: 160) note: 'malt liquor brand names such as Steel Reserve, High Gravity, Hurricane, Magnum, and Panther are used by the alcohol industry to connote power and machismo and attract young adults to the market.' This furthered the debate that high-strength, low-cost products were targeting low-income black people.

During this time, the price of malt liquor also fell. Tremblay and Tremblay (2009: 147) note that Schlitz Malt Liquor, which was once a leading brand, saw steadily declining sales in the 1980s due to its 'image problems' and, as such, lost its status as a premium brand. Product image most certainly played a role in the decline of malt liquor. As Milgrom and Roberts (1986) contend, when consumers are unsure about quality, they tend to use price as a marker of quality and malt liquor's lower price signaled to would-be consumers that the product was of a lesser quality. Additionally, McConnell (1968) notes that the strategy a firm employs when pricing a product influences the consumer's perception of that product. In the case of malt liquor, consumers associated the beverage with inferiority and low quality due to its lower cost, as well as, and perhaps more importantly, due to its association with the black community. Warner (2010: 44) also contends that there was a shift to more 'lifestyle consumption' in the 1970s and 1980s, which led to 'the emergence of the "educated class" or the white collar meritocracy' of the 1990s. This class of white consumers would eventually become craft beer drinkers.

## Racism in marketing

> Even with tobacco and alcohol, the fact that these products are differentially targeted toward minorities is not sufficient evidence for attributing a racist motivation to the marketers. Part of a marketer's job is to target specific segments of the population, find out exactly what those segments desire, and fulfill those desires. (Moore et al 1996: 92)

As previously mentioned, malt liquor advertising and marketing was shifted to African-Americans after middle-class white people rejected the lower-quality beverage. Therefore, one must ask the question: 'Why target the black community, rather than stop producing malt liquor?'

The simple answer is that malt liquor was cheap to produce and offered an opportunity for second- and third-tier producers to claim market share lost to the first-tier producers. Further, Moore et al (1996: 92) report that 'As a result of this natural tendency of a marketer to go after the most attractive segments, proponents of target marketing often mention First Amendment rights and the protection of commercial speech, the inappropriateness of paternalistic protection by the government, and freedom of consumer choice to support their arguments.' The problem with this defense is that it denies the existence of structural barriers within the industry itself. White marketers and white producers are, in effect, producing, marketing, and distributing a product that is perceived as 'less than' by white consumers. Additionally, they are constructing a narrative which would suggest that black people choose malt liquor because they prefer it over other beers, when, in fact, malt liquor was historically intended to appeal to white middle-class affluence and black emulation of middle-class consumption, black masculinity and sexual prowess, and the objectification of black women, being marketed by cultural tastemakers such as rappers and movie stars. In effect, the 'choice' of malt liquor is a forced option that limits the buying power, and the available cultural capital, of black beer drinkers. The brewing industry rejects this position and insists that 'malt liquors have always been highest among minority drinkers; therefore, the brewing companies are merely serving a group of consumers who already have a preference for the product' (Moore et al, 1996: 93).

By marketing products in these ways, producers are able to keep African-Americans 'in their lane,' and to effectively whitewash the regular beer market. This also creates a synonymous image of malt liquor and blackness as less than regular beer and whiteness. Similarly, Gwaltney (1980) and Steele (1989) suggest that black people of all social locations share a *black cultural essence* that represents the lives of lower-class black people as representative of all black people. As May and Chaplin (2007: 58) suggest, 'being black became contrary to being middle class.' Critics of this view have contended that restrictions on minority-targeted marketing would, in effect, suggest that minority consumers must be told what to purchase and are not able to make their own decisions about what products to purchase (Wildausky, 1990). However, as Warner and Goldenhar (1992) argue, advertisers and producers should determine the power of advertising and its effects on minority ethnic groups. Whether or not marketing campaigns are intentionally racist may be inconsequential. Moore et al (1996: 93) suggest that 'it is important to acknowledge that target marketing efforts may have unintended, spin-off effects and consequences that are exactly the same as if the motivation had been racist.' Patricia echoes these sentiments and suggests that craft beer, and beer in general, needs to repair the relationship between black consumers and beer:

> 'I think craft beer doesn't just have to win over existing beer drinkers; it probably has to win over people who were just turned off. So, in terms of people of color, the malt liquor moment in the 60s and 70s really did a number on the relationship between urban blacks and beer specifically. The larger contention has been that the relationship between malt liquor and urban black masculinity set a precedent that turned a lot of upwardly mobile blacks, who were not wanting to represent that specific type of urban blackness, away from beer altogether.' (Patricia, black, female, industry insider)

While the beer industry has not made significant efforts to entice minority drinkers, the craft beer industry has been somewhat blindly exclusionary. There have been no real efforts on the part of either industry to reach out to diverse drinkers.

## Cultural appropriation

As with almost all other forms of black culture, Hip-Hop, the forty, and malt liquor have been appropriated by white, college-age audiences. According to McGuiness (2016), the hard image associated with the beverage 'softened as malt liquor was co-opted by young, white, college-aged men who flocked to gangsta rap and rushed out to buy the iconic 40s.' The forty was particularly popular with college students, in part, because of the low cost and higher strength but also as a form of appropriation of Hip-Hop culture. Just as Bradford (2018) contends:

> Like most things popularized by the black community, it was inevitable that white people would co-opt the trend. References to 40s and malt liquor began appearing in punk music, including records by Leftover Crack and Sublime—whose album *40oz to Freedom* has pretty much become the soundtrack for Southern California beach bros.

College students flocked to the forty, as Bradford (2018) notes: 'for college students, artists, beach bums and countless other cash-strapped demographics, the 40 represents cheap fun.' The forty even became the centerpiece of drinking games such as 'Edward 40-Hands,' a binge-drinking game in which 'two 40s are duct taped to someone's hands and not removed until both have been finished' (Rodell, 2013).

The fondness of forties among white males has become somewhat of an internet phenomenon. Fans of malt liquor have created Facebook groups and YouTube channels dedicated to 'chugging' and celebrating malt liquor. McGuiness (2016) describes the 'prototypical malt liquor fanboy' and other 'members of this movement' as 'almost exclusively male and mostly Caucasian.' One such 'fanboy,' named Steeleworldwide, appears in videos praising Donald Trump and other conservative political figures, to which McGuinness (2016) comments: 'the irony of drinking malt liquor from a bottle with the smiling face of Billy Dee Williams on the label while singing the praises of a man whose campaign has earned the seal of approval from white supremacists like David Duke appears to be lost on Steeleworldwide.' Online fandoms are just the tip of the iceberg. Industry insiders and lifestyle journalists have even touted the forty as 'the most patriotic drink in America' (Glass, 2014).

In an article for the online lifestyle magazine *Thrillist*, Jeremy Glass (2014) argues that the 40 oz bottle of malt liquor is one of the most iconic beverages in the US; in his words, the forty 'embodies every aspect of American life: cheap pleasure without the hard work.' While some readers may view this as tongue-in-cheek, his statement is deeply laden with classist assumptions and a color-blind racist view of a product that has been widely regarded as a bane for the black community. In support of his argument that the forty is patriotic, Glass (2014) outlines the finer qualities of the forty, asserting that 'they're dirt cheap' and 'they're xenophobic' (citing the fact that malt liquor is rarely exported overseas), 'they reek of independence, 40s aren't for sharing ... the dude with a 40 is an autonomous unit of successful drunkenness.' Glass (2014) further contends that:

> Celebrities love them [forties]. Along with the indisputably wonderful Billy Dee Williams, it seems like celebrities cannot get enough of the 40oz. 2-Pac, E-40, Ice Cube, N.W.A., Cypress Hill, Eazy-E, Dr. Dre, Snoop Doggy Dogg, Wu Tang Clan, Warren G, Nate Dogg, Tha Dogg Pound, The Notorious B.I.G., and Eminem. Damn son.

Of course, the list of celebrities 'who love malt liquor,' which was compiled from a Wikipedia search, are all rappers, over half of which are deceased and all but one are black.

Lastly, Glass (2014) passionately describes the forty as being an equal opportunist, 'the 40oz is America at its finest. Affordable, attainable, and built for everyone. … Anyone, rich or poor, can enjoy a 40. Boom—that's how you end the class war.' These statements play directly into the 'bro culture' trope. 'Bros,' much like Steeleworldwide, celebrate the brashness of white male masculinity, patriotism, xenophobia, overindulgence, color-blind racism, classism, sexism, and the consumption of black culture, particularly Hip-Hop, as if it defines their lived experience. To say that malt liquor could 'end the class war' is on the surface absurd, though also deeply offensive and ignorant. That the 40 oz bottle of malt liquor is 'America at its finest' rings in the ear of the uninitiated as a testament to the high potency and low cost of the beverage. However, it also completely ignores the racist advertising, the deeply embedded historical and contemporary industry exclusion of black people, and the health and social issues that resulted from increased alcohol consumption within the black community, and whitewashes these issues into a form of 'nostalgia' for a demographic who were mostly not even born when forties were being rapped about, and who, through appropriation, have co-opted black culture and ignored any sort of structural issues of racism, inequality, or privilege.

The craft industry has even gotten in on the malt liquor craze. Breweries around the country are brewing new 'crafty' malt liquors. As Rodell (2013) notes: 'in 2004, Dogfish Head [a white-owned brewery in Delaware] announced it would put out a high-class 40 called Liquor de Malt, capitalizing on the nostalgia many of us feel for the 40 while also appealing to the fact that many ex-40 drinkers are now into craft beer.' To some drinkers, 'the 40 also represents an antidote to the insufferable elitism that permeates the craft beer scene' (Bradford, 2018). Yet, the trend still continues. Beer bars have even started selling forties, 'complete with brown paper bag,' at a 500 per cent markup (Pereira, 2016). One of the many issues with this trend is that white people are engaging in the 'nostalgic' consumption of malt liquor from a position of racial and class privilege. The history of malt liquor and the black community is one of racist marketing, inferior products, alcoholism, violence, and other serious social issues. White people consuming malt liquor because they think that it is 'cool' are engaging in the appropriation of black culture while also turning a blind eye to the structural issues that allowed malt liquor to pervade black communities across the US. When white people drink malt liquor in an attempt to be ironic, they further racist and classist stereotypes about black people. However, white consumption of malt liquor is not the only issue of appropriation facing the beer industry, in particular, the craft beer industry.

In addition to celebrating the 'nostalgia' surrounding malt liquor, the craft beer industry has also been guilty of appropriating black culture, as well as the culture of other racialized minorities. Breweries across the US have used rap lyrics, Hip-Hop iconography, black cultural references, and even the #BlackLivesMatter movement to market trendy craft beers to white millennials. For example, take Lakeville Brew Crew, a white-owned and -operated brewery in Indiana. Prior to their planned opening in 2018 (the brewery is still not open), Lakeville Brew Crew released the names of several of their beers. The names included, 'Black Beer Matters,' 'Flint Michigan Tap Water,' and 'White Guilt.' In an interview with the *South Bend Tribune*, the owners, both of whom are white males, acknowledge that the names are 'likely to create a reaction from people' but, according to one owner, 'at least people will be talking about current issues' (Shown, 2018b). In a classic act of deflection and tone-deafness, one owner viewed the beer names as a means to raise awareness of social issues, saying:

> The way I look at it—with the 'Flint Michigan Tap Water'—if you're going to get mad about that beer name, you should focus your anger more toward the people that are letting that happen to Flint. … If I can bring some attention to that, whether it be negative attention toward me, it still brings attention to that issue. (Shown, 2018a)

When asked about 'Black Beer Matters,' the owners suggested that the brew was inspired by the fact that stouts and porters (dark beers) 'are good beers and they matter' (Jordan, 2018). After initially doubling down on their position, less than a week later, the owners began to backpedal and issued a written apology, stating:

> During this time, we have had numerous conversations about the best way to move forward with the partnership. The first thing that we had to do was accept that we made mistakes. We neglected to put ourselves in the shoes of other people. As a result of ongoing conversations, the list of beer names has been wiped clean. (Shown, 2018b)

Another example of co-opting the #BlackLivesMatter movement, and, as some would argue, a display of outright racism, is that of Reckless Brewing. In early 2019, the owner and head brewer of

Reckless Brewing, a white male, took to social media to claim 'I have something very serious to talk to you about today. It's about the discrimination that I have observed in the craft beer industry. Specifically, the discrimination against black beers' (Wolinski, 2019). The brewer then continues the diatribe by mocking Dr Martin Luther King Jr's 'I have a dream' speech, proclaiming: 'I have a dream of a world where beers are judged not by their color but by the content of their character' (Wolinski, 2019). The now-deleted post concluded with, 'I [owner and brewer] am renaming Sultry Black [a black lager]—Black Lagers Matter'—and signed off using the moniker: 'the most woke brewery in town' (Wolinski, 2019). The backlash against the comments was swift and effective. Reckless Brewing closed its doors not long after the post was deleted. The brewer, in much the same fashion as the brewers at Lakeville Brew Crew, initially viewed his comments as a joke. He issued a form of apology, saying that 'people can't take a joke,' suggesting that his comments and mocking of Dr King's speech were no big deal. After the social media backlash, the owner issued a lengthy apology, saying that he was 'incredibly sorry,' he 'would do anything to take it back,' and 'the fact that people are calling me a racist is hurting me to the bone' (Wolinski, 2019). He also noted that it 'didn't occur to [him] that it would be harmful or offensive' (Wolinski, 2019). Much like Lakeville, Reckless's owner only relented and 'apologized' after being confronted with his racism, being called out on social media, and the business's bottom line being threatened.

A Seattle-based brewery came under fire after releasing two IPAs whose cans featured blue and red bandanas—the colors of the gangs The Crips and The Bloods, respectively—and the names 'Snitch Blood' and 'Where you From?' (Suzanne-Mayer, 2019). This prompted a rapid response from the black-run beer collective Beer Kulture, who tweeted the brewery, saying: 'Those new beers y'all are releasing is a dub. Y'all are entitled, non creative Kulture vultures that deserve to fail, hard & fast. Fuck all the politeness, people have died over that shit you're trying to use to be down & kool. FUCK Y'ALL' (quoted in Suzanne-Mayer, 2019). Corey echoes these sentiments, saying: "there is a culture of Bloods and Crips that means a lot to some people beyond just the violence … and [for breweries] to utilize terms that are very sensitive was offensive to me." Tony also suggests that brewers who use blatantly controversial elements of black culture do so "because they wanted to cause a stir, they wanted some publicity, and some attention … being naive is no longer an excuse."

While these examples represent the more extreme end, there is also a gray area where cultural appropriation is more subtle. Several breweries, most notably, Monkish Brewing in Southern California and J. Wakefield Brewing in Southern Florida, have co-opted lyrics from popular rap songs to use as names for their beers. Some examples include: 'It was all a dream' from J. Wakefield Brewing, a reference to the Notorious B.I.G. song 'Juicy'; 'Socrates Philosophies and Hypotheses' from Monkish, a reference to the WuTang Clan song 'Triumph'; and the more explicit and self-referential 'Insert Hip-Hop Reference Here,' a collaboration between Monkish Brewing and Trillium Brewing, which makes reference to the increasing number of beers being named after Hip-Hop lyrics and other cultural references. To some extent, it is not surprising that breweries would employ these naming devices. After all, their audience is well documented to have appropriated other forms of black culture, though Hip-Hop in particular seems to be the most popular. The comparisons between the history of the craft beer industry and the history of Hip-Hop are few and far between. Yet, white journalists and bloggers see things a bit differently. According to Heil (2016):

> Hip-Hop and craft beer have a lot in common. Both industries grew out of a need for something different, a creative outlet that goes against the mainstream grain. Both were built on the backs of passionate crazies that gambled on talent and drive to make it big ... that, and all of them just love getting turnt.

Let us unpack this. First, craft beer scholars and Hip-Hop scholars will probably agree that both industries offer a different and unique product. However, the circumstances under which these industries emerged could not be more opposed. Craft beer emerged as a response to the changing tastes of middle-class white people, 'on the backs of' educated white males with access to homebrewing equipment and social capital, and entrepreneurs such as Jim Koch who could afford to take a large financial risk. Hip-Hop emerged as a response to structural and institutional racism, social issues in black and urban communities, and as a creative outlet for lower-class black youths. Second, the notion that early Hip-Hop artists gambled on talent and drive in the same way that craft brewers may have completely denies issues of access to recording equipment, record contracts, exposure and marketing, and start-up costs. Furthermore, the author's usage of the word 'turnt' is appropriation in and of itself. Heil (2016) further suggests that the only difference between rappers and craft brewers is that 'Rappers are, by definition, straight ballers while brewers are massive, undeniable nerds. That's why a handful of these boozy fanboys have been brewing up bomb-ass Hip-Hop inspired beers in honor of their cooler, badder older bros.' Hip-Hop no doubt played a major role in exposing white college students to the forty, and perhaps brewers see this as a viable strategy for marketing to 21- to 34-year-old middle-class white males. However, as Corey contends, this is highly problematic:

> 'When you think about the lack of diversity in this community, the lack of, up until recently, the lack of inclusion or opportunity, an industry that found it absolutely okay to take these monikers and these iconic images, and to incorporate it into their brand when not one person in their brewery could recite one of the lyrics from the song that they use, that's an issue.' (Corey, black, male, influencer/organizer)

Tony also suggests that the appropriation of black culture, particularly Hip-Hop, is indicative of a greater problem in the industry:

> '[Appropriation] was so rampant in the industry, where our culture was making profits, but nobody from our culture was making any profit off of it. So, when I see a WuTang reference, but no black person was paid for the label design, or for any part of the brew, that's what's wrong with the industry.' (Tony, black, male, influencer/organizer)

As Corey asserts: 'When that culture is not steeped in your brewery, either in the background and the heritage of the brewers, or anybody on your staff, that's the issue. When we see brewers utilizing culture, and they have no familiarity with it outside of pop culture, to capitalize on it' (Corey, black, male, influencer/organizer). Further, as Tony suggests:

> 'Ask yourself "Why are you using this label?" Are you just another flannel-wearing, bearded white dude that has a couple of records and maybe a black friend … if you're doing it just to sound cool and sell more product, but not actually empower the actual culture that you're taking from, then it's not okay. … I just feel like if you are going to use

> rap lyrics on a label, or any type of black culture on a label, you should be paying someone black.' (Tony, black, male, influencer/organizer)

Some Influencers, for example, like Tony and Corey, have varying levels of tolerance when it comes to appropriation. As Corey suggests:

> 'If the industry were more diverse, it would make more sense ... given the fact that out of 7,000+ breweries, about 50 of them are black-owned ... look at the appropriation versus the effort to actually bring in any people of color, it's as if they just want the references [rap lyrics, cultural iconography], they just want the culture, but don't want any of the people. That's America in general, people love our culture and they love our style, but they don't love us.' (Tony, black, male, influencer/organizer)

On the other hand, Corey contends that if a brewer has connections to Hip-Hop, or is a genuine fan of the music, they are allowed to use the symbols and references. When asked about Hip-Hop references, specifically Monking Brewing, Corey had the following to say:

> 'Let's be clear, Monkish is owned by Henry and Adriana Nguyen [Asian-American brewers/owners], and they love Hip-Hop. They are also brown people in the craft beer community. Now, I know they don't wave that flag ... but what they do is different from other breweries, they don't just put the obvious Hip-Hop line on a label, they put the line that only a Hip-Hop enthusiast would know. That's different from just plastering Biggie Smalls's face on a can.' (Corey, black, male, influencer/organizer)

Using images and lyrics for branding and marketing seems to be alright under the right circumstances. To some, appropriation is tolerated when a person of color is involved in the creative process or when something is given back to the community.

Issues of appropriation and the co-opting of black culture are a problem for the craft beer industry and culture. As several influencers have suggested, simply hiring or asking a person of color if something is appropriation, or if something is racist, is a step in the right direction. Ultimately, having more representation in the industry, at all levels, would combat these issues. While Hip-Hop has been used inappropriately by the craft beer industry, there are inroads being paved. In Chapter 6, we will examine the role of craft beer in gentrification, how gentrification has displaced minorities and created spaces and places for white consumption, and the craft brewery as a 'white space' and the exclusion of black people from these spaces.

6

# Gentrification and the Making of Craft Beer White Spaces

## Introduction

A central question motivating this book is: 'Why do black people not drink craft beer?' When you visit a brewery, or a beer festival, why are there so few black people? Simply put, historically excluded black people and other contemporarily racialized and oppressed groups do not go where they do not feel welcome, or represented. Craft beer spaces and places are typically located in gentrified areas (Mathews and Picton, 2014), which, as we argue, have become signifiers of gentrification and middle-class consumption. Further, we argue that craft breweries socially and culturally construct authentic identities that reflect middle-class values. In this chapter, we will explore the ways in which gentrification and craft beer are entangled, and the processes whereby such beer gentrification leads to the creation of 'white spaces.' Using interview data, we examine how these spaces discourage and exclude black people and other minorities from participating in craft beer cultures, and therefore its consumption.

## Gentrification in three waves

While gentrification does not have a widely agreed-upon definition, it generally refers to 'the process of middle-class professionals moving to disinvested central city neighborhoods, upgrading housing, and attracting new businesses that cater to the new neighborhood clientele' (Barajas et al, 2017: 158). This process also 'coincides with the displacement of current residents and businesses, who tend to be poorer and from racial and ethnic minority groups' (Barajas et al,

2017: 158). Kirkland (2008: 18) contends that gentrification is 'often a fundamentally racial transformation: the pre-gentrified neighborhood is inhabited mostly by African Americans or other people of color, and the in-movers are typically white.' Despite this conceptualization of gentrification, which places race at the forefront, 'many academic depictions of gentrification ... either omit reference to the racial dimensions of the phenomenon, or acknowledge race and ethnicity but forgo examination' (Kirkland, 2008: 18). Lees (2000: 389) further suggests that 'black/ethnic gentrification—race and gentrification'—are 'wrinkles' in the literature that deserve further scholarly attention.

According to Smith (2002), gentrification in the US and Europe has occurred across three 'waves.' The first wave, which started in the 1950s and ended in the mid-1970s, defined gentrification as a sporadic process in which there is an invasion of working-class neighborhoods by the upper and lower-middle classes (Glass, 1964). As Smith (2002: 438) notes, this definition 'captured the novelty of this new process whereby a new urban "gentry" transformed working-class quarters.' Glass (1964: xviii) contends that, 'once this process of "gentrification" starts in a district it goes on rapidly until all or most of the original working-class occupiers are displaced and the whole social character of the district is changed.' This period also ushered in the rise of state-led gentrification (Hacker and Smith, 2001). State involvement in gentrification was 'often justified through the discourse of ameliorating urban decline' (Hacker and Smith, 2001: 466). Both local and national governments justified gentrification as they 'Sought to counteract the private-market economic decline of central city neighborhoods. Governments were aggressive in helping gentrification because the prospect of inner-city investment was still very risky ... the effect was of course highly class specific' (Hacker and Smith, 2001: 466). As a result of this government intervention, conditions generally worsened for the urban working class (Smith, 1996). Harvey (1985) suggests that the economic downturn of the 1970s encouraged a shift in capital investment that led to reinvestment in central city office, recreation, retail, and residential activities, which would become central signifiers of gentrification in later waves.

The second wave, which lasted up until the late 1980s, is when gentrification became 'anchored' in divested neighborhoods as a state-sponsored strategy for urban redevelopment. According to Smith (2000: 440), gentrification 'became increasingly entwined with wider processes of urban and economic restructuring.' The changes in the gentrification process during this wave are related to 'larger economic and political restructuring,' including 'the return of heavy state intervention' (Hacker and Smith, 2001: 464). Hacker and Smith (2001: 465) suggest that 'When depressed markets began to revive in the late 1970s, gentrification surged as never before. New neighborhoods were converted into real estate "frontiers," and cities that had not previously experienced gentrification implemented far-reaching strategies to attract this form of investment.' As such, this wave of gentrification is characterized by 'the integration of gentrification into a wider range of economic and cultural practices at the global and national scales' (Hacker and Smith, 2001: 467–8). As Hacker and Smith (2001: 467) point out, one mechanism for the shift is the 'anchoring,' or implanting, of the process in 'hitherto disinvested central city neighborhoods.' Additionally, during this time, gentrification was correlated with the emergence of the arts community, which Hacker and Smith (2001: 467) contend served to 'smooth the flow of capital into neighborhoods like SoHo, Tribeca, and the Lower East Side.' Intense political struggles also emerged during this time over concerns about the displacement of the poorest residents (Hacker and Smith, 2001).

Lees (2000: 16) contends that 'gentrification today is quite different to gentrification in the early 1970s, late 1980s, even the early 1990s.' Indeed, during the third wave, amid a sense of hope that degentrification was occurring on a large scale, gentrification became more closely linked to large-scale capital, particularly as large developers began to 'rework entire neighborhoods, often with state support' (Hacker and Smith, 2001: 467). In part, this is due to the recession of the late 1980s, which 'constricted the flow of capital into gentrifying and gentrified neighborhoods, prompting some to proclaim that a "degentrification" or reversal of the process was afoot' (Hacker and Smith, 2001: 467). In reality, gentrification was still occurring; in fact, it was becoming more pervasive as developers began to gentrify entire neighborhoods (Hacker and Smith, 2001). During this period, the process of gentrification began to be viewed as 'thoroughly generalized as an urban strategy' in which 'the impulse behind gentrification is now generalized; its incidence is global, and is densely connected into the circuits of global capital and cultural circulation' (Smith, 2002: 427). Gentrification has become part of cultural policy, or, as Miller and Yudice (2002: 1) define it, the 'institutional support that channel both aesthetic creativity and the collective ways of life.' Butcher (2006: 28) and others argue that cultural policy often incorporates the 'subordination of one group of people by the elites, and hence regard challenges to this as potentially empowering for minorities or even majorities excluded from official manifestations of culture' (see also Miller and Yudice, 2002). The general trend in the gentrification process has been a gradual increase in the level of state involvement, with capital investment becoming more and more concentrated in the state and members of the upper class; additionally, the scope and reach of developers has moved beyond storefronts and individual businesses, to encompass entire neighborhoods.

## Gentrification, craft beer, and tourism

At a fundamental level, gentrification involves several key processes: the influx of affluent individuals; the displacement of poorer individuals; reclaiming a place as 'their own'; and transforming the place to reflect middle-class values and interests—all reminiscent of the settler colonialism that marked the establishment of the US some 400+ years ago. Proponents of gentrification often refer to the process as 'revitalization' or 'rebuilding' a community. Most of the extant literature on gentrification acknowledges race but views class as the main area of focus as gentrification affects not *just* black people, but other lower-income and racialized groups as well. Gentrification disproportionately affects lower-class individuals, and black people and Latinxs are disproportionately represented in the lower class, with little to no wealth compared to white people (Killewald et al, 2017; Oliver and Shapiro, 2013). Gentrification and revitalization projects often involve cultural policy and other institutional supports (Miller and Yudice, 2002) which, as Butcher (2006: 22; see also Throsby, 2000) asserts, 'May be regarded as the ways in which governments support, or fail to support, artistic output, and output that is considered part of a place's "cultural capital," referring to a place being perceived as exhibiting positive cultural connotations, and hence being attractive to prospective cultural tourists.' One defense of gentrification is that it injects capital into a neighborhood and creates local jobs. As Barajas et al (2017: 172) contend, 'today's wave of urban revitalization efforts has been viewed by supporters as a way to increase a city's wealth and economic opportunities,' while critics consider it 'gentrification with better marketing.' As Paulsen and Tuller (2017) note: 'While much of the focus on craft beer and place has come from cultural geographers, a number of sociologists have examined the role of bars and similar consumption spaces in remaking place. Bars are often among the first commercial establishments associated with gentrification.' Ocejo (2017: 3) reinforces this view, stating that bars operate as 'both signposts and catalysts' of gentrification, and that bars and other 'new, hip commercial establishments generate local buzz in a neighborhood and signify it is transforming.' Additionally, Ocejo (2017: 3) suggests that 'bars have a mutually reinforcing relationship with gentrification; new businesses like bars accommodate the needs of middle-class residents at the same time as they attract new ones.' This would suggest that bars, in this case, craft beer bars (Paulsen and Tuller, 2017), meet the needs of new middle-class residents by signaling change but also attract new residents as the presence of bars is an almost-universal signifier that gentrification is occurring in a given area.

However, as Barajas et al (2017: 156) argue, 'seeking to capitalize on a new market of place-based consumers, newer and smaller brewers may not be *catalysts* of urban revitalization so much as *respondents* to changing neighborhood demographics.' Further, Barajas et al (2017: 156) offer keen insight into how urban planners and developers look to craft breweries 'as an opportunity for neighborhood revitalization, economic development, and tourism.' As Zukin (2010) also suggests, consumption is a key component in the transformation of neighborhoods from working-class into gentrified areas. Additionally, 'Craft beer has become intertwined with city planning of the past decade for two related reasons. First, it is increasingly seen as an engine of local economic development and neighborhood vitality. Second ... craft beer is readily identified with its place of origin and attracts well-educated, affluent customers' (Barajas et al, 2017: 158). Cocola-Gant (2018: 281) notes that 'tourism tends to overlap with gentrified areas, especially because of the fact that gentrification provides consumption facilities and a middle-class sense of place that attracts future consumers.' In gentrified areas, 'residents and tourists seek out unique experiences to distinguish their buying habits from patterns of mass consumption' (Mathews and Picton, 2014: 338).

Previous studies have shown how developers have focused their initiatives around consumers' desire to purchase local, craft, and historic goods (Donald, 2009; Leslie and Reimer, 2006). Consumer desire for authenticity has come to the forefront in contemporary consumer culture; according to Fine (2003: 153), this desire often leads the consumer on a quest for the 'real' or 'genuine.' However, as Fine (2003: 153) explains, 'these terms are not, however, descriptive, but must be situated and defined by audiences.' Mathews and Picton (2014: 338) note that 'The craft beer industry in North America reflects this trend. Its product design and recipes are geared toward 'authentic' beers that draw on traditional recipes, local histories, and small batch production techniques ... the craft beer industry offers consumers choice, the potential for self-expression and status.' As the craft beer market continues to expand to over 8,000 breweries

(Brewers Association, 2018a), Koontz and Chapman (2019: 354) argue that 'producers must sell the authenticity of their products to stand out in a saturated or an emerging market, while consumers look for the authentic to help make purchasing decisions.' Examining the ways in which authenticity is constructed and consumed can offer insight into consumption trends, as well as illuminate emerging social values.

Erickson (1995: 121) contends that the 'transition from industrial to postindustrial society' has rooted authenticity as a 'pervasive part of our culture, our institutions, and our individual selves.' This notion of authenticity is important to consumers and tourists; according to Koontz and Chapman (2019: 351), 'constructs of craft brewing often define it simply as being "craft" and in opposition to domestic brewing, which also leads to implicit and explicit assumptions about craft beer as inherently authentic.' Further, Koontz and Chapman (2019: 351; see also Peterson, 2013) argue that 'authenticity is a social construct resulting from authenticity work, or the active processes by which individuals, industries, and organizations make authenticity claims.'

Craft breweries and beer bars offer a unique experience, or escape, for tourists—one that they may view as authentic. According to Wang (1999: 351), 'things appear authentic not because they are inherently authentic but because they are constructed as such in terms of points of view, beliefs, perspectives, or powers.' Part of this process involves what Urry (1990) calls 'the tourist gaze.' In this view, tourists employ a 'gaze,' or lens, which colors their experience. The tourist gaze is socially 'constructed through difference ... the gaze in any historical period is constructed in relation to its opposite, to non-tourist forms of social experience and consciousness' (Urry, 1990: 1–2). As Urry (1990: 2) further contends:

> What makes a particular tourist gaze depends upon what it is contrasted with; what the forms of non-tourist experience happen to be. The gaze therefore presupposes a system of social activities and signs which locate the particular tourist practices, not in terms of some intrinsic characteristics, but through the contrasts implied with non-tourist social practices.

We can see evidence that authenticity is prized among consumers as it is often staged as part of cultural tourism (MacCannell, 1973; Urry, 1990). According to Fine (2003: 155), 'authenticity refers to the recognition of difference.' This recognition of difference is key to cultural tourism as tourists enter these spaces in order to escape their normal lives and experience the lives of others. Additionally, as Wang (1999: 350) suggests, 'authenticity is relevant to some kinds of tourism such as ethnic, history or culture tourism, which involves the representation of the Other or of the past.' In consuming these unique and authentic experiences, tourists and residents of gentrified areas employ a process of 'othering,' that is, as Rose (1996: 116) explains, 'defining where you belong through a contrast with other places, or who you are through a contrast with other people.' Further, Aitchison (2001: 136) notes that 'the construction of dualisms or binary opposites is inherently related to the construction of the Other.' As Cixous (1983) suggests, this involves fundamental processes of the simultaneous construction of the 'Other' in contrast with the 'Same,' and affording greater power and status to that which is defined as the Same. In other words, tourists and residents construct the Other and then use the image of the Other to employ the tourist gaze, which leads to a unique experience that is outside of their everyday lived reality. Indeed, these tourists experience a sense of intra-personal authenticity through a process of 'self-making' (Wang, 1999).

Wang (1999: 363) contends that 'the touristic experiences of intra-personal authenticity involve "self-making" or self-identity. Self-making is an implicit dimension underlying the motivation for tourism, particularly for travelling off the beaten track.' In an effort to experience something new and exciting, tourists travel to places where they feel out of their comfort zone. Gentrified areas, particularly those in urban areas undergoing revitalization, present an accessible opportunity for self-making in this way. Therefore, as Wang (1999: 356) asserts: 'tourists are indeed in search of authenticity; however, what they quest for is not objective authenticity (i.e., authenticity as originals) but symbolic authenticity which is the result of social construction.' As such, it 'has little to do with reality … it is more often than not a projection of certain stereotyped images' (Wang, 1999: 356).

Essentially, these gentrifying areas appear exciting, unique, or even somewhat dangerous to tourists and new residents when they visit these areas. The element of danger and risk is most certainly rooted in stereotypes held about the area and its displaced residents, and is further highlighted by the othering of said residents through the deployment of the tourist gaze. As Graham et al (2000) contend, cultural representations of identity, place, and heritage are both produced and consumed by different groups, even when those conflicting groups occupy the same bounded space. The notion of authenticity is therefore socially constructed by tourists through an interpretive process. Bruner (1994) posits that 'authenticity is a label attached to the visited cultures in terms of stereotyped images and expectations held by the members of the tourist-sending society' (Wang, 1999: 355). Authenticity, or inauthenticity, is therefore 'a result of how one sees things and of his/her perspectives and interpretations' (Wang, 1999: 355). Additionally, Wang (1999: 364) suggests that 'Tourists are not merely searching for authenticity of the *Other*. They also search for the authenticity of, and between, *themselves*. The toured objects or tourism can be just a means or medium by which tourists are called together, and then, an authentic inter-personal relationship between themselves is experienced subsequently.' In this way, authenticity is constructed through a shared identity and shared lived experience—one that is defined by sameness and then contrasted with the Other. Gentrification and its brute forces involve creating spaces for white tastes and consumption patterns, replacing communities of color with white bodies, practices, and cultures.

Taking this notion further, when tourists from similar socio-economic or racial/ethnic backgrounds visit gentrified areas, they may experience a sense of what Turner (1973) referred to as 'communitas.' Wang (1999: 364) notes that in 'communitas, structures fall apart, and differences arising out of the institutionalized socioeconomic and sociopolitical positions, roles, and statuses disappear.' The experience of communitas only further solidifies the differences between the Other and the Same. Communitas causes the tourist to experience 'a spontaneous generated relationship between leveled and equal, total and individuated, human beings, stripped of structural attributes' (Turner, 1973: 216). In other words, tourists experience a sense of solidarity with other tourists when in these spaces: they share in their status as Same, and their status as *not* Other.

According to Paulsen and Tuller (2017: 107), 'part of the attraction of bars in gentrifying areas—for both entrepreneurs and patrons—is the distinctive characters of the neighborhoods they occupy.' Previous work by Brown and Patterson (2000) also suggests that consumers prefer authentic experiences, which may sometimes include experiences with an element of perceived risk. In his book, *Upscaling Downtown*, Ocejo (2017: 133) found that upscale bar consumers in Lower Manhattan preferred certain bars in gentrified areas because they 'still felt like New York,' which is often associated with diversity and, perhaps, even danger (Paulsen and Tuller, 2017). Indeed, as Barajas et al (2017: 157) contend, in efforts to appear authentic:

> Many craft breweries tie into local landmarks and lore through their beer names and labels. This can help

> newcomers share in the cultural history of a place through consumption of a distinctly local product (Schnell and Reese, 2003), creating a common narrative of a certain neighborhood history as new residents move in.

In a sense, the narrative of a place changes when new meanings are attached; in some ways, its origin 'evolves' to reflect the new cultural producers. This is similar to the concept of 'emergent authenticity,' which, according to Cohen (1988: 279–80), describes this 'evolutionary process' as 'negotiable': 'a cultural product, or trait thereof, which is at one point generally judged as contrived or inauthentic may, in the course of time, become generally recognized as authentic.' Cohen (1988) also suggests that people from different backgrounds have different needs in terms of their consumption. Further, Chhabra et al (2003: 706) note that 'there may be differences between those who have experienced the "real" culture and those who have not ... differences by gender, income and other socioeconomic variables.' Therefore, what is authentic to one group may not seem 'real' to another group.

Paulsen and Tuller (2017: 107) also contend that 'bar owners' engagement with "authentic" elements of gentrifying neighborhoods is only one example of how qualities of once-distressed places are made to appeal to affluent consumers and residents.' However, as Bruner (1994: 408) asserts, 'no longer is authenticity a property inherent in an object, forever fixed in time; it is seen as a struggle, a social process, in which competing interests argue for their own interpretation of history.' Additionally, in his work on self-taught artists, Fine (2003: 163) contends that biographies, that is to say, histories, 'justify authenticity, serving as a primary criterion of evaluation ... the biography invests the material with meaning.' This would suggest that craft brewers and developers seek to capitalize on the revitalization and new identity of a neighborhood: one that is constructed with the intent to provide an 'authentic experience' that gives the nod to the history of the neighborhood and is tailored to the interests of new residents and tourists; and one that is most certainly a struggle for interpretation and the creation of new meaning.

In the blog post 'Neighborhood brews: craft beer and gentrification in NYC' (Heritage Radio Network, 2015), the authors, contributors to the Heritage Radio Network, interviewed business owners and a 'business gatekeeper' about craft breweries and how they fit in with changing neighborhoods. One such interview was with the Executive Director of the Bedford-Stuyvesant Gateway Business Improvement District, whose job 'places him at the intersection of community and business interests, and city government' (Heritage Radio Network, 2015). The role of such organizations is to 'support economic development by ensuring that the neighborhood is clean, safe, and well-marketed' (Heritage Radio Network, 2015). While this may seem like a community improvement-oriented organization on the surface, what is not brought to the forefront is the usage of dog whistles such as 'clean,' 'safe,' and 'well-marketed.' This implies to a would-be resident or visitor that this neighborhood has undergone a transformation—that before the revitalization, it was 'dirty' or 'unsafe.' Additionally, the use of the word 'well-marketed' seems to suggest a strategic approach of appealing to a certain class of resident or visitor.

When asked about gentrification, the Director says 'the conversation of gentrification gets visceral. Bed-Stuy may be changing, but it hasn't changed. The north side of Bed-Stuy still has a lot of economic development challenges, a lot of vacancies, a lot of social issues' (Heritage Radio Network, 2015). He seems to suggest that the topic of gentrification is one that cuts to the core of residents, developers, and perhaps even displaced former residents. However, he glosses over the potentially damaging effects, or difficult conversations, that come with gentrification. By suggesting that the area still has a lot of 'economic development challenges, a lot of vacancies, a lot of social issues,' the Director is implicitly suggesting that the previous residents are the reason why the area needs to be revitalized. It is similar to ridding a garden of insects: the insects may have decimated the existing garden but, with a lot of hard work, the gardener can salvage the garden and create new growth. The contributing author concludes the interview by saying, 'by supporting locally-owned businesses, the BID [Business Improvement District] strives to create good jobs and encourage money to recirculate, while protecting the neighborhood's heritage' (Heritage Radio Network, 2015).

However, for whom are these jobs being created and to whom is the money being recirculated to? Black people are much less likely to possess the start-up capital (Robb, 2013), or the social networks (Smith, 2000), to open a brewery or similar business, so they are not the ones benefiting from the economic support, nor are they likely to be the consumers who are injecting money into the local economy. Second, as discussed previously, black people and other minorities are not represented in the craft beer industry; therefore, we can assume, they are most likely not the ones receiving these jobs (or who even know about them). Third, given the displacement of racial and ethnic minorities that coincides with gentrification, what heritage is being protected (or constructed)? Is it the heritage of the previous residents, or the co-opted heritage and connection to community of affluent new residents? As discussed earlier, the relationship between craft beer and gentrification is complicated. Gentrification leads to the displacement of lower-class individuals, particularly minorities, and the creation of new 'revitalized' white spaces. In the next section, we will examine the ways in which people 'consume' space and place, and how space and place are constructed as authentic.

## Space, place, and consumption

Space and place are both geographical and cultural constructs, and, as Tuan (1977: 6) contends, 'the ideas of "space" and "place" require each other for definition.' According to Gieryn (2000), place can be defined by three distinct features: geographic location, material form, and investment with meaning and value. First, a place has a location: it 'is a unique spot in the universe. Place is the distinction between here and there, and it is what allows people to appreciate near and far' (Gieryn, 2000: 464). Second, a place has a material form: it 'has physicality. Whether built or just come upon, artificial or natural, streets and doors or rocks and trees, place is stuff. Places are worked by people: we make places' (Gieryn, 2000: 465). Also, as Habraken (1998) points out, social processes of difference, inequality, power, and collective action occur through these material forms—they occur through place. Last, a place is invested with meaning and value: without a name or 'identification, or representation by ordinary people, a place is not a place' (Gieryn, 2000: 465).

Places are physically constructed but they are also interpreted, narrated, perceived, and understood (Soja, 1996). Additionally, as Gieryn (2000: 465) notes: 'in spite of its relatively enduring and imposing materiality, the meaning or value of the same place is pliable—flexible in the hands of different people or cultures, malleable over time, and inevitably contested.' Further, MacLeod (2006: 7) suggests that there are 'multiple contested meanings of place … with regard to interpretations of history, but these can also be used in creative ways to transform and regenerate, or even to create new destinations.' The process of gentrification involves a transformation of place and the creation of a new destination. Cocola-Gant (2018) refers to this process as 'place-based displacement,' during which residents experience a loss of place as new residents and tourists consume a space. Further, it involves the detachment of meaning and displacement of previous residents, as well as the attachment and creation of new meanings for new residents; it creates a new place. Anderson (2015: 11) adds that 'as demographics change, public spaces are subject to change as well, impacting not only how a space is occupied and by whom but also the way in which it is perceived.'

While the two concepts are often intertwined in sociological analysis, place is not the same as space. As Gieryn (2000: 465) suggests, space 'is more properly conceived as abstract geometries (distance, direction, size, shape, volume) detached from material form and cultural interpretation.' Essentially, spaces become places when actors attach meaning to them, or, as Gieryn (2000: 465) describes, 'place is space filled up by people, practices, objects, and representations.' Humans transform spaces into places by attaching meaning, creating material objects, and engaging in ritualistic behaviors. In the words of Tuan (1977: 6): 'what begins as undifferentiated space becomes place as we get to know it better and endow it with value.' Places also possess their own cultural capital, which is transferred to tourists and residents alike. The cultural capital of a place includes 'the nurturing and marketing of an intangible "sense of place"' (Butcher, 2006: 22). This 'sense of place' is what makes the place unique and what makes it a desirable location for tourists and residents. The gentrification process creates new forms of cultural capital that reflect the new meanings attached to a place—its new 'sense of place'—and provide an authentic experience for consumers.

Craft breweries are some of the first businesses to enter gentrifying spaces, often out of necessity (Barajas et al, 2017). As Barajas et al (2017: 158) note: 'larger breweries require expensive equipment and ample space. Inexpensive rent is essential to keep overhead costs low.' Online blogger Cameron Eittreim (2019) agrees and offers his observation: 'Every time I have seen gentrification taking place in an area it is usually accompanied by these little trendy craft breweries, almost as if there is some sort of cult out there that is hell-bent on bringing naturally crafted beers into urban neighborhoods.' Given their status as signifiers of gentrification, it is imperative to understand how these spaces are created and, of equal importance, how they relate to a particular place.

Koontz and Chapman (2019: 358) argue that 'brewers employ authenticating claims of space and place and legitimation of brand identity.' Further, Brown-Saracino (2018: 5) suggests that 'place identities' provide consumers with a framework of how to relate to others in a place, as well as answering questions about an individual's own self-identity. Koontz and Chapman (forthcoming) describe the way in which breweries create these place identities as 'localized authentication.' This process is defined as 'a contextualized and collaborative process, during which interactions between the products, producers (and/or representatives), and consumers result in the situated experience of a "vibe"' (Koontz and Chapman, forthcoming). Thus, place identities serve several key functions: providing a sense of authenticity for consumers; guiding behavior among consumers in that space; creating a vibe or atmosphere; and providing cultural capital, which, in turn, becomes part of consumers' self-identities. How do breweries achieve this, though?

Paulsen and Tuller (2017: 106) note that 'scholarship on the relationship between craft brewing and places emphasizes the industry's reliance on symbols and stories associated with the home places of microbreweries.' Relating space and place to the product is important to the authentication process. In particular, craft breweries operating in gentrified areas must create an authentic experience for consumers. In line with Baudrillard's (1994) work, the aura or essence that is derived from the original place becomes important when demarcating a place as authentic. In order to create an authentic experience or product, industries and individuals engage in 'authenticity,' which distinguishes their work from other commercial products by connecting it with traditions, originality, the creator or craftsman personally, and space and place (Fine, 2006; Koontz, 2010; Koontz and Chapman, 2019; Peterson, 2005, 2013). Baudrillard (1994) suggests that in order to distinguish something as real or authentic, it must be distinguished from the simulacra through narratives of origin. According to Koontz and Chapman (2019: 362), brewers create their own authentic space by 'connecting with nature that cannot be found anywhere else, the history of the place, and regionalism.'

In terms of craft breweries, the authenticity of a place is constructed through a recognition of difference between the new residents and the displaced Other, a reliance on the history of a place that highlights the heritage of the Other, and a reconstructed meaning that reflects the values of affluence and a desire for authentic experience. While the authenticity of a brewery can be constructed in these ways, it must be noted that this process of authentication most certainly involves the further subjugation of black people and other minorities in these gentrified areas, and ignores the structural barriers and social inequality under which these displaced groups lived. In many ways, white people are consuming a whitewashed history of a place and defining it as real. This is similar to the process of 'fabricating authenticity,' which Peterson (2013) suggests involves creating, or fabricating, shared meaning among producers and consumers. The consumption of authentic goods and experiences, as well as authentic places, is an exchange between the producer and consumer in which shared values are made manifest through cultural goods.

Given the prominence of craft breweries and craft beer spaces in gentrified areas, one must consider how concerns of authenticity contribute to the overall experience of a place. When drinking a beer at a brewery or a bar, one is most certainly consuming the space and place as well. The authenticity of these places is constructed out of middle-class values and consumption but at the cost of lower-class and minority displacement. This place displacement (Cocola-Gant, 2018) leaves minorities and lower-class individuals without a 'place.' Their space has been transformed into a new place in which they no longer feel welcome. In the next section, we will discuss the ways in which spaces become places and how authenticity creates an atmosphere or vibe that reflects white middle-class values.

## Breweries *as* white spaces

Places possess a certain 'vibe,' or atmosphere, that is perceived and felt by consumers. These 'affective atmospheres,' as Anderson (2009) describes them, relate to how people interact with spaces, and how these spaces may be emotionally charged. Anderson (2009) furthers the work of Goffman (1997) which suggests that the setting, or place, in which interactions take place possesses pre-established norms and limitations for human interaction. This inherent 'feel' of a space regulates behavior through normative structures and expectations. Michels (2015: 256) suggests that the affective atmosphere of a place describes a certain 'vibration' that is derived from the aesthetics of a place, as well as the emotions that derive from interaction in the place. This feeling, or 'vibe,' is constructed through connections to the history of a place (for example, an old industrial space) and the connection to the new emerging culture of a place (for example, middle-class values). In this way, a vibe is constructed through interpretation and can be perceived as authentic if the connections make sense to the consumer. The vibe of a place also describes the feelings that an individual may experience when in a place, becoming a part of that place, or, in the case of craft beer bars, becoming a regular. The vibe is therefore perceived or felt differently by different consumers. Breweries in gentrified areas may have a welcoming and authentic vibe to white consumers but, at the same time, be unwelcoming or off-putting to black and other minority consumers.

Another contributor to the overall vibe of a place is the exchange of cultural capital and taste evaluations by consumers. Black people have very different tastes than white people, particularly when it comes to craft beer. However, taste valuations are vital to the interpretation of a space and whether or not it possesses the right vibe. According to Trubek (2008: 7), 'taste evaluations must occur through language, a shared dialogue with others.' This further highlights the importance of cultural capital and exposure to craft beer in developing tastes. Black people may feel uncomfortable, or perceive a negative vibe, if they do not possess the requisite cultural capital to interact effectively in craft beer spaces. Individuals who possess large amounts of cultural capital may be perceived as 'snobs,' which, in turn, can turn people away from a space as well. Corey describes a scenario such as this, saying:

> 'It was pretty intimidating. A lot of it [perceiving a negative vibe] would force someone to crawl back into a shell if they were met with someone saying, "You don't know anything about beer" or "Why are you taking a picture of beer?" Beer snobs can be really intimidating. We [Corey and his business partner] almost turned into beer snobs before we realized that we were losing the very people that we were attempting to bring to craft beer. So, I think that snobbery can turn people off and make people not want to explore something deeper. Think about it, if you're the only person in the room that looks like you, and you are curious about craft beer and you don't understand something, then you ask a question and someone gives you a snobby ass response, the likelihood that (1) you're going to stay there is slim, (2) the likelihood that you're going to return is slim, and (3) the likelihood that you're going to celebrate that culture is slim. So, if you just consider that scenario and go into a craft brewery, specifically one that may not be steeped in a community that is full of people of color, you are still going to be the only one [person of color] there.' (Corey, black, male, influencer)

Additionally, the sheer fact that there are no other black people in a brewery can cause black people to avoid entering. Patricia describes a scenario in which a black person may choose not to enter a craft beer space, in this case, a beer garden:

> 'So, if I'm African-American, and I'm walking down the street, and I see I'm walking past a beer garden, and I look over in that beer garden and I don't see one face that looks

> like me, man or woman, I am probably not going to feel comfortable going in there. And it's not because I don't like white people. It's just that African-Americans in this country, we have a long history of feeling unwanted.' (Patricia, black, female, industry insider)

These feelings of unwelcomeness, that is, of being unwanted, are hallmarks of what Anderson (2015) refers to as 'white spaces.' With their relationship to gentrification and their deeply historical relationship with whiteness and white, particularly, white male, sociability, breweries are particularly great examples of white spaces. These spaces can make black people and other minorities feel uncomfortable and also remind them of the history of racism that they have experienced.

According to Anderson (2015: 13), 'white spaces vary in kind, but their most visible and distinct feature is their overwhelming presence of white people and their lack of black people.' Examples of white spaces include gentrified neighborhoods, schools, restaurants, public spaces such as parks, and breweries. Indeed, the entire craft beer industry is a white space. As Ida asserts: "when we think of the craft brew industry, we think of white men." In these spaces, black people are usually not present, not expected to be in that particular space, or marginalized while in the space (Anderson, 2015). Their blackness becomes a master status. Their identity in the brewery is defined by their otherness; it is defined by the differences in culture. Indeed, as Ida laments:

> 'Having been to no less than 150 breweries, I am always, to use your language, "shocked, not shocked," at the blanket of whiteness that's immediately dropped on me approaching the brewery. There's whiteness in the parking lot, whiteness behind the bar, whiteness in the cellar, whiteness being brewed, whiteness on the TV, white music, white culture. I'm overstimulated by hegemony.' (Ida, black, female, brewer/owner)

Black people may feel alienated or threatened by the lack of people that look like them in white spaces. These feelings may lead to the decision not to enter a white space. Tony suggests that the tension felt by black people is, in part, socially constructed through our interactions:

> 'If you look at human dynamics, not many people go to places where they are a rarity. I don't see too many black people in all-white spaces, or vice versa. If it's an

> environment dominated by a particular group, then people who aren't in that group typically don't feel comfortable going there.' (Tony, influencer/organizer)

Even black people who enjoy craft beer may feel uncomfortable in these spaces. Corey describes this tension, saying: "I enjoy craft beer, but I don't see anybody that looks like me [in a brewery], or resembles or sounds like me. I walk into a space and I don't hear anything that resembles my culture." Despite these tensions, and their deep historical, structural, and cultural antecedents in the relationship between race and beer in the US, black people will often decide to enter a white space. When black people and other minorities enter a white space, they negotiate their interactions through a process. In this process, black people will take notice of the racial composition of the space. In doing so, they may look for other black people to interact with. Whiteness may appear in other ways as well, photos on the walls, names on the menu, the programs on the television, and the music playing in the background. If they find that there are enough black people for them to interact with, they may feel more comfortable in the space. If there are not enough black people for them to interact with comfortably, they may judge a space as 'too white,' which can lead them to 'feel uneasy and consider it to be informally "off limits"' (Anderson, 2015: 10). White people occupying a brewery may be oblivious to these contentious feelings. Recalling a visit to a brewery in a gentrified area, Anderson (2015: 18) describes the tension that can exist in these spaces:

> Young blacks walked stiffly as they made their way through the diners occupying tables and chairs on the sidewalk they once thought of as their own. … Others were more direct, scowling as they passed by this crowd. … Meanwhile, the white clientele seemed generally comfortable. Some were oblivious of the mood of these passersby, while others sent snide or angry looks at the black 'interlopers' or passersby who would dare to disturb their meals. Invested in a posture of being at home in this environment, the brewery patrons displayed nonchalance and appeared unaware of the situational irony, their displacement of the previous black inhabitants from what has been historically their space.

When black people enter a white space, they are often stigmatized and associated with danger, crime, and the ghetto (Anderson, 2015).

However, some black people are more tolerated than others in these spaces. As Anderson (2015: 13) notes: 'The most easily tolerated black person in the white space is often one who is "in his place"—that is, one who is working as a janitor or a service person who has been vouched for by white people in good standing.' Black people may also minimize this stigmatization by performing, negotiating, or doing the 'dance' (Anderson, 2015). The 'dance' most certainly varies by place. Some spaces and places require different performances than others. For instance, a restaurant may require black people to present themselves in a different way than at a movie theater or public park. In performing the 'dance,' black people are effectively proving themselves to their white counterparts: they are attempting to show that the ghetto stereotypes held by white people do not apply to them, and to be accepted in the white space (Anderson, 2015). White people in these spaces generally do not take notice of the lack of racial diversity. Anderson (2015: 10) contends that for white people, 'the same settings are generally regarded as unremarkable, or as normal, taken-for-granted reflections of civil society.' Corey echoes this sentiment, saying: "if you can imagine, you know, if you're a white drinker drinking in a white-dominated environment and industry, you don't see a problem because you see your reflection."

Additionally, craft beer is typically not marketed in areas predominantly occupied by black people and other minorities. The gentrification process further exacerbates this by displacing black people from communities and then supplanting white culture and cultural products into the places that they once occupied. The exposure to craft beer is crucial in the development of a taste for craft beer. As we have seen, the craft industry seems to have made little effort to be inclusive of minority drinkers. This combination of industry exclusion and geographic displacement creates an environment and a culture of exclusion. Kevin suggests that this exclusion is, perhaps, a conscious decision on the part of the industry and one that is backed up by business practices in gentrified areas, as well as gentrification itself:

> 'I think the biggest barrier to black and brown people being more avid consumers on a national level of craft beer is the fact that in the past, there has been an intentional decision not to market to certain communities, or it was an intentional write-off. … I think it was more like, "These people don't consume our products so we are just going to completely write this population off and not market goods to them." So, when at a very high level, you're not exposing black and brown people to become consumers,

> and geographically, you're not attracting them to the places that will [expose them], someone had to make that decision.' (Kevin, black, male, brewer/owner)

Exposing black people to craft beer is difficult because craft beer is typically only available in white spaces. As Marcus contends:

> 'This [craft beer] wasn't a thing that was in our community, it wasn't a part of our culture. Nobody that looked like us owned breweries, or had a lot of these opportunities … when all these breweries are popping up … breweries and things [bottle shops and homebrew stores] of that nature, black people weren't really welcome to drink where white folks drank. When it comes to beer, you'll see great beer selections only in white-dominated towns, towns that are majority white, or affluent … all these places it feels they are mostly white.' (Marcus, black, male, influencer)

The craft beer industry is dominated by white males. The lack of representation of minorities in the industry has led many to associate craft as a symbol of white maleness. Betsy describes craft beer as having a 'hipster' persona, where white males with beards and flannel shirts dominate the scene:

> 'The craft industry, in particular, has developed into something that has a persona that is white and male. And it has a look to it, an aesthetic, that is somewhat self-contained in terms of a hipster social look to it. I wonder if places like taprooms will always feel like uncomfortable spaces for people who don't necessarily have that look.' (Betsy, white, female, curator/historian)

Indeed, the persona of the craft beer drinker is extended to the physical space and the beer itself. Kevin also contends that:

> 'If, historically, the industry has not marketed [beer] to be inclusive of ethnicities and cultures, then you can also see how that [lack of inclusion] translates into the cultures and the environments that are created in the spaces that you're now thinking, "Oh, why aren't there more black and brown people in these spaces," right?' (Kevin, black, male, brewer/owner)

Spaces and places possess meanings—they have inherent and often unspoken rules of interaction—and these meanings are negotiated through a process of othering.

In further addressing the question of why black people do not drink craft beer, we must also consider what craft beer and craft breweries represent to the black community. As mentioned previously, craft breweries are signifiers of gentrification. The gentrification process creates white spaces by displacing minority residents and replacing them with middle-class white people. When asked this very question, Tony replied:

> 'Typically, when we're talking about how we get black people into it [craft beer], the question is usually, "How can we get black people to drink [craft beer]?" Nobody's saying, "Well, how do we empower the black community? How do we put a brewery in a black community, and it does not immediately become gentrified?" Because, typically, in a black community, when we see a craft brewery open up, that's the end of us, we might as well find another place because gentrification is gonna come.' (Tony, black, male, influencer/organizer)

Anderson (2015: 18) suggests that 'the brewery appears as a white space in the middle of the ghetto. Its clientele and workforce are overwhelmingly white and drawn mainly from the local neighborhood.' The brewery is a white space that was previously occupied by black people, which 'constitutes a cultural and economic manifestation of [an] ongoing, major shift from a black space to a white space' (Anderson, 2015: 19). Eittreim (2019: 11) describes this tension in recalling visits to breweries in gentrified areas:

> I've visited quite a few areas that have undergone these 'gentrification' periods, and the retail experience, as well as the neighborhood vibe in general, becomes unwelcoming to the original residents. This then creates a double-edged sword, where you have two different walks of life who are trying to co-exist, causing friction and resentment among the original residents.

Now, black people and other minorities are forced to 'navigate the white space as a condition of their existence' (Eittreim, 2019: 11). To poor and working-class black residents, 'the brewery represents the vanguard of a white invasion … [the brewery] is clearly a significant racial symbol' (Anderson, 2015: 18). Displaced residents may come to resent the brewery and most would not entertain the idea of entering a brewery (Anderson, 2015).

Craft beer is loaded with cultural capital (Darwin, 2018). When black people enter these spaces, they must display their cultural capital in order to be perceived as welcome. As such, their identity performances are centered around beer knowledge and cultural taste. Black people in white spaces are assumed to lack the knowledge or cultural taste to appreciate craft beer. Therefore, when performing the 'dance,' they must prove to their white counterparts that they appreciate craft beer. Depending on the space, some black people may forgo the performance. In some cases, the consumption of a particular good may trump any negative feelings. As Kevin contends, the beer is the most important thing in these spaces. The beer itself becomes the focus, not the racial make-up of the physical space:

> 'I don't look at any place and say, "This is not for me," that's just not in my DNA. You can't keep me out of a room if I want to be there. So we spent a lot of time at breweries and attending beer festivals. And while we were at all these places, in some cases, we could be one of a few, or the only, black people there. But it didn't bother us because, again, we're there for the beer. … I think, in general, it doesn't matter whether you're black, white, or whatever. But if you're operating in a space where there's a lot of people that don't look like you in that space, it doesn't matter what you do, people that already occupy that space are going to look at you funny, until you've proven yourself a couple of times.' (Kevin, black, male, brewer/owner)

Previous research on craft beer (Chapman et al, 2018; Darwin, 2018) has shown that in the eyes of many drinkers, beer itself has an inherent gender. If beer is perceived to have a gender, it may also be perceived to have an inherent race. Given this fact, if we presuppose that beer and beer spaces have a 'race,' then we can assume that when black people enter into these spaces, they are negotiating their identity not only in terms of the space and their otherness in relation to white customers, but also in terms of the beer itself. Ida describes negotiating her identity with beer and the space of a brewery:

> 'So, there's a negotiation that has to happen with the beer, just the beer itself, while you're negotiating white space, right? While you're negotiating a white space, that at any time can become highly volatile. As a black, fat, queer person, who is often misgendered as a man, I'm in a space with white people who are drinking. And, historically, those situations have ended in incarceration, death, brutality, fights, conflict, and what have you. So, I'm choosing to land in a place that I know has a great potential reality for violence on some level—whether emotional violence, psychological violence, spiritual violence—while I'm being deeply saturated with white culture while trying to hang out and unplug [relax].' (Ida, black, female, brewer/owner)

Ida's experience illustrates just some of the issues facing black people when entering a white space. As Anderson (2015: 15) notes, in the white space, the anonymous black person's status is uncertain, and they can be subject to the most pejorative regard. Kevin asserts that "Not to say that these places [breweries] are racist or anything like that. But people want to feel welcome. They want to feel like there are other people that look and think like them there also" (Kevin, black, male, brewer/owner). Being in the presence of other people of color is crucial to determining whether or not a black person in a white space feels welcome. This is echoed by Betsy, who posits: "I think ... the space, you know, the setting of the tap room, is it a place where you see people who look like you? Would you feel welcome there?"

As our respondents clearly articulate, while craft beer certainly has a problem with diversity, it also has a serious problem with inclusion. Often, when brewers mention diversity, they are referring to a diversity of beer styles. Rarely, if ever, are brewers concerned or even aware of the lack of diversity in their consumer base. As Julia Herz (2016), Craft Beer Program Director for the Brewers Association, notes:

> One element of the definition of diversity is 'variety.' Craft brewers have mastered variety in brand offerings, styles of beer made, brewery taprooms, brewpub menus, beer labels, and more. However, especially of late, I've found myself fumbling through cringe-worthy interviews on the topic of diversity that have left me lacking confidence in speaking to the subject.

As one New York-based brewer suggests: 'beer is for everyone … beer isn't just made for fat bearded white dudes by fat bearded white dudes. Everyone can appreciate it' (quoted in Heritage Radio Network, 2015). So, how can craft beer become more inclusive? How can craft breweries, particularly those in gentrified areas, become more inclusive spaces, rather than white, exclusionary spaces? How are social media influencers, brewers, industry employees, bloggers, and rappers bringing craft beer to black people across the US, and what does it mean for the future of craft beer? In Chapter 7, we will examine how these individuals are increasing the exposure to craft beer in black neighborhoods and across the internet, collaborating with breweries to produce culturally authentic products that speak to the black craft beer drinker, and crafting a #newnarrative for a more inclusive craft beer industry and culture.

# 7

# #WeAreCraftBeer: Contemporary Movements to Change the Whiteness of Craft Beer

## Introduction

Although the central story of race and beer in the US is one that centers on the production and reproduction of whiteness, there is reason to believe that the racialized social structure of beer might be cracking. This chapter will cover several developments that may indicate critical change in the phenomenon of craft beer. There is no doubt that there are several contemporary currents that are pressing against the whiteness of craft beer, and there is also no doubt that it is all happening *right now*. We will highlight several of these taking place across the country, in minority-owned breweries, in the digital space of social media, and many occurring right in your backyard, in order to get a bird's-eye view of their challenges and resilience in the face of such a structure. We will also report on the few black/Latino/Asian and immigrant enclaves of beer in the country—neighborhoods, areas, brewers, clubs, drinkers, tasting, and so on—where beer is celebrated to its fullest. This will also take us into discussions of cutting-edge festivals like Fresh Fest and High Gravity Hip-Hop, as well as clever collaborations that are challenging the centuries-long relationship between whiteness and beer. Whether the racialized social structure of beer is cracking or not, this chapter highlights the positive developments that may indicate a way forward concerning equality and inclusion in beer, as well as ideas for (re)crafting beer and beer culture. Indeed, as we were writing the final draft of this book, things were moving really quickly.

On September 9, 2019, J. Nikol Jackson-Beckham ('Dr. J'), the Brewers Association's first ever diversity ambassador (appointed in April 2018), tweeted the following from her very active account, which is always abuzz with issues of craft beer and diversity:

> 1. Take selfie.
> 2. Tell us something about your wonderful, complex, individual self.
> 3. Tag your post with #IAmCraftBeer
>
> Let's create a huge enduring reminder of the incredible diversity in our community! Here we go. … (Jackson-Beckham, 2019)

As of the time of writing, almost one month to the day of that tweet, there have been over 200 responses within the thread, it has been retweeted almost 130 times, and it has been liked by almost 500 Twitter users. If one moves outward and looks at some analytics of that tweet, it has received a significant amount of engagement (over 42,000 engagements) and is still going. The resulting thread, the incredibly diverse selfies, and the narratives of these craft beer brewers, drinkers, homebrewers, and the many other ways in which people interact with craft beer, its industry, and its spaces and places is exciting and shows a face and a social space of craft beer that has been incredibly rare in our reading of the history of race and beer in the US. This excitement and promise is shared by our respondents, alongside their recognition of the stark historical and contemporary realities.

This emergent and ongoing Twitter hashtag (#IAmCraftBeer) is by no means indicative of recouping the lost and hidden stories of minorities and beer throughout history, nor is it evidence of an alteration of the structure of the industry and the three-tier distribution system as they function to keep craft beer white and male, nor is it even a symbol of a fundamentally different set of paths, spaces, and places of craft beer, all of which, as we have shown, are created by white people, for white people. However, it *is* one of a set of very contemporary movements to articulate a different view of craft beer and, with time, likely a different structure and culture of craft beer—all with an eye to importing a critical diversity into the very fabric of it.

In the preceding chapters, we have argued that the beer industry, craft beer and its culture, and the tastes of black beer drinkers have been racialized through historical practices of racism and exclusion dating back to the earliest days of the US, the structure of the three-tier distribution system post-Prohibition, discrimination in hiring practices in the industry itself, racialized advertising and targeted marketing, gentrification and displacement, and the appropriation of black culture. Here, we seek to highlight the paths forward shown in our interview data with brewers, industry insiders, beer historians and curators, sales representatives, and others, and as evidenced by our reading of the contemporary strategies and innovations, almost all led by those who have been actively excluded from craft beer. By virtue of hiring a diversity ambassador, the Brewers Association signaled to the craft beer industry and culture that it was time for a change. While this move may be long overdue, it is certainly not too late. Our interview data highlight the efforts of social media influencers, brewers, industry employees, bloggers, and rappers to make the industry, its spaces and places, and its attendant culture more inclusive. In doing so, these individuals have begun to craft a #newnarrative in which craft beer is accessible to, and enjoyed by, all—where, as the African proverb might say in contemporary Twitter-speak, '#IAmCraftBeer because #WeAreCraftBeer.'

## How beer became white, why it matters, and the movements to change it

Before moving on to the exciting contemporary movements to change the whiteness (and maleness) of craft beer, let us quickly revisit where we have been. In Chapter 1, we laid out the ways in which beer and craft beer is a social, cultural, economic, and political signifier of life in a raced, gendered, and classed America. We raised the notion that beer and its attendant cultures appear to fundamentally cater to white men. The chapter highlighted how beer has been (and remains) quite important in the human experience—understanding beer is important in the understanding of ourselves, who we are, and who we can become. The importance of beer as a social and cultural object was highlighted, and our various theoretical approaches to the study of race and beer were outlined for the reader, including the fundamental organizing principle of race, racism, and racial inequality in US institutions, the creation of and reproduction of whiteness within white spaces, the production of cultural objects (like beer) and their organizational, legal, and other constraints, and the contemporary theory (and hope) of critical diversities in an industry like craft beer. We also introduced our methodological approach, our respondents, and our analytic approach to understanding the whiteness of beer, why it matters, and the contemporary movements to change it.

From there, we embarked on an almost 400-year stretch of critical history that traced the ways in which we talk about, understand, and think about the relationship between beer, brewing, and race. Starting with the (white) origin stories of 20th- and 21st-century beer historians, both scholarly and popular, we highlighted the (white) pulse of those 'beer cosmologies' and what they actively make invisible. We saw whiteness crafting its own brewing histories and highlighted that until alternative stories are told, such histories we will be subject to the delusionary cosmology and mythology of beer and brewing that upholds white people as the true originators and heirs to beer. So, we began, just began, telling some stories that have remained hidden: those of tavern culture and its building of whiteness, but also the ways in which it engaged with race; the relationship between regulating, legislating, and socially controlling the racialized population through beer and beer cultures; and the building of taverns as white spaces, designed for white people to communicate with white people, all to support white male sociability. We also dug a bit into the possibility that black and indigenous people owned and/or ran taverns within this culture, and the structures they faced in doing so. Finally, we drew broad strokes in painting the picture of the racist foundations of both the temperance and Prohibition movements in the US—movements that would ultimately raise up a German-immigrant-turned-white-power structure within the brewing industry.

In the wake of the repeal of Prohibition, the brewing industry entered into a period of widespread consolidation at the hands of larger producers, most often referred to as the 'Big Three.' Indeed, the result of the numerous acquisitions and mergers by these large firms was a highly concentrated and oligopolistic industry structure. This created a vacuum in the industry for niche products and allowed craft beer to emerge and fulfill an unmet need. In order for states to tax and regulate alcohol production, the three-tier distribution system was put in place. The three tiers—producer, distributor, and retailer—regulate beer production, handle the marketing and distribution of beer, and the carry out retail sales to consumers, respectively. This system further racialized the white beer industry and put in place structures that would further discourage, and, in some cases, prevent, black people from producing and consuming beer. At the production tier, black people and other minorities were systematically discriminated against and denied access to jobs at all levels of the production process. At the distribution tier, distributors are tasked with delivering beer to retailers and marketing products in retail settings. We have shown that these practices are, more often than not, based on deeply held racial and class stereotypes. This further excludes black people and other minorities from being exposed to a variety of products and has long-term effects on the cultural tastes of black drinkers.

Chapter 4 traced the social, economic, and cultural paths to becoming a brewer and a consumer of craft beer in the US. Our interviews provided a wealth of information about these processes. The paths to becoming a brewer in the contemporary US are rooted in homebrewing and its clubs, communities, and competitions. It is also still very much of an apprentice system, where volunteering at breweries and working within the food and beverage industry may grant access to various social networks within the industry. It is also rapidly changing into a path that is paved with legitimation through brewing schools and educational credentials. All of these are fundamentally grounded in social networks—who you know—and are therefore more available to white people in an industry that is organized around whiteness. As for becoming a craft beer consumer, we find that these paths are also rooted in social networks and access to certain spaces. If you have beer in the family, you are more likely to engage with craft beer. If you have beer in your friendship networks, you are also more likely to be exposed to craft beer. College—more accessible to white people—equals more craft beer exposure, as does access to beer scenes and distribution networks. Potential black and brown craft brewers and consumers have a large (racial) mountain to climb in order to become a part of this industry.

In Chapter 5, we looked closely at the role of marketing and cultural appropriation. The legacy of malt liquor cannot be understated. For nearly three decades, malt liquor was marketed to black people through racially targeted marketing. The use of prominent black celebrities, athletes, and, perhaps most notably, rappers to market these products has had lasting effects on the culture of drinking in the black community, and has shaped the tastes of black drinkers. During the 1990s, a 'forty ounce' culture emerged that promoted the consumption of malt liquor by young black males. This culture reflected and encouraged a hyper-masculine and hyper-sexualized consumer base. In the late 1980s, rappers began composing lyrics that described the perceived effects of malt liquor in graphic detail. After the decline of malt liquor sales in the mid-1990s, white college students began to appropriate malt liquor and other black cultural symbols. Under the guise of 'nostalgia,' white craft beer drinkers and brewers have begun to brew 'crafty' malt liquors. However, this is not the most egregious action on the part of craft producers. As shown in Chapter 5, craft producers have appropriated Hip-Hop lyrics, iconography, and even social justice movements such as #BlackLivesMatter to appeal to a predominantly white male consumer base. These actions have led many in the craft beer community writ large, including black social media influencers and craft beer enthusiasts, to push back and call out these breweries. This has resulted in the amplification of the call for a more inclusive craft beer culture and craft beer spaces.

Chapter 6 examined the effects of gentrification on black communities and craft beer's role in changing the meanings attached to spaces and places of consumption. Gentrification involves the displacing of low-income minority residents and replacing them with more affluent, and typically white, new residents. Craft beer appeals to this demographic in several key ways, which is evidenced by the rise of craft consumption among this group. Breweries have taken notice and attempted to construct authentic identities that reflect a particular place or region. When viewed through the lens of gentrification, this authenticity work leads to the creation of white spaces. We consume spaces and places much in the same way that we consume other cultural goods. They are embedded with meaning and, as such, often require certain amounts of cultural capital to navigate. As we have shown, through social and symbolic exclusion, black people have not been granted access to cultural capital. Like other white spaces, breweries discourage black consumption of craft beer and discourage black participation in craft beer culture.

Throughout this book, we have demonstrated the importance of exposure to, access to, and knowledge about craft beer. Indeed, our interview respondents also contend that exposure to craft beer is one of the largest barriers in preventing and excluding black people from craft beer consumption. As the Brewers Association reported in their annual address, the craft beer industry has a diversity problem. In the following sections, we highlight the efforts of individuals to make the industry and culture more inclusive by increasing black and minority exposure to craft beer, creating spaces and building community, owning breweries, and using social media platforms to educate people about craft beer.

## Increasing exposure: bringing the beer to the people

In Chapter 3, we outlined the role of the distributor in the three-tier system. These individuals, who are mostly white males, have major control over the marketing of beer. They can limit exposure to a particular product based on the perceived market potential of an area. We also show that these perceptions are often shaped by racial and class stereotypes. Simply put, if you do not have craft beer in your area, you are not exposed to it and you cannot develop a taste for it—and if you are unable to do those things, you cannot participate in craft beer culture. By limiting the beverage options for black drinkers and marketing lesser-quality products, distributors have socially and symbolically excluded black people and other minorities from craft beer consumption. As noted previously, lower-class individuals' taste preferences are often developed out of necessity, rather than actual preference for a good. In other words, if you have a limited variety of products available to you, and you are economically unable to consume higher-quality goods, lesser-quality products (that is, malt liquor) become your preference. Corey discusses the importance of exposure and how social media influencers and black craft beer drinkers have worked to increase the exposure of craft beer to black people by hosting beer-tasting and bottle-share events in black spaces:

> 'We started doing events throughout California, then other places in the United States. We did pop-up craft beer tastings in the back of barbershops. We were able to do that because Governor Davis signed a law so you could pour up to a pint of beer or a glass of wine in a barber shop or a salon. So, that gave us an opportunity to give tastings of craft beer. We did 3 oz tastings of several different styles of beer [at the barbershops and salons].' (Corey, black, male, influencer)

Events such as these not only increase the exposure of craft beer, but also grant access to cultural capital by educating new craft drinkers about various styles, tasting notes, and so on. Taking craft beer outside of white spaces and into black spaces makes beer and the culture more accessible.

In Chapter 5, we discussed the ways in which black culture has been appropriated in the craft beer industry. In particular, we highlighted the ways in which Hip-Hop culture and iconography are used to market craft beer. Hip-Hop's history with craft beer is certainly complex. Several of our interview respondents viewed appropriation as a serious problem in the industry, particularly as it further excludes black people from participating in the craft beer culture, though also in that it limits exposure as well. Black people and other minority consumers are much less likely to consume a product if they view that product as offensive or racist. When asked about how to fix the problem of appropriation, our respondents all agreed that the easiest way is to hire black people to work in the industry and to engage in community outreach. From the perspective of some black craft beer drinkers, brewers should stop trying to use black culture and Hip-Hop to market to white drinkers, and should focus on ways to support the community. Jack echoes this, saying:

> 'They're not out in the streets, and they're not out in the community doing things for the community because if they were, those communities and those people would be more exposed to beer. I think, a lot of times, the culture is taken advantage of by certain breweries and slapped onto a can just to make a quick buck because, honestly, suburban America is one of the largest supporters of Hip-Hop music.' (Jack, black, male, sales/marketer)

As Tony suggests, brewers are also becoming more aware of the damage that these types of labels can cause to their brand:

> 'But in general, I think that as you start to see the industry hitting this plateau, and they're looking for ways to grow, that you're going to see more diversity and things of that nature. Those little gimmicks [appropriating black culture] and things of that nature are just going to hurt a brand more than they help the brand.' (Tony, black, male, influencer/organizer)

A few instances of cultural appropriation received backlash from the online craft beer community. In almost all of these instances, the brewers issued half-hearted apologies and claimed either that 'it was just a joke' or that they 'didn't think it was offensive.' When asked about these instances in particular, Tony responded that he is 'hopeful' that things will change. He continued, saying:

> 'Naivety is no longer an excuse. And that's where it starts. The reason why we have taboos and political correctness is because some people just aren't exposed to these things. They don't know why it's wrong. We need the community to react and come together and say, "Hey, this isn't what we want." But I think you're going to see more of that—more of these kinds of shock labels—because anytime you change a culture, then you have this counterculture backlash. People are going to seize the opportunity to grab

headlines, even if the beer never comes out.' (Tony, black, male, influencer/organizer)

Community outreach and hiring black people and other minorities will increase the exposure of beer, but what about changing the culture? Marcus discusses his efforts to change the culture through his status as a social media influencer:

> 'This is what I've been trying to do. Trying to broaden the scope of who drinks beer and who's exposed to it. I have this thing I talked about. It's called the "three E's." It's really four E's now. Education, experience, exposure, and, now, enlightenment because people become enlightened through exposure to the three others. So, that's the result. That's what I tried to teach with beer, those three E's. And now the fourth, which is enlightenment, which is the ultimate goal.' (Marcus, black, male, influencer)

In Marcus's view, craft beer can be a vehicle for cultural change. If we educate brewers and drinkers, and expose them not only to beer, but also to people of different races, we can enlighten the craft beer culture and become more inclusive and diverse. We will highlight the role of social media influencers later in this chapter. For now, we turn our focus to other efforts to change the culture.

Rappers and Hip-Hop artists are entering into the craft beer culture through collaboration brews with breweries and concert performances at beer festivals. Given the tumultuous history of Hip-Hop and beer, who could be better spokespeople for change than rappers and Hip-Hop artists? Jen Price, an Atlanta-based beer educator, believes that 'craft brewers could benefit from having Hip-Hop culture appreciate what they do, and vice versa' (quoted in Harling, 2018). Patricia comments on the role of rappers and Hip-Hop artists in changing the culture of craft beer, saying:

> 'I think their work is as important as it could possibly be because I have been studying this kind of cultural history and its impact for years and wondering "How do we get past this history?" … as Hip-Hop artists, this is really, really critical for them to be doing this. And I am really excited. And it's really exciting to see the creativity and the energy they bring to brewing because I think it's really similar to

> the kind of energy that they've always brought to music.' (Patricia, black, female, industry insider).

The first Hip-Hop and craft beer collaboration took place in 2007 at Sixpoint Brewery when the Hip-Hop duo Junk Science brewed a limited run of 'Gran'Dad's Nerve Tonic,' a nod to an album of the same name (Mylnar, 2019). Hip-Hop record-label owner Jesse Ferguson came up with the idea to promote Junk Science's 2007 album. He recalls the idea as follows:

> At that point the music industry was falling apart and nobody was selling albums. I thought this would be a good way for artists to monetize their brands and a good way for breweries to get exposure in the music industry. I see the two as very similar markets in terms of niche lifestyle marketing. (Mylnar, 2019)

The similarities between the industries, and indeed the production processes and artistic creativity and variety of products within each industry, are drawing more and more Hip-Hop artists into craft beer. Fish Scales of Nappy Roots, one of the more prominent faces in the craft beer and Hip-Hop game, describes the relationship as follows: 'craft beer is something you have to get up and do every day. It's an independent way of thinking, an artistic way of thinking, and that's the same with Hip-Hop' (Mylnar, 2019).

Recently, Nappy Roots brewed their newest beer in a series of limited edition collaborations with prominent Southern craft breweries (Stuart, 2019). The group sees their love of craft beer and their music as a way to bring communities together, as well as to merge the craft beer and Hip-Hop industries: 'anyone who's influential in the Hip-Hop game, they can get turned on to craft beer' (Stuart, 2019). Nappy Roots member Fish Scales had the following to say: 'You take a person who doesn't like beer and take them to a brewery, I guarantee they will find something they like. One of our main targets is to introduce the black community to craft beer. That relationship hasn't happened yet, but we want to build that bridge' (quoted in Poole, 2018). Nappy Roots is doing just that—and in some very creative ways. According to the group's official webpage, they are embarking on what they are calling the 'Great American Beer Run,' a beer-tasting music tour sponsored by some of their brewer friends and collaborators (Nappy Roots, 2019). Each stop on the tour features a performance by the group and then a tasting event at a local brewery. Nappy Roots, who formed their group in Bowling Green, Kentucky, 'started their venture into the craft beer industry a little over two years ago' while looking for ways to connect their brand of 'country fried Hip-Hop' with communities in the South (Stuart, 2019). Their most recent stop in Birmingham, Alabama, was a product of 'months of conversations and meetings' with a Birmingham-area bartender and blogger who goes by the moniker 'Beered Black Man' (Stuart, 2019).

The success of the collaboration brews and the 'Beer Run' tour has been well received by audiences and craft drinkers alike. As Fish Scales notes, 'people have really believed in our journey as Hip-Hop artists into craft beer' (Stuart, 2019). In addition to their tour and new album, Nappy Roots are producing their own television show, '40 Akerz and a Brew,' which is a 'docu-style reality series about their ventures into the world of craft beer' (Stuart, 2019). The show features the group as they navigate the contours of the brewing industry and learn the business; most importantly, it shows the world that 'craft beer is not just a white man's game anymore' (Stuart, 2019). Marcus, a black, male influencer who has worked with Nappy Roots 'since their early days in the industry,' had the following to say:

> I'm taking them seriously and everybody else should as well. These brothas are not just doing it as a fad, jumping in and out. They really know their shit, man. And they're realizing that there is a void to fill. And out of all the groups and people in Hip-Hop [who are in] craft beer, they're at the top of the list. And they're well on their way. (Quoted in Stuart, 2019)

Nappy Roots envision a future where Hip-Hop and craft beer go hand in hand. Fish Scales describes their vision, saying: 'we want to create a platform for black people and artists to do beer' (quoted in Stuart, 2019).Other artists are doing just that: Atlanta rapper Ludacris recently opened a craft beer bar and restaurant called 'Chicken + Beer'; brands such as 'High Gravity Hip Hop' are launching the first ever Hip-Hop beer festival; New York-based brand 'Kicks and Kegs' are merging sneaker culture with craft beer; and 'Bier Wax' is a vinyl record craft beer bar that is also bringing craft beer to new audiences (Stuart, 2019). The Hip-Hop duo Run the Jewels has brewed several collaborations with prominent breweries across the US. El-P and Killer Mike of Run the Jewels recognize the parallels between the two industries: 'it became really clear to us that the whole beer community is as passionate and creative about their craft as we are about ours' (quoted in Mylnar, 2019).

The craft beer industry is also taking notice. Craft beer has a diversity problem but creating cultural change takes time and effort, and as 808 Blake and Fish Scales from Nappy Roots suggest, craft beer is culture for everyone:

> I don't think you can just go in there and say, 'hey, I'm Hip-Hop, I'm going to break the stigma. You have to ingratiate yourself into the whole situation, meet people, and become part of the community. Craft beer is part of who we are just like everybody else. We're not culture vultures. We're not just in this for a new market. This is part of us and we do it just as well. This is part of our culture. And we've got to own it. (Quoted in Stuart, 2019)

When prominent artists such as Run the Jewels and Nappy Roots become involved in craft beer, 'authentic relationships and foundations are being forged' (Mylnar, 2019). These relationships are the result of outreach into the community by brewers and an embracing of cultural tastemakers, such as rappers, celebrating craft beer and its culture. While these collaborations are making huge strides in bridging the gap between cultures, there is still much work to be done. In Chapter 6, we examined how breweries function as white spaces that socially and symbolically exclude black people and other minorities. In order to become truly diverse and inclusive, craft breweries, and indeed all craft beer spaces, need to become open spaces. Also, as our respondents have insisted, there need to be black spaces for craft beer consumption that have been created by black people.

## Minority-owned breweries, Fresh Fest, and creating space

> 'I'm starting to see more black and brown people at some of these beer gardens and other places. And when we go there, a couple people with us will say, "I've never been to this place and I pass it all the time." Or, "This place is great!" On the flip side, I've had some people say, "Is this place even for us?"' (Kevin, black, male, brewer/owner)

More and more black-owned breweries are popping up across the US. These breweries are being opened and operated in black communities by black people. Take Corey, for example, who was in the process of opening a brewery at the time of writing this book:

> 'We are opening a brewery in Inglewood, which is a traditional neighborhood of black and brown people. Once you see someone that looks like you and reflects you doing something [opening a brewery], it's much easier for you to see yourself doing it as well. And, and if you look at the fact that less than 1 per cent of breweries in this country are owned by people of color, you could perceive that as a barrier because, again, if you don't see your reflection, if you don't see your culture represented, then it looks like something that may not be an option for you.' (Corey, black, male, influencer)

This echoes the sentiments of our respondents in earlier chapters, who said that simply seeing another person that looks like you in a white space (that is, a brewery) sends a message to the would-be craft beer drinker signaling that a space is welcoming:

> 'We're located in El Segundo, which is nowhere near the community where we live. Being in El Segundo put me in a place to have a conversation with someone who owned a brewery, you see what I'm saying? So, if your community doesn't support things or have places that would put you in a scenario to share a common thread with someone in a craft beer community, then the likelihood that an organic relationship that is going to allow you to have these conversations is far and few between.' (Corey, black, male, influencer)

Additionally, when minority brewers are able to bring their craft to the stage of craft beer, they are creatively synthesizing their cultural experiences into the beer:

> 'In really small circles, you have some brewers—black brewers, who have a kind of Caribbean connection—who maybe are not necessarily thinking about different techniques, but are trying to introduce ingredients that are maybe less common here, but may be more common to African or Caribbean climates. Which is timely right now. Honestly, because fruited beers are still quite popular. So, people are working with things like that. And, I would say with Latino brewers, you see two interesting trends there. Same thing, people playing with ingredients, especially if

> you go to Southern California and in the Southwest, you'll see a lot of folks playing with Horchata beers and different kinds of cactus ingredients, or prickly pear, just playing with different types of ingredients.' (Patricia, black, female, industry insider)

Further efforts on the parts of brewers, influencers, and organizers have highlighted the need to strengthen existing communities, or, in some cases, to build a new community. Beer festivals are a common occurrence in the craft beer industry. Typically, a beer festival involves brewers from a given region, or from all across the US, together in a space that is solely devoted to bringing people together around craft beer. However, beer festivals can also constitute a white space. Festivals are cultural sites where ritualized displays of cultural capital symbolize a racialized hierarchy of consumption and taste. In order to encourage black drinkers to attend beer festivals, festival organizers must create a safe space. Tony, an organizer of the first black beer festival, Fresh Fest, recalls his experience of creating such an event:

> 'With the festival, we thought we could bring in people from around the country to come in, and we could have some representation. Then there's a safe space. People don't feel comfortable going into places where they're going to be the only person there. With a festival, you can create a safe space, and you can see more people like that.' (Tony, black, male, influencer/organizer)

In creating a black beer festival that highlighted black brewers and other minority brewers, Fresh Fest organizers sought to create a more inclusive space and culture, while still celebrating black culture. It is vital for black consumers to feel represented in craft beer. In highlighting black culture and black brewers (for example, music, art, black-owned businesses, issues concerning the black community, and so on), Fresh Fest itself became a representation of the community, as well as shed light on the overall lack of representation in the industry:

> 'And the whole purpose at its core, the whole reason for the brew fest, is to bring more black and brown people in and expose them to craft beer. I was actually talking to [the festival organizer] and she was telling me how the whole festival came about, it was [festival organizer] that reached

> out and said "Hey, we were noticing that there's a lack of diversity in our brewery. And we want to help you."' (Jack, black, male, sales/marketer)

Corey echoes the need to increase representation, saying: "And that's where it happened. I thought, 'Well, maybe we could use this medium as a way to get people in [involved in craft beer].' So, the questions were, 'Why aren't there more black people in the industry?' A large part of that is [the lack of] representation" (Corey, black, male, influencer). While Fresh Fest was billed as the first black beer festival, not all breweries in attendance were owned by black people. For one, there are simply so few black-owned breweries that the festival would have been too small to attract craft beer drinkers. Also, while Will, a podcaster, agrees that there is a need for inclusive spaces such as Fresh Fest, the reception of such events may be misguided:

> 'So, let's take Fresh Fest for instance. It is something that needs to be done. I love that. But I wonder if people will look at that just be like, "Well, that seems racist. What if it was an all-white brewery or an all-white beer festival?" And my response to that would be, is that they [those who view it as racist] are kind of innocent. They don't necessarily come out and say that. But what something like fresh Fest is saying is: "This is the first black or African-American beer festival." Right? Boom, that's what it says. Now, what exactly does that mean? Does that mean that only black people can come? No, that is not, that's not what that means. What that means is, it's a celebration of diversity and inclusiveness in an industry that may not, for the most part, look like them.' (Will, black, male, podcaster)

Kevin attended Fresh Fest and shares his thoughts on the experience:

> 'Fresh Fest last year was amazing. Most of the people, and it's funny, because most people thought, "Oh, well, there is this black beer festival, are we allowed to come?" It's a beer festival, everyone's allowed to come. It's just being organized by predominantly black people and people that you don't normally see. Three quarters of the people [attendees] there were not black. I think you're going to

> see more of a half-and-half split this year. I know people traveling from all over the country that are coming. But most of the people there were white, and to see their faces, and not in a, not in a disrespectful way, but in a truly like, "Oh my god, I just found something amazing, right?"' (Kevin, black, male, brewer/owner)

Making Fresh Fest an open space for all craft beer drinkers not only exposes black people to craft beer, but also exposes white people to black drinkers. This is crucial in order to bridge the cultural and social gap between white and black craft drinkers. Further, it exposes white craft drinkers to black-owned breweries and beer. It helps to shift perceptions that craft beer is only for white people and only brewed by white people:

> 'You've got all these people making all this great beer. Just to see the look on people's faces. You could tell that they were surprised. They were surprised at not only the beers and the quality of the beers, but the character of the brewers and the overall event in general. It was just done really, really well.' (Kevin, black, male, brewer/owner)

When we started the research for this book on race and beer, the story that came up again and again was the short-lived People's Brewing Company in Oshkosh, Wisconsin, and black entrepreneur Theodore Mack (Harry, 2019). The issues that were emblematic in the Mack case and People's Brewing Company was the story of racism, capitalism, mergers, and exclusion in the white-dominated industry—all the things that we have found in our research for this book. Now, we can celebrate Ida Beatty, Kofi Meroe, Ceasar Marron, Shyla Sheppard and Melissa Bergay, L.A. McCrae, and a host of other black and brown, indigenous, and female, lesbian, and gay brewers. Their stories (all publically available) are echoes of what we have found in this book, and are also part of the movements to change the whiteness of craft beer. While craft beer festivals can certainly bring people together (Fresh Fest's attendees were majority white), craft beer enthusiasts, educators, social influencers, and others interested in bringing the broader diversity of the craft beer community together have found social media and podcasts to be the most effective way to create new narratives, new stories, and new possibilities for the craft beer community—and to help people find each other.

## New narratives, new stories, and new possibilities for craft beer

Before 'Dr. J' took to the twitterverse to highlight the diversity within the craft beer scene across the US, several now-prominent hashtags, podcasts, social influencers, and online communities were using the new technologies and their unprecedented reach to gather the black and brown craft beer communities. Teo Hunter (and his partner in community-building, Biny) created the hashtag #blackpeoplelovebeer, and the offshoot #brownpeoplelovebeer, in their effort to bring together the diversity that exists in the community, as well as to organize stridently against the many exploits and exploitations of the beer industry that have impacted black and brown people's production of, engagement with, and consumption of its products. In 2017, Teo announced, via Crown & Hops, Dope & Dank's family initiative:

> It is in the spirit, the DOPE & DANK family compels all beer drinkers to support local craft beer and rebuke cheap mass produced 'pig-trough' beverages. In addition, DOPE & DANK champions diversity within the craft beer industry so that our breweries look as diverse as the communities they reside in. (Hunter, 2017)

These hashtags have created a flurry of activity over the years and, in many ways, served as the social media fulcrum upon which our understanding of the movements within the scene center. For instance:

> 'This becomes a resource for people of color that were interested in getting employment or finding jobs in craft beer. There were people, women and men of color both, who would ask, "How do I get this? How do I gain entry? How do I accomplish this?" And we're able to connect them with breweries, brewers, and homebrewers. We're able to give them more context in their direct community. So, exposure is everything.' (Corey, black, male, influencer)

Combine Crown & Hops's important engagement with the online presence of craft beer celebrities and social influencers like Ale Sharpton, Day Bracey, Mike Potter, Teo Hunter, and Beny Ashburn, as well as blogs and podcasts like Beered Black Man, and one has a revolution—certainly a reckoning that the craft beer industry would do well to acknowledge, and then do something about. It is infuriating that racialized minorities always have to come to the rescue of industries that have mistreated them for so long and build their own interventions; however, yet again, this is happening.

Two other hashtags have been invoked on social media (Twitter, Facebook, Instagram) in order to bring the conversations together—#newnarrative and #somethingsbrewing. These hashtags are used to highlight the ways in which social media influencers and brewers are making progress in diversifying the craft beer industry and culture. We encourage all readers to follow these threads if they are interested in understanding the realities of craft beer on the ground for the broader community beyond bearded white men. Marcus summarizes this moment in many ways:

> 'It's slowly happening where more breweries are starting to understand that, "Hey, these different races, or these women, actually have a different way of bringing different flavor profiles to beer." Let's say a woman is making something that might fill her friends will love, or her family, or bringing whatever her experiences that are missing in the beer industry. That particular woman is going to say, "Y'all need to do this." And it's the same with African-Americans, or Puerto Ricans, or Latina. I befriended an Asian-American who owns a brewery called Hop Sticks. And he is using his life experiences to flavor his beers. He was from the Indonesian street culture and adapted that to the beer, adding lemon grass and chrysanthemum, and all these different things. So, I think that's what beer has to do. I think it might be an economical thing. We need to broaden the scope of different types of beer. So, why not make sure we provide opportunities for minorities who can share their experiences? So, it's happening. And this is what I've been trying to do, is to broaden the scope for who drinks beer and who's exposed to it.' (Marcus, black, male, influencer)

There is a recognition that the stories that have been told, that the experiences that have been highlighted, that the identities that have been marketed to positively, and that the communities where brewing, beer, and beer culture has been highlighted have been significantly limited. Yet, there is a new desire to reclaim the histories, the stories, and the experiences that more fully describe brewing and the culture surrounding beer in the US. Conscientious and intentional education is a part of creating the conversations that will develop (and recover) the (new) narratives:

> 'My role is to teach people that beer is for everybody. It's not a white man's beverage. It's not a heavy-set bearded guy's beverage. It's not all these different stereotypes. It's not the stereotypical drinker that thinks that all beers are bitter. So, these are things that the more and more I learn about them, the more I want to teach about them.' (Marcus, black, male, influencer)

Many of these social influencers see their role as not only to educate, but also, with that education, to more fully empower their communities *through* craft beer—an important approach in a society that has historically and contemporarily used beer against racialized minority communities. As Tony fully articulates:

> 'It's not only trying to get black people to drink more beer, but to also be empowered by the beer. ... So, I think the goal is to get black people to drink craft beer. The goal is to get people to see the value in them investing in the craft beer industry. Let them see what they are going to get out of it. Can they get a job out of this? Can my kids get some kind of benefit from this? A large portion of the flak that I get from grant organizations when I try to pitch ideas [like an all-black beer festival] is, "Well, its alcohol." This is not just alcohol. This is STEM (science, technology, engineering, and mathematics], there are lessons that you can teach children about engineering, biology, chemistry, how to own a business, and networking opportunities. They [grant organizations] don't see it as that; they just see it as alcohol, this product that has caused a lot of harm to our community. It is seen as these "new guys" who are coming into the community and trying to sell us a higher-priced beverage. People respond, "I'm good, I've been working this job for ten years, I may have US$20 to US$30 bucks to my name, and I want to spend it all on a good time." They are not going to take a chance, but if you say, "Hey, buy this, and this will help your life in some way," then they are more inclined to maybe spend some money on that and see some opportunity there and go out and try that.' (Tony, black, male, influencer/organizer)

For the majority of our respondents, they see the importance of critical diversity within the industry as related to the liberation of their people: diversify craft beer across the fullness of its historical (and contemporary) hierarchy (ownership, brewers, distributors, marketers, consumers) and liberate the communities.

There is also a desire to reclaim histories that have been hidden and to reclaim representational realities within the industry. This includes the reclamation of early American craft brewing:

> 'He [slave owned by Thomas Jefferson] brewed beer for Thomas Jefferson. He wrote the recipes and everything like that. And hearing stuff like that is really cool to me because it says that, a long time ago, we were the ones that were brewing beer and had the knowledge about brewing.' (Jack, black, male, sales/marketer)

However, it also includes new representations that combat the old narratives and images supported by national organizations like the Brewers Association, which has historically had no interest in the diversity of its community:

> 'I think, if you take something as simple as posting to social media about this beer festival, here you have a picture of people drinking your beer, having a good time, you have three or four black faces in there, three or four Asian faces, three or four white faces, so that everybody thinks, "Oh, what's going on in this picture, all these people look like they're having a good time?" So, I think that's one way. The Brewers Association is making a really good push to do that as well. I would love to see more colleges offering programs in brewing. I went to an HBCU, a historically black college and university, that wasn't a thing there. I'm sure I would have been interested in doing that had it been available when I was in college.' (Will, black, male, podcaster)

Patricia reminds us all that it is the marginalized craft beer *consumers* who have been at the forefront of bringing the breadth and depth of the community together, and who have been most urgently articulating the needs, pushing for new narratives, and blasting the clarion call that something is indeed brewing in the scene:

> 'When you look at the landscape of people who are pushing those efforts, in terms of trying to racially diversify ... most of those hashtags, and those efforts you're talking about are, coming from folks who are largely on the consumer side. So, fans and consumers probably all started this by saying, "I am a huge fan of this industry, and I don't see myself represented in it," or "I tried to get into this industry and there wasn't space for me to find my way in." So, I would say that, right now, you have four or five people and a few groups who are really pushing and gaining a lot of visibility. And they are using all kinds of different strategies and tactics to create change, or make inroads into the industry, which is really interesting to watch. Ultimately, I think this critical mass that they're creating with this diversity of tactics is a really great thing.' (Patricia, black, female, industry insider)

Only time will tell where these social media movements will take us but their very existence and the growing number of followers suggests that change is indeed on the horizon.

These online social media hashtags and movements have led to the real on-the-ground building of the ever-important social networks that have structured the (white) industry for hundreds of years. These movements are entering the fray in real ways, from their virtual connection and digital community-building, through podcasts, leading to real connections:

> 'And then we got to actually hang out and do a live podcast with [brewery], another brewery out here. They had just wrapped up the podcast event and said, "You know, you guys are great. You guys should go hang out with [networked brewers]." We had just finished this event with them, and we thought, "Wait, you mean if we hang out with you guys, we can hang out with other people [brewers]?" And they said, "Yeah, everybody's cool. We can all play in the same sandbox." And then it blew up from there. Now, every time we work with a brewery, they would suggest another brewery that we should work with. And we started to see the camaraderie that was in the brewing industry and how it was leading to their success.' (Tony, black, male, influencer/organizer)

Many of our respondents made a point of clearly letting us know how much the internet and social media, whether through hashtags, podcasts, or other online initiatives, have served as a structural and discursive leveling of the playing field within the craft beer industry. Consider Will:

> 'We started a podcast in an attempt to draw more traffic to our website because we both held nine-to-five jobs and it was kind of hard to travel places every weekend and do the podcast. So, we were trying to think of creative and cool ways to travel and do the podcast. We came up with this idea of creating a YouTube channel about beer. We would take a beer from some country and then pair it with an album, kind of like a wine and cheese sort of thing. We did a few episodes of that, just messing around, trying to do something creative and it thrust us into the industry.' (Will, black, male, podcaster)

With the emergence of more diverse spaces and places being built, as discussed earlier, minority brewers are more likely to be able to find each other and to build those social networks that are so important in the industry and culture—more networks, more experiences; more experiences, more stories; more stories, more narratives.

## Who has the next round?

It is clear that there is a *lot* going on in the contemporary movements to change the brewing of, distribution of, and consumption of craft beer in the US—virtually *all* of these movements are being pushed by black, Latinx, indigenous, Asian-American, women, and other individuals and communities who have been actively excluded from and marginalized within US beer and craft spaces and processes for centuries and generations. All of this happening as the other two arms of the three-tiered distribution system—production/brewing and distribution/retailing—are *very slowly* lumbering toward the recognition of the fundamental whiteness that undergirds their entire enterprise. Indeed, #somethingisbrewing in the 21st century as these pioneers of color are clearly finding new ways to expose their communities to the brewing of and the myriad possibilities of craft beer for their communities. They are able to more effectively do this than ever before due to the availability of modes of communication that link people across space and place, like social media and the various vehicles within that medium (for example, podcasts, hashtags, various platforms), creating social networks of craft beer that are beginning to look very different from those of the first 400+ years of brewing and beer in US society. These pioneers are creating new spaces, new places, and new narratives of craft beer. As they do so, they are crafting new techniques, new networks, new structural and cultural supports for craft beer communities of color, and new beers for us all to enjoy and share.

Some of these pioneers see the very full, complex, structural, political, economic, and cultural web that has been the beer industry as it has interfaced with their black and brown communities for generations—rarely, if ever, in a positive light, and never with the empowerment of black and brown communities front and center. Yet, due to understanding the *real* and *complex* story of beer, there are those who can innovate at a whole other level. Consider Tony's vision:

> 'My goal is to cultivate the first black brewery here. We don't have a middle-class black neighborhood here in [city with 300,000 population, 2 million metro-wide, 34 per cent minority], which is kind of odd for a major city in America. Cleveland, DC, Philly, they all have strong middle-class black neighborhoods with black businesses. And we don't have that here in [city], we don't have a black radio station, no black TV station, we don't have a black newspaper. We just lack so many things as a black culture here. So, I would like to see more outreach and investing in folks wanting to get into brewing. Education about the stages of owning a brewery, or looking for spaces, or looking for loans. So, the idea of a black-owned brewery [here] is now a thing that everybody's waiting to happen. So, hopefully, if that happens, we can actually build a middle-class neighborhood around that. Given the economic power that you typically tend to bring to neighborhoods with black businesses, it can also attract outside black investment, which is something that we don't have here. Most people come here to earn a degree, then leave immediately, or they get stuck here and they spend all their free time and money traveling elsewhere. So, it will be nice to attract some outside black interest that the community will see as a pillar.' (Tony, black, male, influencer/organizer)

Tony certainly has a dream here: minority-owned breweries *as* the seed for black community development in his city. For him, investing in a black-owned brewery in his community might be the catalyst for increasing investment for the community, for growing black cultural institutions, for building a black middle class that stays, for all of these things and more. Such a vision is not yet a reality in the US, but the pioneers that we have described in the chapter, and their work, are slowly building new social and cultural infrastructures and making possible the new, more inclusive and representative grammar with which to tell new stories. This is exciting, and as the excitement grows, it will be important to ensure that the next wave of more diverse and inclusive craft beer in the US will have shed its whiteness, and will also need to watch itself very closely to ensure that it, itself, is creating spaces to include women and women of color, and LGBTQ (Lesbian, Gay, Bisexual, Transgender, and Questioning) people and LGBTQ people of color. Otherwise, there is a chance to *reproduce* the structure in a particular way that continues to exclude and cut off paths to the industry, to the beer, in problematic and unequal ways.

All of these movements are also *slowly* encouraging those who have benefitted from the world and culture of beer (that is, white men) to excavate and attempt to integrate old hidden stories of beer in order to grapple or attempt to grapple with the facts of racism, sexism, classism, heteronormativity, and empire (to name a few) that have created the structure of brewing, beer, and its attendant cultures in the US. As they begin to acknowledge and attempt a recognition of these histories that built the contemporary realities of craft beer (for example, Dogfish Head Brewing's uncovering of ancient beer recipes that became the basis of a historical beer series), and as they start to wake up to the reality that race and racism are fundamentally woven into the fabric of the story of beer in the US, perhaps beer can live up to its mythical status as that cultural object that really 'brings people together.' After research and writing this book, we share the pioneers' hope but also their pessimism. The whiteness and maleness of the craft beer enterprise is not going to give up easily after 400 years of benefitting. As with many such structures, we again see black and brown folks come to the rescue, having to 'prove themselves' to the white structure *after* that structure actively excluded them, their voices, and their experiences. Theodore Mack and People's Brewing Company? Mack had the 'entrepreneurial spirit' that many of our white respondents and the mythic origin story of beer says is required but the *system* kept him down. The so-called pioneers of American beer—all white and all male, as the stories currently go—were propped up by the system. The whiteness of craft beer has therefore been no accident; it has been an ongoing accomplishment through a bringing together of the white public. It has created white sanctuaries (Embrick et al, 2019). The black and brown pioneers are the hope for craft beer; white people will have to reckon with their myths, which have created their (and others') realities. We are excited that this book—with all of its strengths and weaknesses, with all of its partial answers and posing of even more questions, and with all of its cynicisms and hopes across its argumentation and evidence—has spent its pages fundamentally calling out the white system of beer and craft beer, historically and contemporarily. While we see those who have previously been marginalized and actively excluded from the industry beginning to reclaim their rightful heritage and contemporary place within the brewing industry, we are hopeful that white people will take their part in initiating an acknowledgment of their past and contemporary wrongs, take it upon themselves to learn the real history of beer, apologize to the communities that they have erased in that history, and begin a discussion akin to reparations for the brewing industry, for much was erased, stolen, and profited from in the making of the whiteness of beer.

In seeking the answer to the question 'Why don't black people drink craft beer?,' this book has highlighted the deep structures of racism and white supremacy in the beer industry and craft beer culture. While this question is much deeper and more nuanced than its innocent naive tone would suggest, there are some basic and fundamental, surface-level issues that are uncovered. Indeed, this work has shed light on many issues surrounding race and beer, theorized about race and consumption, and helped to fill in deep theoretical holes in the sociology of race and taste; however, this work has also uncovered many other holes. For every question answered, seemingly endless new questions have arisen. Thus, the task of this book was not simply to answer the question, but to problematize it, to unpack it, and to engage with it across disciplines. It is our intention that this book will be the beginning of a conversation, a dialogue between scholars, and a way to bring issues of race and racism to the forefront of cultural studies and indeed sociology. We look forward to the future of craft beer in the US.

APPENDIX A

# Respondents to the Semi-Structured Interviews

| Pseudonym | Position | Race/ethnicity | Gender |
|---|---|---|---|
| Marcus | Influencer | Black | Male |
| Juan | Brewer/owner | Latinx | Male |
| Tony | Influencer/organizer | Black | Male |
| Albert | Brewer | White | Male |
| Jack | Sales/marketer | Black | Male |
| Patricia | Industry insider | Black | Female |
| Will | Podcaster | Black | Male |
| Kevin | Brewer/owner | Black | Male |
| Ida | Brewer/owner | Black | Female |
| Karina | Curator/insider | Latinx | Female |
| Matt | Sales rep | White | Male |
| Scott | Sales rep | White | Male |
| Layla | Sales rep | White | Female |
| Corey | Influencer/organizer | Black | Male |
| Betsy | Curator/historian | White | Female |

APPENDIX B

# Interview Protocol

- How does one become a brewer?
- How did you become a wholesale rep?
- How does one break into the brewing industry?
- What are the most fulfilling aspects of your job?
- What are the challenges of your position?
- What do people look for in a beer?
- What can you tell me about the history of brewing in this area?
- Who tends to brew beer? Is there a typical background to a brewer in your experience?
- Who tends to rep beer? Is there a typical background in your experience?
- What are some parts of beer and brewing history that make you proud?
- What are some parts of beer and brewing history that you are not so proud of?
- What is the future of beer? Brewing? The industry?
- Do any of your answers differ if we are discussing craft beer and the craft brewing industry?
- Why do you think there are so few minorities in the business? As reps? As brewers? As homebrewers? As drinkers?
- Why do you think there are so few women in the business? As reps? As brewers? As homebrewers? As drinkers?

# References

Acitelli, T. (2013) *The Audacity of Hops: The History of America's Craft Beer Revolution*, Chicago, IL: Chicago Review Press.

AHA (American Homebrewers Association) (2019) 'Homebrewing statistics,' American Homebrewers Association. Available at: www.homebrewersassociation.org/membership/homebrewing-stats/ (accessed September 27, 2019).

Aitchison, C. (2001) 'Theorizing other discourses of tourism, gender and culture: can the subaltern speak (in tourism)?,' *Tourist Studies*, 1(2): 113–47.

Alexis, M. (1970) 'Patterns of black consumption 1935–1960,' *Journal of Black Studies*, 1(1): 55–74.

Allen-Taylor, J.D. (1997) 'The malt-liquor industry, drunk on high-octane sales to the black Hip-Hop nation, has set its sights on the Latino youth market,' *Sonoma County Independent Newspaper*. Available at: www.metroactive.com/papers/sonoma/10.02.97/latino-drinking-9740.html (accessed August 30, 2019).

Anderson, B. (2009) 'Affective atmospheres,' *Emoticon, Space and Society*, 2(2): 77–81.

Anderson, E. (2015) 'The white space,' *Sociology of Race and Ethnicity*, 1(1): 10–21.

Appiah, K.A. (2018) *The Lies that Bind: Rethinking Identity*, New York, NY: Liveright Publishing Corporation.

Arai, S. and Kivel, B.D. (2009) 'Critical race theory and social justice perspectives on whiteness, difference(s) and (anti)racism: a fourth wave of race research in leisure studies,' *Journal of Leisure Research*, 41(4): 459–72.

Arcaya, M.C., Schwartz, G., and Subramanian, S.V. (2018) 'A multi-level modeling approach to understanding residential segregation in the United States,' *Environment and Planning B: Urban Analytics and City Science*, 45(6): 1090–105.

Arthur, J.W. (2014) 'Beer through the ages: the role of beer in shaping our past and current worlds,' *Anthropology Now*, 6(2): 1–11.

Baker, P. (1983) 'Baker on beer,' *All About Beer*, 4(3): 17.
Barajas, J.M., Boeing, G., and Wartell, J. (2017) 'Neighborhood change, one pint at a time: the impact of local characteristics on craft breweries,' in N. Chapman, S. Lellock, and C. Lippard (eds) *Untapped: Exploring the Cultural Dimensions of Craft Beer*, Morgantown, WV: West Virginia University Press, pp 155–77.
Baron, S. (1962) *Brewed in America: A History of Beer and Ale in the United States*, New York, NY: Arno Press.
Baudrillard, J. (1994) *Simulacra and Simulation*, Ann Arbor, MI: University of Michigan Press.
Becker, H. (1982) *Art Worlds*, Berkeley, CA: University of California Press.
BI (Beer Institute) (2011) 'Beer Institute advertising and marketing code.' Available at: www.beerinstitute.org/assets/uploads/BIdCode-5-2011.pdf (accessed February 18, 2015).
BI (2019) 'Annual report, 2018.' Available at: www.beerinstitute.org/wp-content/uploads/2018/12/Beer-Institute-Annual-Report-2018.pdf (accessed August 20, 2019).
Bellant, R. (1991) *The Coors Connection: How Coors Family Philanthropy Undermines Democratic Pluralism*, Boston, MA: South End Press.
Benjamin, R. (2019) *Race after Technology: Abolitionist Tools for the New Jim Code*, New York, NY: John Wiley & Sons.
Benner, C. (2015) 'Racial and gender occupational segregation in the restaurant industry.' Available at: http://rocunited.org/wp-content/uploads/2015/10/RaceGender_Report_LR.pdf (accessed October 8, 2019).
Bennett, L.A. and Ames, G.M. (eds) (1985) *The American Experience with Alcohol: Contrasting Cultural Perspectives*, Boston, MA: Springer.
Berger, P.L. and Luckmann, T. (1991[1967]) *The Social Construction of Reality: A Treatise in the Sociology of Knowledge*, London: Penguin.
Bonilla-Silva, E. (1997) 'Rethinking racism: toward a structural interpretation,' *American Sociological Review*, 62(3): 465–80.
Bonilla-Silva, E., Goar, C., and Embrick, D.G. (2006) 'When whites flock together: the social psychology of white habitus,' *Critical Sociology*, 32(2/3): 229–53.
Bourdieu, P. (1977) *Outline of a Theory of Practice*, New York, NY: Cambridge University Press.
Bourdieu, P. (1984) *Distinction: A Social Critique of the Judgment of Taste*, Cambridge, MA: Harvard University Press.
Bourdieu, P. and Passeron, J.C. (1977) *Reproduction in Education, Culture and Society*, London: Sage Publications.

Bowles, J.P. (2001) 'Blinded by the white: art and history at the limits of whiteness,' *Art Journal*, 60(4): 38–43.

Bradford, R. (2018) 'Is it time to embrace the 40oz? A hard look at the bro-preferred bottle, its troubled history and why craft beer isn't using it,' *San Diego City Beat*. Available at: http://sdcitybeat.com/special-issues/beer-issue/is-it-time-to-embrace-the-40-oz/ (accessed September 4, 2019).

Braidwood, R.J., Sauer, J.D., Helbaek, H., Mangelsdorf, P.C., Cutler, H.C., Coon, C.S., Linton, R., Steward, J., and Oprenheim, A.L. (1953) 'Symposium: did man once live on beer alone?,' *American Anthropologist*, 53(4): 515–26.

Brewers Association (2015) 'Beer franchise law summary.' Available at: www.brewersassociation.org/wp-content/uploads/2015/06/Beer-Franchise-Law-Summary.pdf (accessed August 7, 2019).

Brewers Association (2018a) 'Number of breweries.' Available at: www.brewersassociation.org/statistics/number-of-breweries/ (accessed August 28, 2018).

Brewers Association (2018b) 'Shifting demographics among craft drinkers.' Available at: www.brewersassociation.org/insights/shifting-demographics-among-craft-drinkers (accessed September 21, 2018).

Brewers Association (2019a) 'National beer sales and production data.' Available at: www.brewersassociation.org/statistics-and-data/national-beer-stats/ (accessed August 6, 2019).

Brewers Association (2019b) 'Who we are.' Available at: www.brewersassociation.org/who-we-are/ (accessed September 25, 2019).

Brown, S. and Patterson, A. (2000) 'Knick-knack paddy-whack, give the pub a theme,' *Journal of Marketing Management*, 16: 647–62.

Brown-Saracino, J. (2018) *How Places Make Us: Novel LBQ Identities in Four Small Cities*, Chicago, IL: The University of Chicago Press.

Bruner, E.M. (1994) 'Abraham Lincoln as authentic reproduction: a critique of postmodernism,' *American Anthropologist*, 96: 397–415.

Brunsma, D.L., Brown, E.S., and Placier, P. (2013) 'Teaching race at historically white colleges and universities: identifying and dismantling the walls of whiteness,' *Critical Sociology*, 39(5): 717–38.

Brunsma, D.L., Chapman, N.G., and Lellock, S.L. (2016) 'Racial ideology in electronic dance music festival promotional videos,' in J.A. Smith and B.K. Thakore (eds) *Race and Contention in Twenty-First Century U.S. Media*, New York, NY: Routledge, pp 148–61.

Bryson, B. (2002) 'Symbolic exclusion and musical dislikes,' in L. Spillman (ed) *Cultural Sociology*, London: Blackwell Publishers, pp 108–19.

Butcher, J. (2006) 'Cultural politics, cultural policy and cultural tourism,' in M.K. Smith and M. Robinson (eds) *Cultural Tourism in a Changing World: Politics, Participation and (Re)Presentation*, Clevedon: Channel View Publications, pp 21–35.

Byrd, W.C. (2017) *Poison in the Ivy: Race Relations and the Reproduction of Inequality on Elite College Campuses*, New Brunswick, NJ: Rutgers University Press.

Campbell, C. (2005) 'The craft consumer: culture, craft and consumption in a postmodern society,' *Journal of Consumer Culture*, 5(1): 23–42.

Carney, J.A. and Rosomoff, R.N. (2009) *In the Shadow of Slavery: Africa's Botanical Legacy in the Atlantic World*, Berkeley, CA: University of California Press.

Carrington, B. (2013) 'The critical sociology of race and sport: the first fifty years,' *Annual Review of Sociology*, 39: 379–98.

Chapman, N.G. (2015) 'Craft beer in the US: a production of culture perspective,' doctoral dissertation, Virginia Tech, USA.

Chapman, N.G., Lellock, J.S., and Lippard, C. (eds) (2017) *Untapped: Exploring the Cultural Dimensions of Craft Beer*, Morgantown, WV: West Virginia University Press.

Chapman, N.G., Nanney, M., Lellock, J.S., and Mikles-Schluterman, J. (2018) 'Bottling gender: accomplishing gender through craft beer consumption,' *Food, Culture, and Society*, 21(3): 296–313.

Chhabra, D., Healy, R., and Sills, E. (2003) 'Staged authenticity and heritage tourism,' *Annals of Tourism Research*, 30(3): 702–19.

Childress, C. (2017) *Under the Cover: The Creation, Production, and Reception of a Novel*, Princeton, NJ: Princeton University Press.

Cixous, H. (1983) 'The laugh of the Medusa,' in E. Abel and E.K. Abel (eds) *The Signs Reader: Women, Gender and Scholarship*, Chicago, IL: Chicago University Press.

Coates, R.D., Ferber, A.L., and Brunsma, D.L. (2017) *The Matrix of Race: Social Construction, Intersectionality, and Inequality*, Thousands, CA: Sage Publications.

Cocola-Gant, A. (2018) 'Tourism gentrification,' in L. Lees and M. Phillips (eds) *Handbook of Gentrification Studies*, Cheltenham: Edward Elgar Publishing, pp 281–93.

Cohen, E. (1988) 'Traditions on the qualitative sociology of tourism,' *Annals of Tourism Research*, 15: 29–46.

Collins, P.H. (1998) 'It's all in the family: intersections of gender, race, and nation,' *Hypatia*, 13(3): 62–82.

Collins, R.L., Bradizza, C.M., and Vincent, P.C. (2007) 'Young-adult malt liquor drinkers: prediction of alcohol problems and marijuana use,' *Psychology of Addictive Behaviors*, 21(2): 138–46.

Coward, K. (2015) 'When Hip-Hop first went corporate,' *The Atlantic*. Available at: www.theatlantic.com/business/archive/2015/04/breaking-ad-when-Hip-Hop-first-went-corporate/390930/ (accessed November 9, 2018).

Daniels, J. (2013) 'Race and racism in internet studies: a review and critique,' *New Media & Society*, 15(5): 695–719.

Darwin, H. (2018) 'Omnivorous masculinity: gender capital and cultural legitimacy in craft beer culture,' *Social Currents*, 5(3): 301–16.

Davis, A., Gardner, B.B., and Gardner, M.R. (1941) *Deep South*, Chicago, IL: University of Chicago Press.

Desmond, M. (2019) 'Slavery and capitalism,' *New York Times*. Available at: www.nytimes.com/interactive/2019/08/14/magazine/slavery-capitalism.html (accessed September 9, 2019).

Doane, A.W. and Bonilla-Silva, E. (eds) (2003) *White Out: The Continuing Significance of Racism*, London: Psychology Press.

Donald, B. (2009) *From Kraft to craft: Innovation and Creativity in Ontario's Food Economy*, Working Paper Series: Ontario in the Creative Age, Toronto, ON: Martin Prosperity Institute, Rotman School of Management, University of Toronto.

Downard, W.L. (1980) *Dictionary of the History of the American Brewing and Distilling Industries*, Westport, CT: Greenwood Press.

Du Bois, W.E.B. (1903) *The Souls of Black Folk*, New York, NY: Oxford University Press.

Edwards, P.K. (1936) 'Distinctive characteristics of urban Negro consumption,' unpublished D.C.S. dissertation, Harvard University, USA.

Eittreim, C. (2019) 'Why do craft beer and gentrification go hand-in-hand?,' *Medium*. Available at: https://medium.com/@eittreimcameron/why-do-craft-beer-and-gentrification-go-And-in-hand-630d53224f64 (accessed September 13, 2019).

Embrick, D.G., Weffer, S., and Dómínguez, S. (2019) 'White sanctuaries: race and place in art museums,' *International Journal of Sociology and Social Policy*, 39(11/12): 995–1009.

Erickson, J. (1987) *Star Spangled Beer: A Guide to America's New Microbreweries and Brew Pubs*, Reston, VA: RedBrick Press.

Erickson, R.J. (1995) 'The importance of authenticity for self and society,' *Symbolic Interaction*, 18: 124–44.

Fahey, D.M. (2015) *Temperance and Racism: John Bull, Johnny Reb, and the Good Templars*, Lexington, KY: University Press of Kentucky.

Feagin, J.R. (2012) *White Party, White Government: Race, Class, and US Politics*, New York, NY: Routledge.

Feagin, J.R. (2013) *The White Racial Frame: Centuries of Racial Framing and Counter-Framing*, New York, NY: Routledge.

Fine, G.A. (2003) 'Crafting authenticity: the validation of identity in self-taught art,' *Theory and Society*, 32(2): 153–80.

Fine, G.A. (2006) *Everyday Genius: Self-Taught Art and the Culture of Authenticity*, Chicago, IL: University of Chicago Press.

Fiske, J. (1992) 'Cultural studies and the culture of everyday life,' in L. Grossberg, C. Nelson, and P. Treichler (eds) *Cultural Studies*, New York, NY: Routledge, pp 154–73.

Geller, J. (1993) 'Bread and beer in fourth-millennium Egypt,' *Food and Foodways*, *5*(3): 255–67.

George, N. (2001) *Buppies, B-Boys, Baps, & Bohos: Notes on Post-Soul Black Culture*, Cambridge, MA: Da Capo Press.

Gieryn, T.F. (2000) 'A space for place in sociology,' *Annual Review of Sociology*, 26: 463–96.

Glass, J. (2014) 'The 40oz. is the most patriotic drink in America, and here's why,' *Thrillist*. Available at: www.thrillist.com/vice/the-colt-45-40-oz-is-the-most-patriotic-drink-in-amerCa (accessed August 30, 2019).

Glass, R. (1964) *London: Aspects of Change*, London: Centre for Urban Studies and MacGibbon and Kee.

Glenn, E.N. (2015) 'Settler colonialism as structure: a framework for comparative studies of US race and gender formation,' *Sociology of Race and Ethnicity*, 1(1): 52–72.

Goetz Brewing Company (1955a) 'The new party brew (backyard barbecue),' magazine advertisement.

Goetz Brewing Company (1955b) 'The new party brew (dinner party),' magazine advertisement.

Goffman, E. (1997) *The Goffman Reader* (eds C. Lemert and A. Branaman), Malden, MA: Blackwell.

Gordon, A.F. (2008) *Ghostly Matters: Haunting and the Sociological Imagination*, Minneapolis, MN: University of Minnesota Press.

Graham, B., Ashworth, G., and Turnbridge, J. (2000) *A Geography of Heritage: Power, Culture and Economy*, London: Arnold.

Granovetter, M.S. (1977) 'The strength of weak ties,' *Social Networks*, January 1: 347–67.

Graves, L. (2019) 'Slaves and indentured servants were vital to Virginia's colonial beer making,' *Virginia Craft Beer*. Available at: https://virginiacraftbeer.com/slaves-and-indentured-servants-were-vital-to-virginias-colonial-beer-making/ (accessed September 6, 2019).

Gray, K.L. (2014) *Race, Gender, and Deviance in Xbox Live: Theoretical Perspectives from the Virtual Margins*, Boston, MA: Routledge.

Greer, D.F. (1998) 'Beer: causes of structural change,' *Industry Studies*, 2: 28–64.

Gwaltney, J.L. (1980) *Drylongso: A Self-Portrait of Black America*, New York, NY: Random House.

Habraken, N.J. (1998) *The Structure of the Ordinary*, Cambridge, MA: MIT Press.

Hacker, G.A. (1987) *Marketing Booze to Blacks: A Report from the Center for Science in the Public Interest*, Washington, DC: Center for Science in the Public Interest, Department PD/EDRS.

Hacker, J. and Smith, N. (2001) 'The changing state of gentrification,' *Tijdschrift voor economische en sociale geografie*, 92(4): 464–77.

Hall, S. and Jefferson, T. (1993) *Resistance Through Rituals: Youth Subcultures in Post-War Britain* (Vol. 7), London: Psychology Press.

Harling, D. (2018) 'Craft beer and Hip-Hop: it's complicated,' *October*. Available at: https://oct.co/essays/craft-beer-and-hip-hop (accessed October 9, 2019).

Harry, J. (2019) 'The People's Brewing Company,' *Voyageur*, Summer/Fall.

Hartfiel, R. (1991) 'Regional brewing: by definition,' *All About Beer*, 12(5): 18–19, 47.

Harvey, D. (1985) *The Urbanization of Capital: Studies in the History and Theory of Capitalist Urbanization*, Baltimore, MD: The Johns Hopkins University Press.

Hawkins, A.M. (2004) 'Raising our glass: a history of saloons in Toledo from 1880–1919,' doctoral dissertation, University of Toledo, USA.

Hebdige, D. (1979) *Subculture: The Meaning of Style*, London: Routledge.

Heil, M. (2016) 'Beers brewed for (Hip) Hop heads,' *Thrillist*. Available at: www.thrillist.com/drink/nation/craft-beers-inspired-by-Hip-Hop-artists (accessed September 5, 2019).

Heritage Radio Network (2015) 'Neighborhood brews: craft beer and gentrification in NYC,' *Huffpost*. Available at: www.huffpost.com/entry/neighborhood-brews-craft-beer-and-gentrificatio-in-nyc_b_8433080 (accessed September 10, 2019).

Herring, C. and Henderson, L. (2012) 'From affirmative action to diversity: toward a critical diversity perspective,' *Critical Sociology*, 38(5): 629–43.

Herz, J. (2016) 'Embracing diversity in the beer biz,' Brewers Association. Available at: www.brewersassociation.org/communicating-craft/embracing-diversity-ber-biz/ (accessed September 24, 2019).

Herz, J. (2019) 'The diversity data is in: craft breweries have room and resources for improvement,' Brewers Association. Available at: www.brewersassociation.org/communicating-craft/the-diversity-data-s-in-craft-breweries-have-room-and-resources-for-improvement/ (accessed September 24, 2019).

Hicks, S. (1979) 'America sees the light,' *All About Beer*, 1(1): 3.

Hilt, P.J. (1991) 'Alcohol ads criticized as appealing to children,' *The New York Times*. Available at: www.nytimes.com/1991/11/05/us/alcohol-ads-criticized-as-appealing-to-cIldren.html (accessed November 9, 2018).

Hindy, S. (2014) *The Craft Beer Revolution: How a Band of Microbrewers is Transforming the World's Favorite Drink*, New York, NY: Palgrave McMillan.

Horvat, E.M. (2003) 'The interactive effects of race and class in educational research: theoretical insights from the work of Pierre Bourdieu,' *Penn GSE Perspectives on Urban Education*, 2(1): 1–25.

Hunter, M.A. and Robinson, Z. (2018) *Chocolate Cities: The Black Map of American Life*, Berkeley, CA: University of California Press.

Hunter, T. (2017) 'Death of the 40 ounce.' *Crown and Hops*. Available at: https://crownsandhops.com/blogs/craft-culture/death-of-the-40-ounce

Infante, D. (2015) 'There are almost no black people brewing craft beer. Here's why,' *Thrillist*. Available at: www.thrillist.com/drink/nation/there-are-almost-no-black-people-brewing-craft-beer-heres-why

Infante, D. (2016) 'The sleazy and spectacular history of malt liquor,' *Thrillist*. Available at: www.thrillist.com/drink/nation/malt-liquor-history-sleazy (accessed November 8, 2018).

Iroquois Brands (1970) 'Celebrate nothing,' magazine advertisement.

Iroquois Brands (1979) 'Champale: the ultimate experience,' magazine advertisement.

Itzigsohn, J. and Brown, K. (2015) 'Sociology and the theory of double consciousness: W.E.B. DuBois's phenomenology of racialized subjectivity,' *DuBois Review: Social Science Research on Race*, 12(2): 231–48.

Jackman, M.R. (1994) *The Velvet Glove: Paternalism and Conflict in Gender, Class, and Race Relations*, Berkeley, CA: University of California Press.

Jackson, M. (1977) *The World Guide to Beer: The Brewing Styles, the Brands, the Coutries*, Upper Saddle River, NJ: Prentice Hall Publishing.

Jackson, M. (1991) *New World Guide to Beer*, Philadelphia, PA: Running Press.

Jackson, M. (1997) *The New World Guide to Beer*, Philadelphia, PA: Running Press.

Jackson-Beckham, N. (2019) September 9. Available at: https://twitter.com/jnikolbeckham/status/1171173904611729410 (accessed October 7, 2019).

Jacobson, M.F. (1999) *Whiteness of a Different Color: European Immigrants and the Alchemy of Race*, Cambridge, MA: Harvard University Press.

Johnson, G.D., Thomas, K.D., Harrison, A.K., and Grier, S.A. (eds) (2019) *Race in the Marketplace: Crossing Critical Boundaries*, New York, NY: Springer.

Jones-Webb, R. et al (2008) 'Alcohol and malt liquor availability and promotion and homicide in inner cities,' *Substance Use & Misuse*, 43: 159–77.

Jordan, J. (2018) 'Midwest brewery faces backlash for "Black Beer Matters,"' *Detroit Metro Times*. Available at: www.metrotimes.com/table-and-bar/archives/2018/07/19/midwest-brewer-faces-backlash-for-black-beers-matter (accessed September 4, 2019).

*Journal of Material Culture* (2019) 'Home page.' Available at: https://journals.sagepub.com/home/mcu (accessed August 20, 2019).

Joyner, H. (2016) '5 steps to becoming a Master Brewer,' *Zippia*. Available at: www.zippia.com/advice/become-a-master-brewer/ (accessed September 30, 2019).

Kaplan, V. (2006) *Structural Inequality: Black Architects in the United States*, Lanham, MD: Rowman & Littlefield.

Kelley, R.D. (2015) *Hammer and Hoe: Alabama Communists During the Great Depression*, Chapel Hill, NC: University of North Carolina Press.

Kendall, J. (2019) 'Power hour: Nielsen shares 2019 craft beer consumer insights,' *Brewbound*. Available at: www.brewbound.com/news/power-hour-nielsen-shares-2019-craft-beer-cNsumer-insights (accessed September 24, 2019).

Killewald, A., Pfeffer, F.T., and Schachner, J.N. (2017) 'Wealth inequality and accumulation,' *Annual Review of Sociology*, 43: 379–404.

Kirkland, E. (2008) 'What's race got to do with it? Looking for the racial dimensions of gentrification,' *The Western Journal of Black Studies*, 32(2): 18–30.

Klonoski, B. (2013) 'More and more ladies enjoying beer, especially craft brews,' *Ryot*. Available at: http://dev1.ryot.org/more-and-more-ladies-enjoying-beer-especially-craft-brews/100209 (accessed July 1, 2016).

Koontz, A. (2010) 'Constructing authenticity: a review of trends and influences in the process of authentication in consumption,' *Sociology Compass*, 4(11): 977–88.

Koontz, A. and Chapman, N.G. (2019) 'About us: authenticating identity claims in the craft beer industry,' *The Journal of Popular Culture*, 52(2): 351–72.

Koontz, A. and Chapman, N.G. (forthcoming) 'Crafting community and drinking local: constructing authenticity and identity in the craft beer culture,' in D.C. Harvey, E. Jones, and N.G. Chapman (eds) *The Microgeographies of Craft Beer*, Fayetteville, AR: University of Arkansas Press.

Kritzer, H.M. (2007) 'Toward a theorization of craft,' *Social and Legal Studies*, 16(3): 321–40.

La Barre, W. (1938) 'Native American beers,' *American Anthropologist*, 40(2): 224–34.

Lacey, M. (1992) 'Marketing of malt liquor fuels debate: consumption: sales of the high-alcohol beverage soar in inner cities,' *Los Angeles Times*. Available at: http://articles.latimes.com/1992-12-15/news/mn-2228_1_malt-liquor-market (accessed November 9, 2019).

Ladson-Billings, G. (2003) 'Lies my teacher still tells,' in G. Ladson-Billings (ed) *Critical Race Theories Perspectives on Social Studies: The Profession, Policies, and Curriculum*, Greenwich, CT: Information Age Publishing, pp 1–11.

Lees, L. (2000) 'A re-appraisal of gentrification: towards a "geography" of gentrification,' *Progress in Human Geography*, 24(3): 389–408.

Lena, J.C. (2012) *Banding Together: How Communities Create Genres in Popular Music*, Princeton, NJ: Princeton University Press.

Leonardo, Z. (2009) *Race, Whiteness, and Education*, New York, NY: Routledge.

Leslie, D. and Reimer, S. (2006) 'Situating design in the Canadian household furniture industry,' *Canadian Geographer*, 50(3): 319–41.

Lewis, A.E. (2003) *Race in the Schoolyard: Negotiating the Color Line in Classrooms and Communities*, New Brunswick, NJ: Rutgers University Press.

Loewen, J.W. (2018) *Sundown Towns: A Hidden Dimension of American Racism* (2nd edn), New York, NY: The New Press.

MacCannell, D. (1973) 'Staged authenticity: arrangements of social space in tourist settings,' *American Journal of Sociology*, 79(3): 589–603.

MacLeod, N. (2006) 'Cultural tourism: aspects of authenticity and commodification,' in M.K. Smith and M. Robinson (eds) *Cultural Tourism in a Changing World: Politics, Participation and (Re)Presentation Vol.* 7, Bristol, UK: Channel View Publications, pp 77–190.

Malkin, R. and Hanke, A. (2018) 'How to do business in a franchise state,' *SevenFifty*. Available at: https://daily.sevenfifty.com/how-to-do-business-in-a-franchise-state/ (accessed August 8, 2019).

Marable, M. (2015 [1983]) *How Capitalism Underdeveloped Black America: Problems in Race, Political Economy, and Society*, Chicago, IL: Haymarket Books.

Marriott, M. (1993) 'For minority youths, 40 ounces of trouble,' *The New York Times*. Available at: www.nytimes.com/1993/04/16/nyregion/for-minority-youths-40-ounces-of-Trouble.html (accessed August 30, 2019).

Mathews, V. and Picton, R.M. (2014) 'Intoxifying gentrification: brew pubs and the geography of post-industrial heritage,' *Urban Geography*, 35(3): 337–56.

Matias, Cheryl E. (2016) *Feeling White: Whiteness, Emotionality, and Education*, Leiden, Netherlands: Brill Sense.

May, R.A.B. and Chaplin, K.S. (2007) 'Cracking the code: race, class, and access to nightclubs in urban America,' *Qualitative Sociology*, 31: 57–72.

McConnell, J.D. (1968) 'The price–quality relationship in an experimental setting,' *Journal of Marketing Research*, 5(3): 300–3.

McGirr, L. (2015) *The War on Alcohol: Prohibition and the Rise of the American State*, New York, NY: WW Norton & Company.

McGirr, L. (2019) 'How Prohibition fueled the Klan,' *New York Times*. Available at: www.nytimes.com/2019/01/16/opinion/prohibition-immigration-klan.html (accessed September 17, 2019).

McGovern, P.E., Zhang, J., Tang, J., Zhang, Z., Hall, G.R., Moreau, R.A., Nuñez, A., Butrym, E.D., Richards, M.P., Wang, C.S., and Cheng, G. (2004) 'Fermented beverages of pre- and proto-historic China,' *Proceedings of the National Academy of Sciences*, 101(51): 17593–8.

McGovern, W. (1980) 'Cartwright Portland beer wheels down West Coast,' *All About Beer*, 2(2): 4.

McGuiness, C. (2016) 'Hoisting a 40 with malt liquor's rabid online fanboys,' *New York Magazine*. Available at: http://nymag.com/article/2016/05/malt-liquor-fan-online-youtube.html (accessed August 30, 2019).

McIntosh, P. (1988) 'White privilege: Unpacking the invisible knapsack.' Available at: www.racialequitytools.org/resourcefiles/mcintosh.pdf (accessed June 22, 2020).

McNeil, M.A. and Letschert, V.E. (2005) 'Forecasting electricity demand in developing countries: a study of household income and appliance ownership,' European Council for an Energy Efficient Economy, Summer Study, Mandelieu, France, LBNL 58283, 85:90.

Michels, C. (2015) 'Researching affective atmospheres,' *Geographica Helvetica*, 36(3): 255–63.

Milgrom, P. and Roberts, J. (1986) 'Price and advertising signals of product quality,' *Journal of Political Economy*, 94(4): 796–821.

Miller, T. and Yudice, G. (2002) *Cultural Policy*, London: Sage.

Mills, C. (1997) *The Racial Contract*, Ithacaca, NY: Cornell University Press.

Mills, C. (2007) 'White ignorance,' in S. Sullivan and N. Tuana (eds) *Race and Epistemologies of Ignorance*, Albany, NY: State University of New York Press, pp 11–38.

*Mintel* (2012) 'Craft Beer—US—November 2012.' Available at: https://infogram.com/who-drinks-craft-beer-the-infographic-1g143mn741n42zy (accessed August 9, 2019).

Mittleman, A. (2008) *Brewing Battles: A History of American Beer*, New York, NY: Algora Press.

Moore, D.J., Williams, J.D., and Qualls, W.J. (1996) 'Target marketing of tobacco and alcohol-related products to ethnic minority groups in the United States,' *Ethnicity and Disease*, 6: 83–98.

Moore, W.L. (2007) *Reproducing Racism: White Space, Elite Law Schools, and Racial Inequality*, Lanham, MD: Rowman & Littlefield Publishers.

Morris, J. (2013) 'Why espresso? Explaining changes in European coffee preferences from a production of culture perspective,' *European Review of History: Revue européenne d'histoire*, 20(5): 881–901.

Morrison, T. (1993) *Playing in the Dark: Whiteness and the Literary Imagination*, New York, NY: Vintage Books.

Moseley, M.E., Nash, D.J., Williams, P.R., DeFrance, S.D., Miranda, A., and Ruales, M. (2005) 'Burning down the brewery: establishing and evacuating an ancient imperial colony at Cerro Baúl, Peru,' *Proceedings of the National Academy of Sciences*, 102(48): 17264–71.

Motl, K.A. (2018) 'Dashiki chic: color-blind racial ideology in EDM festivalgoers' "dress talk,"' *Popular Music and Society*, 41(3): 250–69.

Mr. Beer (2018) 'Mr. Beer celebrates 25 years of industry-leading homebrew kits.' Available at: www.mrbeer.com/blog/post/mr-beer-celebrates-25-years-industry-leading-homebrew-kits (accessed September 27, 2019).

Munn, C.W. (2017) 'The one friend rule: race and social capital in an interracial network,' *Social Problems*, 65(4): 473–90.

Musick, M.A., Wilson, J., and Bynum, W.B., Jr (2000) 'Race and formal volunteering: the differential effects of class and religion,' *Social Forces*, 78(4): 1539–70.

Mylnar, P. (2019) 'A brief history of Hip-Hop craft beers,' *CraftBeer.com*. Available at: www.craftbeer.com/craft-beer-muses/hip-hop-craft-beers (accessed October 9, 2019).

Nappy Roots (2019) 'Beer run.' Available at: https://nappyroots.com/beer-run (accessed October 9, 2019).

NBWA (National Brewery Wholesaler Association) (2019a) 'Industry fast facts.' Available at: www.nbwa.org/resources/industry-fast-facts (accessed August 20, 2019).

NBWA (2019b) 'What is a beer distributor.' Available at: www.nbwa.org/about/what-beer-distributor (accessed August 9, 2019).

NCES (National Center for Education Statistics) (2019) 'Status and trends in the education of racial and ethnic groups, indicator 27, educational attainment.' Available at: https://nces.ed.gov/programs/raceindicators/indicator_RFA.asp (accessed September 27, 2019).

Neuman, S. (2019) 'The Napa Valley of Beer: Boulder's best breweries,' *Trip Savvy*. Available at: www.tripsavvy.com/top-boulder-breweries-419255 (accessed September 28, 2019).

Nickles, S. (2002) 'More is better: mass consumption, gender, and class identity in postwar America,' *American Quarterly*, 54(4): 581–622.

Ocejo, R.E. (2017) *Masters of Craft: Old Jobs in the New Urban Economy*, Princeton, NJ: Princeton University Press.

*October* (2018) 'Theresa McCulla Smithsonian craft beer historian.' Available at: https://oct.co/essays/theresa-mcculla-smithsonian-craft-beer-historian (accessed October 15, 2018).

Ogle, M. (2006) *Ambitious Brew: The Story of American Beer*, San Diego, CA: Harcourt.

Oliver, M. and Shapiro, T. (2013) *Black Wealth/White Wealth: A New Perspective on Racial Inequality*, New York, NY: Routledge.

Papazian, C. (2014) *The Complete Joy of Homebrewing: Fully Revised and Updated*, New York, NY: William Morrow Paperbacks.

Patterson, M. and Hoalst-Pullen, N. (eds) (2014) *The Geography of Beer: Regions, Environment, and Societies*, New York, NY: Springer Science & Business Media.

Paulsen, K.E. and Tuller, H.E. (2017) 'Crafting place: craft beer and authenticity in Jacksonville, Florida,' in N.G. Chapman, J.S. Lellock, and C.D. Lippard (eds) *Untapped: Exploring the Cultural Dimensions of Craft Beer*, Morgantown, WV: West Virginia University Press, pp 105–23.

Pegram, T.R. (1997) 'Temperance politics and regional political culture: the Anti-Saloon League in Maryland and the South, 1907–1915,' *The Journal of Southern History*, 63(1): 57–90.

Pereira, A. (2016) 'California bar reportedly selling 40oz bottles of Colt 45 with brown bag for $15,' *SFGATE*. Available at: www.sfgate.com/food/article/Calif-bar-selling-40-oz-bottles-of-Colt-45-with-10806519.php (accessed September 4, 2019).

Perry, S.L. (2012) 'Racial habitus, moral conflict, and white moral hegemony within interracial evangelical organizations,' *Qualitative Sociology*, 35(1): 89–108.
Peterson, R. (1982) 'Five constraints on the production of culture: Law, technology, market, organizational structure and occupational careers,' *Journal of Popular Culture*, 16(2):143.
Peterson, R. (1990) 'Why 1955? Explaining the advent of rock music,' *Popular Music*, 9(1): 97–116.
Peterson, R. (2005) 'In search of authenticity,' *Journal of Management Studies*, 42(5): 1083–98.
Peterson, R. (2013) *Crafting Country Music: Fabricating Authenticity*, Chicago, IL: University of Chicago Press.
Peterson, R. and Anand, N. (2004) 'The production of culture perspective,' *Annual Review* of *Sociology*, 30: 311–34.
Piperno, D.R., Ranere, A.J., Holst, I., Iriarte, J., and Dickau, R. (2009) 'Starch grain and phytolith evidence from early ninth millennium B.P. maize from the Central Balsas River Valley, Mexico,' *Proceedings of the National Academy of Sciences of the United States of America*, 106(13): 5019–24.
Platts, T.K. (2013) 'Locating zombies in the sociology of popular culture,' *Sociology Compass*, 7(7): 547–60.
Poole, S. (2018) 'Grammy-nominated Nappy Roots ferments passion for craft beer,' *Atlanta Journal Constitution*. Available at: www.ajc.com/lifestyles/grammy-nominated-hip-hop-group-nappy-roots-fements-passion-for-craft-beer/H8f77yZ1ajKDYVqyUaSfkK/# (accessed October 9, 2019).
Prior, N. (2011) 'Critique and renewal in the sociology of music: Bourdieu and beyond,' *Cultural Sociology*, 5(1): 121–38.
Quinn, E. (2004) *Nuthin' but a 'G' Thang: The Culture and Commerce of Gangsta Rap*, New York, NY: Columbia University Press.
Ray, V. (2019) 'A theory of racialized organizations,' *American Sociological Review*, 84(1): 26–53.
Reid, P.V.K. (1997) 'Wholesale distributors: the beer industry's hidden hand,' *All About Beer*, 18(2): 12.
Robb, A. (2013) *Access to Capital Among Young Firms, Minority-Owned Firms, Women-Owned Firms, and High-Tech Firms*, Washington, DC: Office of Advocacy, US Small Business Administration.
Roberston, J.D. (1984) *The Connoisseur's Guide to Beer*, Ottowa, IL: Jameson Books.
Rockquemore, K.A. and Brunsma, D.L. (eds) (2007) *Beyond Black: Biracial Identity in America*, Thousand Oaks, CA: Sage Publications.

ROC (Restaurant Opportunities Centers) United (2015) 'Race and gender report.' Available at: http://rocunited.org/wp2015b/wp-content/uploads/2015/10/RaceGender_ReportLR.pdf (accessed August 9, 2019).

Rodell, B. (2013) '40 ounces to freedom,' *Punch*. Available at: https://punchdrink.com/articles/40-ounces-to-freedom/ (accessed August 30, 2019).

Rodgers, D.M. and Taves, R. (2017) 'The epistemic culture of homebrewers and microbrewers,' *Sociological Spectrum*, 37(3): 127–48.

Roediger, D.R. (1999) *The Wages of Whiteness: Race and the Making of the American Working Class*, London: Verso.

Rose, G. (1996) 'Place and identity: a sense of place,' in D. Massey and P. Jess (eds) *A Place in the World? Places, Cultures and Globalisation*, Milton Keynes: Open University Press.

Salinger, S.V. (2004) *Taverns and Drinking in Early America*, Baltimore, MD: JHU Press.

Sanders, C. and Vail, D.A. (2009) *Customizing the Body: The Art and Culture of Tattooing*, Philadelphia, PA: Temple University Press.

Satran, J. (2014) 'Here's how a six-pack of craft beer ends up costing $12,' *Huffpost*. Available at: www.huffpost.com/entry/craft-beer-expensive-cost_n_5670015 (accessed September 28, 2019).

Scherer, F.M. and Ross, D. (1990) *Industrial Market Structure and Economic Performance*, New York, NY: Houghton Mifflin.

Schille, W.S. and Geyser, S.A. (1991) 'G. Heileman Brewing Company (A): power failure at PowerMaster,' *Harvard Business School Case*, 592(017): 1–12.

Schnell, S.M. and Reese, J.F. (2003) 'Microbreweries as tools of local identity,' *Journal of Cultural Geography*, 21(1): 45–69.

Scott, T. (2015) '40oz beats: a brief history of malt liquor in Hip Hop,' *Noisey: Music By Vice*. Available at: www.vice.com/en_au/article/rjxak4/40oz-beats-a-brief-history-of-malt-liqur-in-Hip-Hop (accessed August 30, 2019).

Serrano, S. (2015) *The Rap Year Book: The Most Important Rap Song from Every Year Since 1979, Discussed, Debated, and Deconstructed*, New York, NY: Abrams Image.

Shepherd, W.G. (1967) 'What does the survivor technique show about economies of scale?,' *Southern Economic Journal*, 34(1): 113–22.

Shown, M. (2018a) 'Will beer names bring the right kind of attention to New Lakeville Brewery?' *South Bend Tribune*. Available at: www.southbendtribune.com/news/business/marketbasket/will-beer-name-bring-the-right-kind-of-attention-to/article_e4a03341-997c-5205-98ae-1042fddef69a.html (accessed September 4, 2019).

Shown, M. (2018b) 'Lakeville Brew crew retracts contentious beer names,' *South Bend Tribune*. Available at: www.southbendtribune.com/news/business/marketbasket/lakeville-brew-crew-retracts-contentious-beer-names/article_ce5f7c6b-36a9-57e8-96c1-0cf97a91e01d.html (accessed September 4, 2019).

Shulman, R. (2012) *Eat the City: A Tale of the Fishers, Foragers, Butchers, Farmers, Poultry Minders, Sugar Refiners, Cane Cutters, Beekeepers, Winemakers, and Brewers Who Built New York*, New York, NY: Broadway Books.

Silberberg, E. (1985) 'Nutrition and the demand for tastes,' *Journal of Political Economy*, 93(5): 881–900.

Slocum, R. (2011) 'Race in the study of food,' *Progress in Human Geography*, 35(3): 303 –27.

Smith, N. (1996) *The New Urban Frontier: Gentrification and the Revanchist City*, New York, NY: Routledge.

Smith, N. (2002) 'New globalism, new urbanism: gentrification as global urban strategy,' *Antipode*, 34(3): 427–50.

Smith, S.S. (2000) 'Mobilizing social resources: race, ethnic, and gender differences in social capital and persisting wage inequalities,' *The Sociological Quarterly*, 41(4): 509–37.

Soja, E.W. (1996) *Thirdspace: Journeys to Los Angeles and Other Real-and-Imagined Places*, Cambridge, MA: Blackwell.

Stainback, K. and Tomaskovic-Devey, D. (2012) *Documenting Desegregation: Racial and Gender Segregation in Private Sector Employment since the Civil Rights Act*, New York, NY: Russell Sage Foundation.

Steele, S. (1989) 'On being black and middle class,' in G. Wolff (ed) *The Bes American Essays*, New York, NY: Ticknor & Fields.

Sterling, K. (2015) 'Black feminist theory in prehistory,' *Archaeologies*, 11(1): 93–120.

Stuart, S. (2019) 'Craft beer, Hip Hop, and the clout of the Nappy Roots,' *AL.com*. Available at: www.al.com/life/2019/10/craft-beer-hip-hop-and-the-clout-of-nappy-roots.Tml (accessed October 9, 2019).

Sugrue, T.J. (1996) *The Origins of the Urban Crisis: Race and Inequality in Postwar Detroit*, Princeton, NJ: Princeton University Press.

Suzanne-Mayer, D. (2019) 'Seattle brewery cancels release of Crips- and Bloods-themed beers after outcry,' *The Takeout*. Available at: https://thetakeout.com/mirage-brewery-crips-bloods-gang-beers-apology-183505374 (accessed September 5, 2019).

Thornton, S. (1995) *Club Cultures: Music, Media, and Subcultural Capital*, Middletown, CT: Wesleyan University Press.

Throsby, D. (2000) *Economics and Culture*, Cambridge: Cambridge University Press.

Tilly, C. (1998) *Durable Inequality*, Berkeley, CA: University of California Press.

Tremblay, V.J. and Tremblay, C.H. (2009) *The US Brewing Industry: Data and Economic Analysis*, Cambridge, MA: MIT Press.

Trigg, A.B. (2001) 'Veblen, Bourdieu, and conspicuous consumption,' *Journal of Economic Issues*, 35(1): 99–115.

Trubek, A.B. (2008) *The Taste of Place: A Cultural Journey into Terroir*, Berkeley, CA: University of California Press.

Tuan, Y. (1977) *Space and Place: The Perspective of Experience*, Minneapolis, MN: University of Minnesota Press.

Turner, V. (1973) 'The center out there: Pilgrim's goal,' *History of Religions*, 12: 191 –230.

Urry, J. (1990) *The Tourist Gaze: Leisure and Travel in Contemporary Societies*, Thousand Oaks, CA: Sage Publications.

US Census Bureau (2017) 'Educational attainment in the United States, 2017.' Available at: www.census.gov/data/tables/2017/demo/education-attainment/cps-detailed-tables.html (accessed September 27, 2019).

US Census Bureau (2018) 'Income and poverty in the United States, 2017.' Available at: www.census.gov/library/publications/2018/demo/p60-263.html (accessed September 24, 2019).

Veblen, T. (2017) *Theory of the Leisure Class*, New York, NY: Routledge.

Wang, N. (1999) 'Rethinking authenticity in tourism experience,' *Annals of Tourism Research*, 26(2): 349–70.

Warner, A.G. (2010) 'The evolution of the American brewing industry,' *Journal of Business Case Studies*, 6(6): 31–46.

Warner, K.E. and Goldenhar, L.M. (1992) 'Targeting of cigarette advertising in U.S. magazines,' *Tobacco Control*, 1(1): 25–30.

Watson, B. (2018) 'Shifting demographics among craft drinkers,' Brewers Association. Available at: www.brewersassociation.org/insights/shifting-demographics-among-craftdrinkers/ (accessed September 24, 2019).

Weber, M. (1978 [1968]) *Economy and Society* (trans G. Roth and C. Wittich), Berkeley, CA: University of California Press.

Weems, R.E., Jr (1998) *Desegregating the Dollar: African American Consumerism in the Twentieth Century*, New York, NY: New York University Press.

Whitman, J.Q. (2017) *Hitler's American Model: The United States and the Making of Nazi Race Law*, Princeton, NJ: Princeton University Press.

Wildausky, B. (1990) 'Anti-billboard campaign insults blacks' intelligence viewpoint,' *Centre Daily Times*, 12(8).

Withers, E.T. (2017) 'Brewing boundaries of white/middle-class/ male-ness: reflections from within the craft beer industry,' in N.G. Chapman, J.S. Lellock and C.D. Lippard (eds) *Untapped: Exploring the Cultural Dimensions of Craft Beer*, Morgantown, WV: West Virginia University Press, pp 236–60.

Wolch, J., Wilson, J.P., and Fehrenbach, J. (2005) 'Parks and park funding in Los Angeles: an equity-mapping analysis,' *Urban Geography*, 26(1): 4–35.

Wolinski, C. (2019) 'The beer industry grapples with racism, again,' *VinePair*. Available at: https://vinepair.com/articles/beer-industry-racism/ (accessed September 4, 2019).

Yoshihara, M. (2007) *Musicians from a Different Shore: Asians and Asian Americans in Classical Music*, Philadelphia, PA: Temple University Press.

Zerubavel, E. (1993) *The Fine Line*, Chicago, IL: University of Chicago Press.

Zuberi, T. (2001) *Thicker than Blood: How Racial Statistics Lie*, Minneapolis, MN: University of Minnesota Press.

Zuberi, T. and Bonilla-Silva, E. (eds) (2008) *White Logic, White Methods: Racism and Methodology*, Lanham, MD: Rowman & Littlefield.

Zukin, S. (2010) *Naked City: The Death and Life of Authentic Urban Places*, New York, NY: Oxford University Press.

# Index


21st Amendment 60
'40 Akerz and a Brew' show 165

## A

A-1 beer 117
accessibility of craft beer 59, 67–8, 96–8
acquisitions and mergers 49–50, 54–6
advertising 17, 62
  and black people 59, 68–9, 110, 113–16, 119–20, 124
  and malt liquor
    and black people 110, 113–16, 119–20, 124
    celebrity advertising 111, 115, 116, 119, 123
    and sexualization 114, 115
    and white people 111, 112, 123
  and white people 57–8, 111, 112, 123
African Americans *see* black people
age of homebrewers 82
age of malt liquor drinkers 116–17, 119–20
Aitchison, C. 137
Albert, brewer 80, 99–100
alcohol strength 31, 66, 115, 116, 120, 122
  ABV (alcohol by volume) 111, 113
Alexis, M. 55
Allen-Taylor, J.D. 115
American Homebrewers Association (AHA) 19, 82, 83
Anderson, B. 144
Anderson, E. 10, 141–2, 146, 147, 148, 150
Anglo-Americans 34
Anheuser Busch (now AB-Imbev) 2, 46, 47, 49, 50, 54
apprenticeships 86–90, 159
Arnold, Aaron Paxton 117
arts community 133
authenticity 115, 135–9, 142–4

## B

Baker, Patrick 56
banking industry 90
Barajas, J.M. 134, 135, 138, 142
Barber, Pearl 42
barbers shops 161
barley 29, 30
Baron, S, 31
bars 134–5, 138–9
  *see also* saloons; taverns
Baudrillard, J. 143
Bavarian style 56
Becker, H. 18
Bedford-Stuyvesant Gateway Business Improvement District 139–40
beer *see* brewing industry; craft beer industry; malt liquor
beer barons 46–7, 49–50, 81
beer festivals 23, 68, 163–4, 168, 169–70
Beer Institute 21, 119–20
Beer Kulture 126
'beer summit' xi–xii
Beered Black Man 164, 171
Betsy, curator/historian 82–3, 91–2, 149, 152
'Bier Wax' 165
Big Three 50, 54, 158
Birmingham Centre for Contemporary Cultural Studies 118
Black Beer Matters 125
'black codes' 34
black people
  and advertising 59, 68–9
    and malt liquor 110, 113–16, 119–20, 124
  black beer festivals 168, 170
  black culture 127–30, 162–6, 177–8
    cultural appropriation 24, 104, 122–30, 159, 161–2
  black women 121, 178
  as brewers 81, 82, 89, 100–1, 104, 166–70

education/training 76, 85
and brewing industry 46–7, 100–1, 103–4, 107–8, 177
brewery ownership 40–4, 90
craft beer industry 14
employment opportunities 41–2, 89, 90, 104
and labor 42, 55, 58, 65–6, 68, 69, 70–1, 73
and marketing 63–4, 66–9, 127–30, 148–9
and white people 178–9
craft beer drinkers xii–xiii, 15, 63, 93–4, 100
developing taste for craft beer 51, 67–8, 72, 96–8, 145–52, 161, 163–8
and cultural capital 110, 118, 121, 145, 151, 160, 161–2, 168
and distribution system 70, 73, 158
and gentrification 98–9, 132–4, 135, 138–40, 143–53
history of brewing 37–9, 46–7
and taverns 37, 39, 40–4, 59
and homebrewing 59, 77–8, 80–1, 83–4, 90, 93–4, 97–8
and income 58, 59, 67, 89, 98–9, 140
migrants 40, 41–2
and place 143–53, 166, 168–9
and neighborhoods 100, 112, 113, 132–4, 135, 138–40
social class 111–14, 118, 121, 124
and social networks 81, 92–3, 95, 140
status symbols 57, 58, 73
stereotyping of 124–6, 159
*see also* craft beer industry; malt liquor
#BlackLivesMatter movement 125–6, 160
blackpeoplelovebeer hashtag 171
Blue Moon 94–5
Bonilla-Silva, Eduardo xv
Bosman, Willem 30–1
Boston Beer Company 19, 52, 100
Bourdieu, Pierre 91–2, 105–7, 109
Bradford, R. 122–3
breweries
large 12, 49, 53–4, 56
numbers of 1, 49, 53
regional 49, 56, 64
small 49, 50, 59, 60, 64, 87
brewers 29
black people as 81, 82, 89, 100–1, 104, 166–70
indigenous people as 29, 31
women as 30, 31
Brewers Association 15, 19
accessibility of craft beer brewery 96, 98
'Brewers Association Certified' label 20
'Brewery Operations Benchmarking Survey' 16
and diversity 16–17, 21, 160, 174
Diversity Ambassador 17, 118, 156, 157
Marketing and Advertising Code 17
and three-tier system 21, 61, 96
brewery ownership 40–4, 90
Brewery Workers Union 55
brewhouses 29
brewing industry *see* black people; craft beer industry; distribution system; employment opportunities; labor; representation in brewing industry; white people
brewing schools 76, 78, 85, 86
brewpubs 1, 17, 64
brothels 42
Brown, S. and Patterson, A. 138
brownpeoplelovebeer hashtag 171
Brown-Saracino, J. 142
Bruner, E.M. 137–8, 139
Brusyo, Pete 117
Bryson, B. 108
Budweiser 56, 57
Busch *see* Anheuser Busch (now AB-Imbev)
Butcher, J. 133, 134


## C


Campbell, C. 18
capitalism 5, 33–4, 110
Carney, J.A. and Rosomoff, R.N. 30
Catholicism 45
cavemen 28
celebrity advertising 115, 116, 119, 123
champagne 112
Champale 111, 112
Chapman, N.G. 54, 63
with Koontz 136, 142, 143
Chhabra, D. 138
'chocolate cities' 40, 43, 100
Christianization 34
Chuck D 119
churches 36
citizenship 33, 45
Civil Rights Act 1964 6
Cixous, H. 137
Clarke, Edward Young 46
Cocola-Gant, A. 135, 141
Cohen, E. 138
college towns 65, 66
Collins, R.L. 111
colonists, white European 29–30, 32–40, 43–4, 49
Colt 45, 113, 115
Commodores 115

communitas 138
community support and engagement 81–2, 162, 163, 166, 167–9, 173, 175–7
  and diversity 171–2, 174–6
competition 47, 54, 56, 59, 60, 62
competitions, brewing 81
concentration ratios 54
consumer choice 50, 51, 64, 121
consumption 1, 58
  conspicuous 110, 112–13
  cultural 106–7, 108–10
  private 38, 47
  *see also* craft beer drinkers
control, oligopolistic 12, 53–4, 158
Coors 46, 49, 50, 54
copyright law 12
Corey, influencer/organizer 82
  black culture 126, 128, 166–7
  black people 113–14
    and craft beer industry 169, 171
    developing taste for craft beer 145, 147, 148, 161
corn 29, 56
cotton industry 33
Country Club 111, 112
Coward, K. 116
'cracking a beer' xi
craft beer *see* craft beer brewers; craft beer culture; craft beer drinkers; craft beer industry; homebrewing
craft beer brewers 75–90
  black people 81, 82, 89, 100–1, 104, 166–70
    education/training 76, 85
  craft breweries 15, 19–20
  and social networks 77, 78, 88–9, 90, 159
craft beer culture 4, 11–13, 18–19
  developing taste for craft beer 161, 163
  and Hip-Hop 161–2, 163–6
  and homebrewing 12, 90, 91–2, 100
  and middle-classes 52–3, 57, 131
  and white people 9, 157
craft beer drinkers 90–9
  black people xii–xiii, 15, 63, 93–4, 100, 124–30
    developing taste for craft beer 51, 67–8, 72, 96–8, 145–52, 161, 163–8
  and diversity 103–4, 152, 168–9, 174–5
  and gentrification 131, 134–51, 160
  and homebrewing 91–2, 97–8, 100
  and networks, social 91–4, 95, 159
  and social class 65, 120, 131
  and social networking 91–4, 95, 159
  and white people 15–16, 63, 120, 124–30, 160
    'hipster' persona 15, 149
    taste of beer 50–1, 52–3
craft beer industry 1–2, 18–19, 49–73
  authenticity 115, 135–9, 142–4
  and black people 14, 163–9, 171–2
    and black culture 162–3, 166, 177
    cultural appropriation 24, 104, 122–30, 159, 161–2
  and diversity 21–3, 68, 103–4, 155–79
  niche markets 59, 158, 164
  styles of 14, 52, 56–7, 63
    and black people 14, 167–8
    German lagers and pilsners 49, 50, 56
    recipes 49, 56, 135, 172, 178
  and white people 6, 146, 148–9
  *see also* brewing industry; community support and engagement; distribution system; gentrification; marketing
craft beer movements 22–3, 59, 155–79
craft beer scene 89, 94, 96–8
  *see also* community support and engagement; diversity; gentrification
Craft Brewers Conference 2016 16–17
craft products 18
Crawford, TJ 119
Crown & Hops 171
cultural appropriation 24, 104, 122–30, 159, 161–2
cultural capital
  and black people 110, 118, 121, 145, 151, 160, 161–2, 168
  and gentrification/place 134, 142, 143, 144–5, 151, 160
  and social class 106–7, 108, 109
cultural change 163–6
cultural policy 133, 134
cultural taste 18, 105–8, 109, 121, 151, 166
culture, black 124–30
  and craft beer industry 162–3, 166, 177
  cultural appropriation 24, 104, 122–30, 159, 161–2
  and white people 124–30
culture, public 35–6, 39
culture perspective 7, 11–13, 14–15, 118, 122–30

## D

Dale, Jim 115
danger, risk of 137, 138, 140
Darwin, H. 63
Davis, A. 57
Delaware, Lord 29
demography 62, 99
Desmond, Matthew 33
discrimination, interracial 8–9, 71, 72
  *see also* black people
distinction 4, 105, 107, 109, 110, 141

distribution system 47
  *see also* three-tier system
diversity 7, 13–15, 83
  and Brewers Association 16–17, 21, 160, 174
    Diversity Ambassador 17, 118, 156, 157
  consumer 103–4, 152, 168–9, 174–5
  and craft beer movement 22–3, 155–79
  and employment opportunities 68, 173
DJ Pooh 116
Dogfish Head Brewing 124, 178
domination *see* black people; white people
DOPE & DANK 171
drunkenness 30, 38–9, 123

## E

economic development 132, 135, 140–1, 177–8
educational attainment 82, 83, 89, 93–5, 122–3, 159
education/training 76–7, 84–90, 174, 177
  brewing schools 76, 78, 85, 86
'Edward 40-Hands' game 123
Edwards, P.K. 58
Eittreim, Cameron 142, 150
Elhardt, Merlin 51
elites class 33, 34, 36, 37, 40
Emancipation Proclamation xiv
employment opportunities 16–17, 65–6, 85
  and black people 58, 68, 69, 71–2, 89, 90, 104, 108
  and culture 12, 13
  and diversity 68, 173
  and gentrification 134, 140–1
  and social capital 70, 71–2
entrepreneurship 27, 42, 178
Erickson, Jack 28–9
Erickson, R.J. 136
ethnicity *see* black people
eugenics 44, 45
European brewing practices 59
European settlers, white 29, 31, 33, 34
  *see also* German migrants
exclusion 8, 36, 148
  social and symbolic 108–9, 110
exploitation 32–5

## F

'Faces of the American Beer Distribution Industry' slideshow 65
family memories 91–2
favoritism, intra-racial 8
fear of black and indigenous people 37
Ferguson, Jesse 164
Fine, G.A. 135, 139
First Amendment rights 121
Fish Scales 164, 165
Fiske, J. 106, 107
Flint Michigan Tap Water 125
food and beverage industry 70–1, 73, 93
  restaurant industry 88, 93
forty ounce bottle 'forties' 111, 116, 117–18, 122–4, 159
Four Tops soul group 116
Foxx, Redd 115
franchising 60–2
Freemasons 38
Fresh Fest 168–70

## G

gender issues 63, 151
Geneva Club 37–8
gentrification 131–53, 160
  and black people 132–4, 135, 138–40, 143–53
  and craft beer drinkers 131, 134–51, 160
  and danger, risk of 137, 138, 140
  degentrification 133
  and economic development 132, 135, 140–1
  and employment opportunities 134, 140–1
  and heritage 137, 140–1
  and place 141–5
    and bars 134–5, 138–9
    and cultural capital 134, 142, 143, 144–5, 151, 160
  and revitalization of neighborhoods 134, 135, 140–1
  and self-making/self-identity 137, 143
  and social class 135–7
    lower classes/incomes 98, 132, 133, 134, 140
    middle-classes 135, 144
  and white people 132, 138, 146, 150, 160
George, N. 118
Georgia 61
German migrants 42, 43–4, 45, 46–7, 56, 158
Gieryn, T.F. 141, 142
G.I.s 50
Glass, J. 123–4, 132
Goetz Brewing Company 111, 112
Goffman, E. 144
government involvement 132–4
Graham, B. 137
*Gran Torino* (Eastwood) film xii
'Gran'Dad's Nerve Tonic' 164
'Great American Beer Run' 164

Great Chain of Being 7
Greer, D.F. 55
Grossman, Ken 52, 100
Gwaltney, J.L. 121

## H

habitus 92, 105–7
Habraken, N.J. 141
Hacker, G.A. 111, 112–13, 114–15
Hacker, J. and Smith, N. 133
Hall, S. and Jefferson, T. 118
Harris poll 16
Hartfiel, R. 62, 64
*Harvard Business School Case* study 113
Harvey, David 132
Hawkins, Arnette 41, 42, 45
Heil, M. 127–8
Hell Town, Philadelphia 39
heritage 57, 137, 140–1
Heritage Radio Network 139
Herring, Cedric and Henderson, Loren 13–14
Herz, Julia 16–17, 152
Hicks, S. 50
'High Gravity Hip Hop' 165
Hill, Jerry 113
Hip-Hop 116–17, 118, 122–3, 127–30, 161–2, 163–6
'hipster' persona 15, 149
history of brewing 27–47, 174
  black people 37–9, 46–7
    and taverns 37, 39, 40–4, 59
  German migrants 42, 43–4, 45, 46–7, 56, 158
  and recipes 49, 174, 178
  and social class 36–7, 38, 39–40, 44, 45–6
    elites class 33, 34, 36, 37, 40
  and white people 32, 36, 38, 40, 43
    men 28–9, 32, 36, 38, 40, 43
    white supremacy/domination 7–9, 28–35
Homebrewers Act 1978 75, 81
homebrewing 51–2, 79–84
  and black people 59, 77–8, 80, 81, 83–4, 90, 93–4, 97–8
  and craft beer culture 12, 90, 91–2, 100
  educational attainment of homebrewers 82, 83
  as a hobby 51, 76, 77, 78, 97–8
  homebrew clubs 51, 52, 53, 81
  homebrew kits 77, 80, 89
  income levels of homebrewers 82, 83, 89
  and white people 51, 52, 81, 90
    men 52, 80, 81, 83, 90
homogenization 50, 56–7, 59
Hop Sticks brewery 172
Horvat, E.M. 106
H.R. 1337 51
Hunter, Teo 171

## I

IAmCraftBeer hashtag 156
Ice Cube 116
Ida, brewer/owner 88, 89, 146, 151–2
identity
  self-identity 137, 143, 151–2
  white 9, 10
importation of beer 50–1, 56
inclusion, social 7, 14, 128, 149, 152
income 65, 66, 68, 78, 113
  and black people 58, 59, 67, 89
    and gentrification 98–9, 140
  of homebrewers 82, 83, 89
indigenous people 32–3, 34, 37, 39, 44
  as brewers 29, 31
inequality in US society 3, 27, 51, 107
  *see also* black people; educational attainment; income; white people
Infante, Dave 2–3, 110, 111, 117
innovation 50, 57, 177
interaction, social 9, 10, 38, 108, 144, 147
interviews for research 21, 181, 183

## J

J. Wakefield Brewing 127
Jack, sales/marketer 70, 162, 169
Jackson, Michael 28
Jackson-Beckham, J. Nikol ('Dr J') 17, 118, 156
  *see also* Brewers Association
Jefferson, Marth Wayles Skelton 30
Jefferson, Thomas 30, 174
Jim Crow laws 58–9
Jones-Webb, R. 117, 120
*Journal of Material Culture* 5
Joyner, H. 78–9
Juan, brewer/owner 76
  and black people 87
    and homebrewing 77–8, 81, 84
    and social networks 92–3, 95
    and taste for craft beer 96, 98
Junk Science 164

## K

Karina, curator/insider 27, 95
Kevin, brewer and brewery owner 81, 166, 169–70
  and education/training 76, 77, 85
  and homebrewing 77, 80
  and place 148, 149, 151, 152

and taste for craft beer 67, 97–8, 148, 149, 151, 152
'Kicks and Kegs' 165
King Cobra 115
Kirkland, E. 132
knowledge of beer/beer scene 79, 96–7
Koch, Jim 52, 100
Koontz, A. and Chapman, N.G. 136, 142, 143
Kritzer, H.M. 18
Ku Klux Klan 46

## L

labor 33
in brewing industry
and black people 42, 55, 58, 65–6, 68, 69, 70–1, 73
and white people 65, 69, 71–2
and women 65, 70
household 31, 84
Lacey, Marc 113, 115
lager, adjunct 56, 57, 111
lager, German 49, 50
Lakeville Brew Crew 125
Latinx *see* black people
law/legislation 12, 13, 36–7, 39–40, 158
Lawson, Josephine 42
Layla, distributor 71–2
Lees, L. 132, 133
legalization of homebrewing 51
leisure time 57, 59, 89, 112
LGBTQ 178
lived experience 106, 138
*Los Angeles Times* 117
lower classes 111, 134, 161
*see also* income; working classes
Ludacris 165

## M

Mack, Theodore 100, 170, 178
MacLeod, N. 141
Malkin, R. and Hanke, A. 61
malt liquor 110–17
and advertising
and black people 110, 113–16, 119–20, 124
celebrity advertising 111, 115, 116, 119, 123
and sexualization 114, 115
and white people 111, 112, 123
alcohol strength 113, 115, 116, 120, 122
decline 118–20
'forties' 111, 116, 117–18, 122–4, 159
and Hip-Hop 116–17, 118, 122–3, 127–30
and marketing 111, 113–14, 116–17, 159
and sexualization 114, 115, 116
and social class 111–14, 121, 124
and white people 111–12, 113–14, 121, 123
Maltose Falcons 51
Marcus, influencer 86, 101
and diversity 163, 165, 172, 173
and white people 97, 149
marital status of homebrewers 82
marketing 17, 103–30, 164
and black people 63–4, 66–9, 127–30, 148–9
and malt liquor 111, 113–14, 116–17, 159
and middle-classes 111–12, 114
racist 51, 120–2
and three-tier system 62, 65, 99
and white people 63, 67, 77
masculinity/machismo 28–9, 114, 120, 121, 122
Maspee Indians 44
Master Brewers Association 79
Mathews, V. and Picton, R.M. 135
Matt, sales rep 60–1, 64, 65–7, 68–9, 70, 71–2
May, R.A.B. and Chaplin, K.S. 121
McAuliffe, Jack 52, 100
McConnell, J.D. 120
McCulla, Theresa 31
McGirr, Lisa 45–6
McGovern, W. 50
McGuiness, C. 122, 123
McIntosh, P. 7–8
McKenzie River Corporation 116
McNeil, M.A. and Letschert, V.E. 58
men, white 2, 100, 122–4, 146, 157, 178
bearded white man stereotype 2, 15, 128, 153, 172
and history 28–9, 32, 43
and social class 36, 38, 40
and homebrewing 52, 80, 81, 83, 90
three-tier system 60, 63, 67, 69, 77
mergers and acquisitions 49–50, 54–6
Metropolis Brewing 111, 112
Michels, C. 144
microbreweries 1, 56, 59, 64
*see also* craft beer movements
middle-classes 65, 177–8
and craft beer culture 52–3, 57, 131
and gentrification 135, 144
and marketing 111–12, 114
Midnight Dragon 114
migrants 40, 41–2, 43–4, 45, 46–7, 56, 158
*see also* European settlers, white

Milgrom, P. and Roberts, J. 120
Miller, T. and Yudice, G. 133
Miller Brewing Company 50, 54, 117
millet 31
Mills, Charles 7, 34
minority groups *see* black people
mobility, social 110
Monkish Brewing 127, 128
monopolization 47, 60, 108
Montonny's 'negro man' 38–9
Moore, D.J. 120, 121–2
Moore, Wendy 10
morality 36, 44
'more is better' ethos 57
'Mr Beer' kit 80
music, popular 11, 12
  and Hip-Hop 116–17, 118, 122–3, 127–30, 161–2, 163–6
Mylnar, P. 164
mythology of beer 28, 30, 32, 43

## N

'Napa Valley of Beer' 96
Nappy Roots 164–5, 166
National Beer Wholesalers Association (NBWA) 21, 60, 62, 64, 65
National Brewing, Baltimore 113
'Neighborhood brews' blog 139
neighborhoods 41, 99
  and black people 100, 112, 113, 132–4, 135, 138–40
  and gentrification 132–4, 135, 138–40
    and white people 146, 150
New Albion Brewing 52, 100
New Belgium brewery 96
New England 29–30
New York Attorney General's Office 119
newnarrative hashtag 157, 172
niche markets 59, 158, 164
Nickles, S. 57, 58
Nielsen report 16
Noah's ark 29
Northern states 44
nostalgia 124, 125, 159
Notorious B.I.G, 127
Novello, Antonia 119
NWA, rap group 116

## O

Obama, Barack xi–xii
Ocejo, R.E. 134–5, 138
Ohio Supreme Court 42
Olde English 800 113, 115
opportunity hoarding 8
organizational structure 12
Otherness 137, 138, 143

## P

Pabst Brewing Company 46, 47, 49, 54, 115
packaging 99, 112
Papazian, Charlie 28, 52, 100
paternalism 37, 121
Patricia, industry insider 27, 66, 103–4, 163–4, 174–5
  and black people 83–4, 122, 145, 167–8
  distribution system 65, 70
  and employment opportunities 88, 90
  and white people 63, 65
patriotism 123–4
Paulsen, K.E. and Tuller, H.E. 134, 138, 139, 143
Penn, William 37
People's Brewing Company, Oshkosh 100, 170, 178
Peterson, R. 11–13, 53, 59, 143
Philadelphia 37, 39
Pilgrim Fathers 29, 43
place
  and black people 143–53, 166, 168–9
  and gentrification 143–53
    and bars 134–5, 138–9
    and cultural capital 134, 142, 143, 144–5, 151, 160
  and white people 35, 97, 149
plantation owners 36
Pope, Exavier 119
population control 36
poverty 51, 66, 67
Powell, Chick 113, 118
power 107, 109, 120
Price, Jen 163
price of beer 66, 67–9, 121
producers 60–2, 121
  *see also* breweries; craft beer industry
profit 34, 47, 69, 73
Prohibition 21, 43, 44–7, 158
protectionism 61
Protestantism 43, 44, 46

## Q

Quinn, E. 116, 117, 118

## R

'racial contract' 34
racial hierarchy/stratification 7, 33, 39–40, 106, 113, 168
racial institutionalism 7–8, 10, 13, 110, 127
racial segregation 10, 41, 51, 55, 99, 108, 109
recipes 4, 49, 56, 135, 172, 178
Reckless Brewing 125–6

recording industry 53
refrigerators 57, 58
Reid, P.V.K. 62
religious freedom 33–4
representation in brewing industry 103–4, 105, 108, 129, 137, 149, 168–9, 174
research into beer and racism 20–1
restaurant industry 88, 93
  *see also* food and beverage industry
Restaurant Opportunity Centers United (ROC) 70, 71
résumés 85
retailers 60, 62, 64–5, 99
revitalization of neighborhoods 134, 135, 140–1
Robertson, J.D. 110
Robinson, Cedric xv
Rodell, B. 119, 124
Rose, G. 137
Roundtree, Richard 115
rum 31, 37
Run DMC, rap group 116
Run the Jewels 165, 166
rural areas 62, 65, 66

## S

sales figures 63
Salinger, S.V. 35, 36, 37–40
saloons 41–3, 44, 45–6, 47, 59
  *see also* bars; taverns
Samoset people 29
Samuel Adams Boston Lager 52, 100
Satran, Joe 99
Scherer, F.M. and Ross, D. 54
Schille, W.S. and Geyser, S.A. 114
Schlitz Malt Liquor 46, 47, 115, 120
scientific knowledge 77, 78, 84, 89
Scott, sales rep 70, 78, 93, 99, 116
Sedgwick, Captain 29–30
self-making/self-identity 151–2
  and gentrification 137, 143
Serrano, S. 117
sexualization of malt liquor 114, 115, 116
Shepherd, W.G. 54
Shown, M. 125
Shulman, R. 45
Siebel Institute of Technology, Chicago 86
Sierra Nevada Brewing Company 19, 52, 94–5, 100
Simmons, William 46
Sixpoint Brewery 164
slavery 30–1, 33–4, 36, 37, 174
Smith, N. 132
Snitch Blood 126
snobbery 145
social capital 52, 53, 66, 110
  and employment opportunities 70, 71–2
social class 105–8
  black people 111–14, 118, 121, 124
  and cultural capital 106–7, 108, 109
  and gentrification 98, 132, 133, 134, 135–7, 140, 144
  and history 36–7, 38, 39–40, 44, 45–6
    elites class 33, 34, 36, 37, 40
  lower classes/incomes 98, 111, 132, 133, 134, 140, 161
  and malt liquor 111–14, 121, 124
  middle-classes 65, 177–8
    and craft beer culture 52–3, 57, 131
    and gentrification 135, 144
    and marketing 111–12, 114
  racial hierarchy/stratification 7, 33, 39–40, 106, 113, 168
  white people 120
    history of brewing 36, 38, 40
    and malt liquor 114, 121
    working classes 37, 43, 57
  working classes 37, 43, 45–6, 57, 118, 132, 133
social control 44–5
social media 23, 68, 123, 156, 171–7
social networks
  and black people 81, 92–3, 95, 140
  and craft beer brewers 77, 78, 88–9, 90, 159
  and craft beer drinkers 91–4, 95, 159
social object, beer as 4–6
socialization 106, 107, 108
somethingsbrewing hashtag 172, 176
South African Breweries 54
Southern states 44
Southern Sun brewery 96
space 141–53, 166–70
  *see also* gentrification; place
St. Ides malt liquor 116, 119
status, socio-economic 36, 57–8, 62–3, 67–8, 73, 108
Steele, S. 121
Steeleworldwide 123
stereotyping 69, 80, 137
  bearded white man 2, 15, 128, 153, 172
  of black people 124–6, 159
  and three-tier system 73, 109
stigmatization of black people 147–8
'strength of weak ties' 92
Stuart, S. 163–6
students 66, 95, 122–3, 159
styles of beer *see* craft beer industry
suburban areas 57, 65, 162
Sugrue, T.J. 55, 72

## T

'tap takeovers' 68
taste of beer

cultural 18, 105–8, 109, 121, 151, 166
developing taste for craft beer 71, 72, 90, 91, 96–8, 161
black people 51, 67–8, 72, 96–8, 145–52, 161, 163–8
and diversity 161, 163–8, 171–3
homogenization of taste 50, 56–7, 59
and place 144–5, 148–9
regional 56–7
white people 50–1, 52–3
tastings, free 68, 98, 161
tavern culture 35–40
tavern owners 40–4
taverns 35–42, 158
and black people 37, 39, 59
and law/legislation 36–7, 39–40
and population numbers 36, 41
and slavery 36, 37
as social hubs 37, 41, 43
taxation 33, 60, 64, 99
technologies, new 12, 13
temperance movement 43, 44–7, 158
Thomas, Rufus 115
three-tier system 49, 59–69, 158
and black people 70, 73, 158
and Brewers Association 21, 61, 96
and marketing 62, 63, 65, 67, 77, 99
producers 60–2, 121
retailers 60, 62, 64–5, 176
and stereotyping 73, 109
and taxation 60, 64, 99
and white people 53, 77
and white men 60, 63, 67, 69
and wholesale distributors 60, 61, 62, 65–9
tied houses 42–3
Tilton, John B. 42
Toledo, Ohio 40–4
Tony, influencer/organizer
becoming a brewer 78, 89, 100–1, 104
and black culture 126, 128–9, 162–3, 177
and community engagement 173, 175, 177
and homebrewing 83, 90, 93–4
and place 146–7, 150, 168–9
and taste for craft beer 96–7, 150
tourism 135–8
trade unions 43, 55
travel, international 50, 51
travelers 35, 36
Tremblay, V.J. and Tremblay, C.H. 50, 54, 56, 59, 120
Trigg, A.B. 112–13
Trillium Brewing 127
Trubek, A.B. 144–5
Trump, Donald 123
Tuan, Y. 141, 142
Turner, V. 138
Tyler, Elizabeth 46

## U

urban areas 66, 97, 132–3
Urry, J. 136
US Bureau of Labor Statistics 21

## V

Veblen, T. 112–13
vibe 143, 144–5
Virginia 29, 30
volunteering 86–7, 159

## W

Wang, N. 136, 137, 138
Warner, A.G. 56, 120
Warner, K.E. and Goldenhar, L.M. 121
Watson, Bart 16, 17, 63
WeAreCraftBeer hashtag 155–79
*see also* community support and engagement; diversity
Weber, M. 108
Weems, R.E. 114
Where you From? 126
white Anglo-Saxon protestants (WASPs) 43–4
white people
and advertising 57–8, 111, 112, 123
and brewing industry 42, 158
and craft beer industry 6, 146, 148–9
craft brewers 75–90, 100
labor 65, 69, 71–2
and craft beer culture 9, 157
and craft beer drinkers 15–16, 63, 120, 124–30
'hipster' persona 15, 149
taste of beer 50–1, 52–3
and diversity 170, 178–9
and gentrification 132, 138, 146, 150, 160
neighborhoods 146, 150
and history of brewing 28–9, 32, 36, 38, 40, 43
white supremacy/domination 7–10, 28–35, 45–6
and homebrewing 51, 52, 80, 81, 83, 90
identity 9, 10
and institutionalism, racial 7–8, 10, 110
and malt liquor 111–12, 113–14, 121, 122–30
and place 35, 97, 149
social class 120
and history 36, 38, 40

and malt liquor 114, 121
working classes 37, 43, 57–8
and space 75, 144–53
and status, socio-economic 36, 57–8, 67–8
and three-tier system 53, 60, 63, 67, 69, 77
white men 2, 100, 122–4, 146, 157, 178
bearded white man stereotype 2, 15, 128, 153, 172
and history 28–9, 32, 36, 38, 40, 43
and homebrewing 52, 80, 81, 83, 90
three-tier system 60, 63, 67, 69, 77
wholesale distributors 60, 61, 62, 65–9
Will, podcaster 169, 176
Williams, Billy Dee 115, 123
Williamson, Fred 115
Winthrop, John 29
Wolinski, C. 125–6
women 112
and beer drinking 15, 38, 63
black women 121, 178
as brewers 30, 31
and homebrewing 83, 90
and labor in brewing industry 65, 70
in taverns 36, 42
working classes 45–6, 118
and gentrification 132, 133
white people 37, 43, 57–8
World War II 55
WuTang Clan 127

**Y**

youth culture *see* Hip-Hop

**Z**

Zukin, S. 135

CPSIA information can be obtained
at www.ICGtesting.com
Printed in the USA
BVHW040028031020
590243BV00001B/1